P9-CRR-860

The Lion Companion to Church Architecture

Copyright © 2008 David Stancliffe
This edition copyright © 2008 Lion Hudson

The author asserts the moral right
to be identified as the author of this work
A Lion Book
an imprint of
Lion Hudson plc
Wilkinson House, Jordan Hill Road,
Oxford OX2 8DR, England
www.lionhudson.com
ISBN 978 0 7459 5190 4

First edition 2008
10 9 8 7 6 5 4 3 2 1 0

Text acknowledgments
All scripture quotations are from the Revised Standard Version published by HarperCollins Publishers,
copyright © 1989 by the Division of Christian Education of the National Council of the Churches of Christ in
the USA, and are used by permission. All rights reserved.

Picture acknowledgments
Alamy Ltd: p. 62 ALIKI SAPOUNTZI/aliki image library (right); p. 217 William Owens; p. 224 Bildarchiv
Monheim GmbH (right bottom); p. 259 Robert Holmes (top); p. 267 LOOK Die Bildagentur der Fotografen
GmbH (top). *Art Archive*: p. 151 Galleria Nazionale dell'Umbria Perugia/Alfredo Dagli Orti (left top). *Paul
Bevan*: p. 201 (bottom); p. 203 (left top); p. 207 (both); p. 209 (top); p. 220 (left); p. 224 (left centre); p.
226 (top); p. 229 (left); p. 232 (right top); p. 241 (left bottom and right top); p. 242 (right top); p. 243 (left
top); p. 250 (both). *Hugh Bonsey*: p. 238 (left inset and top). *Corbis*: p. 121 Michael S. Yamashita; p. 128
Dennis Marsico; p. 129 Chris Bland; Eye Ubiquitous; p. 269 KNA-Bild Radtke/dpa/. *John Crook*: p. 8; p, 11
(right top); pp. 12-13 (bottom centre); p. 14 (left); p. 16 (centre); p. 29 (centre top); pp. 28-29 (bottom
centre); p. 37 (bottom); p. 47 (centre); p. 48 (left); p. 53 (right); p. 67; p. 72 (right top); p. 73 (right); p.
75 (left); p. 76 (left centre); p. 78; p. 84 (both); p. 89 (left); p. 97 (top); p. 100 (right inset); pp. 100-101
(centre, main picture); p. 102 (right); p. 103; p. 104 (right); p. 105 (centre top); p. 105 (right centre); p. 107
(left); p. 107 (left centre); p. 115 (right); p. 117; p. 124 (left); pp. 130-1 (top centre); p. 134; p. 138 (right);
p. 139; p. 140 (left); p. 141 (left); p. 148; p. 158 (left); p. 160; p. 221 (left); p. 231 (left bottom);
p. 233 (left inset). *Anthony Feltham-King*: p. 241 (left top). *Getty Images*: p. 10 Hulton Archive;
p. 42 Martin Gray/National Geographic; p. 45 Robert Harding/Digital Vision (left); p. 69 IIC/ Axiom (left);
pp. 152-3 Altrendo Travel (centre, main picture); p. 182 De Agostini Picture Library (centre); p. 183 Petr
Svarc/Iconica (top). *Richard Giles*: p. 267 (bottom). *Michael Hsu*: p. 185 *Ben Stancliffe*: p. 189 (right); p. 190
(left); p. 242-3 (centre). *Jonathan Roberts*: p. 218 *Scala Archives*: p. 26 Piero della Francesca (1415/20-1492):
Legend of the True Cross: Constantine's Dream. Arezzo, Church of San Francesco. © 2003. Photo Scala,
Florence. *Wallace Collection*: p. 126 by kind permission of the Trustees of the Wallace Collection (right).
All other photos are from the author's personal collection.

All diagrams by Richard Watts at Total Media Services apart from those listed below. Every effort has been
made to trace and contact copyright holders. We apologize for any inadvertent errors or omissions which may
remain, and would ask those concerned to contact the publishers, who will ensure that full acknowledgment
is made in the future.
pp. 21 and 29 taken from *Art in the Christian World: 300-1500: A Handbook of Styles and Forms* by Yves Christe
et al. Published by Faber & Faber, 1982; pp. 55 and 65 taken from *Byzantine Architecture* (History of World
Architecture series) by Cyril Mango. Published by Faber & Faber 1986; p. 63 taken from *Early Christian and
Byzantine Architecture* (Pelican History of Art series) by Krautheimer. Published by Penguin, 1965; pp. 76 and
87 taken from *Carolingian and Romanesque Architecture* (Pelican History of Art series) by K J Conant. Published
by Penguin, 1959; p. 176 taken from *Temples, Mosques and Churches* by J G Davies. Published by Blackwells,
1982. Permission granted by Blackwells; p. 186 taken from *Modern Churches of the World* by Robert Maguire
and Keith Murray published by Studio Vista, 1965; p. 251 taken from *Liturgy and Architecture* by Peter
Hammond. Published by Barrie and Rockcliffe (Random House), 1960. Permission granted by David Higham
Associates Limited; p. 257 permission granted by Gibberd Architectural Practice.

A catalogue record for this book is available
from the British Library

Typeset in 10.5/14 ITC Berkeley Oldstyle BT
Printed and bound in China

The Lion
Companion
to

David Stancliffe

Church

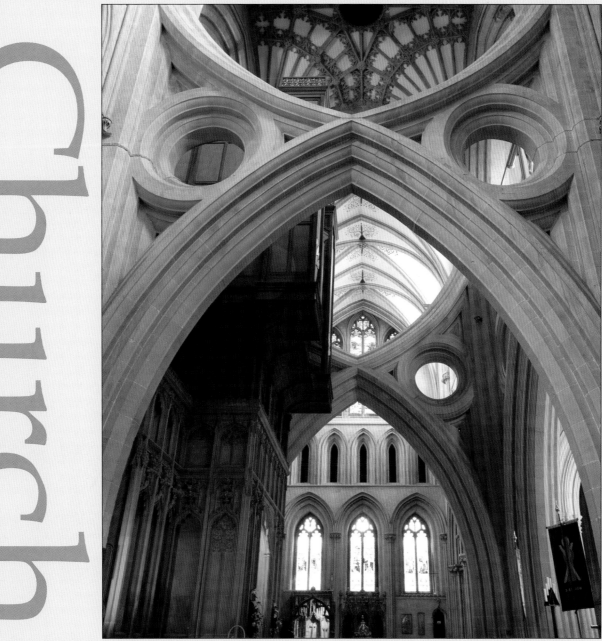

Architecture

In thanksgiving for
Staunton Harold
where passion proved as fierce as the grave
and hope triumphed over despair.

Many waters cannot quench love,
neither can the floods drown it.

Contents

Salisbury Cathedral.

Preface

My starting point is that understanding the development of church architecture involves significantly more than tracing the development of various styles of architectural expression – discovering the beginnings of Gothic in the attempts to vault significant spaces in stone, for example, or tracing the first fan vaults chronologically. There are books that do that, such as Sir Bannister Fletcher's classic *History of Architecture on the Comparative Method*. It is also enormously important to understand both the potential and the limitations of building materials that are available in any one region at any time, as described in Alec Clifton-Taylor's *The Pattern of English Building*, and also to engage with the challenges to human ingenuity needed to overcome them.

Nor is it simply a matter of understanding the functional requirements of the church's worship as it develops. The history of the development of the church's worship is indeed vital for understanding the changes that are demanded as a worshipping community 'makes the offering', (as the Eucharistic liturgy was once known): it tells you, for example, why baptismal fonts became smaller – as the majority of those baptized were no longer adults but children. But it does not answer questions about the sense of God and our relationship to him that the particular building was designed to evoke.

For these questions we need to look beyond both the technical possibilities and the liturgical functions to ask why, for example, a building like Salisbury Cathedral is the size it is, given that the congregation for which it was built comprised the bishop with his chapter of forty canons and their attendants. Even more basically, we need to understand – difficult in our utilitarian age – that all building was once held to be sacred: in other words, the way you built your house and lived in it echoed something of what you believed was true about the world you lived in and your relationship to the one who created it.

If that was once true even of domestic buildings, then how much more so of the specifically religious buildings. Even the humblest chapel was a bit of 'heaven on earth', as the eighth-century bishop, Germanus, described the church. The great Gothic cathedrals still tower over even modern cities such as Strasbourg, Milan or Cologne, and much of a community's life and longing were invested in such buildings. This is hardly echoed today, even in the great cathedrals of power and wealth, the temples of today's corporate giants. What were the aspirations of the great church-builders, and how did they understand and then express their changing relationship to God?

All these questions are interrelated, and each chapter of this book addresses not only the significant shift in architectural style but also the historical, theological and liturgical contexts that frame it. My hope is that those who read this book may learn to 'read' the churches they visit not merely as stunning examples of the architects' and craftsmen's skill, but as continuing signs of that 'heaven on earth'.

Editor's note: Terms marked with an asterisk (*) in the text are defined in further detail in the Glossary found at the back of the book.

The chapel of St Michel d'Aiguilhe crowns a basalt pinnacle in Le Puy-en-Veley, France.

Sacred Space

Where Heaven and Earth Touch

Human experience operates within two distinct time frames, the cyclic and the linear. The major human experiences of birth and death, marriage and childbearing, toil and leisure, growth and decline offer both a cyclic and a linear experience. To the individual, the experiences of a succession of events in any one human life seem linear; we construct imaginative reflection out of the events of our life as it develops. We remember the experiences of childhood – a birthday party or the first day at school – and we link these with the memory of joys and sorrows, of successes and failures, and impose on that a linear pattern of cause and effect to give it some shape. But there is also a sense that our experience is cyclic. The seasons of the year repeat; our memories of the bulbs in successive springtimes or the carols at Christmastide slide together. With 'the ever-circling years' comes the sense that the patterns repeat themselves, and, like the succession of the seasons of the year, there is always new life, and there is always death.

Alongside these different ways of reflecting on our experience lie the different ways we receive that experience itself. At what point do we consciously become aware that discovering who we are in relation to the other is conditioned by the space we inhabit, and that we can shape that

environment to some extent? Much of the time we take our relationship to the world outside or beyond us for granted. It is just there. But at other times we find ourselves reflecting consciously on our external environment: in a domestic sense, the rooms in our house, the pictures on the walls and the views from the windows; the smells and sights of the kitchen as food is prepared; the warmth of our beds and the sights that greet us as we wake. Partly, as with our homes, we have consciously fashioned that environment; partly, as with the streets of the place where we were brought up, or the walls of the schoolroom where we were taught, or the interiors of the churches where we worshipped as children, the environment has fashioned us.

WHAT IS SACRED SPACE?

In every case, the natural environment has a profound effect on what we experience and who we are becoming. There is *place* – the given environment around us, which is a physical reality made up of natural objects, fashioned and arranged by human ingenuity – and there is *space*, the frame within which we live and grow. Place may have a natural resonance that can be enhanced, but space is something we long for, and that helps us grow into what we are becoming. We call space sacred when we sense that our environment is either naturally or consciously created to hold us in relationship with the beyond, with something greater than ourselves that is gently shaping us, or even radically changing us.

High Places and Caves in the Earth

Such intimations of how place gives us space are common to human experience. Few people are unmoved by climbing a mountain. It is not just the view from the summit but the whole effort of getting there that provides what is generally recognized as a near 'religious' experience. High places have been associated with the home of the gods from the dawn of human consciousness. The peaks, where the sky gods lived in the mysterious, cloud-capped regions on the mountain tops and from which they hurled their thunderbolts,

were identified as the archetype of the male, the aggressive, the beyond, the other; while the caves and folds in the earth, where the soft rains fell and made the earth fertile, were the archetype of the female, the soft, the womb-like, the interior.

Little wonder then that both mountain tops and caves have been endowed with spiritual significance, and that both have been thought of as places of religious importance. Where there were no mountains, no high places, people built pillars or ziggurats. The story of the Tower of Babel in the Old Testament is a witness to the long tradition of trying to reach the home of God, to get in contact, of the desire to build upwards that some of the great Hindu temples in India emulate. Nor is this a 'primitive' idea: the spire of Salisbury Cathedral, for example, bears witness to the human desire to reach up beyond ourselves. Similarly, the claustrophobic confines of a cave have been

THE TOWER OF BABEL

'Now the whole earth had one language and few words. And as men migrated from the east, they found a plain in the land of Shinar and settled there. And they said to one another, "Come, let us make bricks, and burn them thoroughly." And they had brick for stone, and bitumen for mortar. Then they said, "Come, let us build ourselves a city, and a tower with its top in the heavens, and let us make a name for ourselves, lest we be scattered abroad upon the face of the whole earth." And the Lord came down to see the city and the tower, which the sons of men had built. And the Lord said, "Behold, they are one people, and they have all one language; and this is only the beginning of what they will do; and nothing that they propose to do will now be impossible for them. Come, let us go down, and there confuse their language, that they may not understand one another's speech." So the Lord scattered them abroad from there over the face of all the earth, and they left off building the city. Therefore its

name was called Babel, because there the Lord confused the language of all the earth; and from there the Lord scattered them abroad over the face of all the earth.' (Genesis 11:1–9)

The Tower of Babel (1563), Peter Bruegel, Kunsthistorisches Museum, Vienna.

Below: A rock-cut tomb, north of Jerusalem, showing a stone door rolled away.

Bottom left: A natural waterfall near Figaleia, Greece, feeding the River Neda.

Below: The grotto at Lourdes, the site of the apparition.

Bottom right: Channelled water flowing down a picnic table at the Villa Lante, near Viterbo, Italy.

recognized as a place in which to explore the inward journey or the interior life. In the Classical world, caves gave birth to rivers, and in Greece many places laid claim to being the mouth of hell, the place where you leave this earth to journey into the underworld; others, as at Delphi, housed the oracle.

near miraculous. In some famous gardens, such as the garden of the Villa Lante near Viterbo, Italy, water plays a huge part, as it does in Rome and other Classical cities. Sometimes a grove of trees with their over-arching boughs and soft indirect light can give a magical feel to a space both private

In our time few caves are as well known as the grotto at Lourdes, but others – such as the cave where the archangel Michael appeared at Monte San Angelo in the Gargano peninsula in southern Italy – are equally venerated. What gives caves and rock-cut tombs their primary significance in the Christian tradition is their association with the burial and resurrection of Christ.

But it was not only natural phenomena or human endeavour on a large scale that provided this kind of experience. Sometimes a natural spring could be harnessed and provide a captivating setting, and in places where water was scarce, the effective use of such a life-giving sign could seem

and yet superhuman in scale; in England the missionaries had residual suspicions of the ancient power of the yew groves.

The reuse of pagan sites and shrines by the Christian church in England has an interesting history. After Pope Gregory sent Augustine to England in 597 to convert the inhabitants to the faith, he also wrote a letter to the Bishop of London, Mellitus, with wise advice. Rather than destroying the heathen temples as he had originally advocated, Gregory now advised him to convert them into churches, destroying the idols and sprinkling them thoroughly with holy water. He had in mind a gradual softening of the 'savage

The massive Doric columns of a Greek temple set into the walls of Syracuse Cathedral, Sicily, show how the Christian faith incorporated the old pagan world.

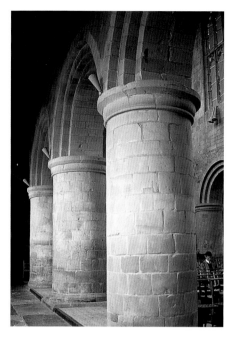

Left: The heavy drums of the Romanesque nave of Great Malvern, like those of Gloucester nearby, contrast sharply with the airy Gothic superstructure.

Below: The Great Mosque at Cordoba, Spain, where Muslims and Christians once worshipped side by side.

hearts' of the people, who might be won over to the new faith if their familiar buildings were given a continuing use, adding that the usual animal sacrifices could be converted into a Christian feast to celebrate the name day of the martyr, whose relics would consecrate the new church.

Nor is this taking over of recognized holy places confined to the early period of the church's life. The adaptation of the Great Mosque at Cordoba in southern Spain by the church is a breathtaking example of the reuse of a building. There the Christian architects of the fifteenth century cleared a large cruciform space in the centre of the huge forest of *pillars that formed the prayer-hall, and raised a Late Gothic structure in its heart. The contrast between the low arches of the mosque, which form the outer *aisles, and the soaring Gothic of the Christian cathedral is enormous, echoed in England by the experience of moving from the Norman *nave of Gloucester Cathedral, with its heavy, drum-like *columns like those of the church at nearby Malvern, into the airy Gothic of the *choir, with its gilded angel minstrels flying in the apex of the vault, raised up through the solid Romanesque of the *ambulatory that surrounds it.

Another large building, this time dating from Classical Rome, is the former temple known as the

Left: The interior of the dome of the Classical Pantheon, Rome.

Right: The Cosmati pathway in the Basilica of San Clemente, Rome, leads worshippers from the atrium to the altar in a swaying movement.

Pantheon. This astonishing circular building in the heart of the old city is covered by what was for a long time the largest known *dome in the West. A structural marvel, the Pantheon has a history of continuous use as a place of worship. Different in scale and construction are the layers of building beneath the Basilica of San Clemente not far from the Pantheon. The lowest level included rooms dedicated to the sun god Mithras, a cult popular with Roman soldiers and probably brought back from the Near East. Central to the initiation rites of the Mithraic Mystery religion was the slaughtering of a bull, so that its blood flowed down though a grating over the initiates below. On top of this, and providing the middle layer of this three-tier construction, is an early Christian *basilica, in use until the building of the upper church in the eleventh century. Perhaps the most evocative reuse of a pagan building today is the conversion of the Doric temple in Syracuse – the significant seaport on the east side of Sicily – into a cathedral. The great Doric columns of the temple are clearly visible, embedded within the walls of the new church.

But religious experience is not to be had only on high mountains or in deep caves, gained by testing the limits of human endurance; there is also the journey inwards. In Classical times,

13

Above: The Dome of the Rock, standing on the original site of the Temple in Jerusalem.

Right: The Temple of Garni at Kotak, Armenia, illustrates the popular image of a Classical temple, with a cella surrounded by pedimented arcades.

this had been expressed in the story of the hero Theseus' journey, following Ariadne's thread, into the heart of the maze to encounter and slay the Minotaur. In the Christian tradition specifically, treading the maze has been developed as a model of the interior journey – encountering the darkest depths of our human sense of isolation and loss. This liminal journey is that experienced by *catechumens (those preparing for the sacrament of baptism at Easter) in their Lenten preparation and accounts for the number of mazes on the floors of Medieval cathedrals, such as Chartres, or on the walls, such as the cathedral at Lucca, Italy, where Lenten penances were performed. But the journey is not only inwards and downwards; it is also upwards and outwards. On at least one of these mazes, at Auxerre, France, complex Easter dances were performed by the canons of the cathedral as a ball – the *pilota* – was tossed from one to the other while the Easter sequence, *Victimae paschali laudes*, was sung. In the centre, the dean trod the maze and tossed the ball – possibly representing in origin the ball of pitch Theseus is said to have stuffed into the Minotaur's mouth – like some Medieval baseball pitcher. The same model of the descent into hell to encounter death and win back the souls from their captivity is seen on Orthodox icons of the *Anastasis and

was known in Medieval England as the Harrowing of Hell. This descent into the underworld to win back his betrothed, who had been seized by death, is the heart of the Orpheus myth, and may account for the identification of Orpheus as a Christ figure. As the church began to craft a theology of baptism in the context of a society in which Classical mythology provided the religious framework, this model provides the classic pattern for baptism as a passage through a place of non-being to the emergence as a different person, new-born in Christ, to take their place in the dance of life. In Classical Greek tragedy, the liturgical reflection on the drama was provided by the chorus, who chanted their verses rhythmically as they danced solemnly on the orchestra, the circular dancing floor of the Greek theatre.

Sometimes, these natural sites are what are known as 'thin places', where people have sensed that another world is close to breaking through. They may be the site of a life-changing vision, dream or encounter, or an episode in the life of a saint, such as the island of Iona off the coast of Scotland. Such thin places are often sites of great natural beauty, but they did not remain just that. These were the places where an encounter with the divine was marked with a temple or a shrine. The original temples were not the towering constructions of

Classical Athens, with columns and *pediments outlined against the blue sky of the Mediterranean; they were precincts, marked or cut out from the surrounding chaos by a boundary, such as Romulus created when he drove a ploughshare round the area that was to become Rome, so marking out an area within which law and order were to reign.

Left: The maze, or labyrinth, by the door of the Cathedral of St Martin, Lucca, in Italy, which worshippers might trace with their fingers.

Above: The Greek theatre, with its central orchestra, or dancing floor, at Segesta, Sicily.

A space like this is marked out, set apart and consecrated to be a sign of the engagement between the human and the divine. The word temple comes from the Greek verb *temno*, 'I cut'; and early temples were sacred precincts dedicated, like a tennis court or football pitch, to an ordered encounter between polar opposites – in this case between the human and the divine.

Later, more permanent structures were erected to witness to the significance of the space. An obvious example is the Acropolis in Athens, and a more atmospheric one used to be the temple of Bassae, situated in a fold between two peaks in the heart of the Peleponnese in Greece, before it was wrapped in a gigantic polythene bag to 'protect it'; some of the best examples are in Sicily.

Such temples not only marked places of serious encounter; they were also the shrine or home of the god they were built to honour. The elaborate *portico of a Classical temple was the gateway to the *cella, the inner room in which the statue of the god – often a rich work of art adorned with precious metals – was housed. The doors were frequently orientated towards the rising sun so that its rays would strike the image, and give it a new, bright life. In this way, Classical temples were the houses of the gods as well as places of encounters. Altars on which cereal or animal sacrifices were offered stood in open ground before the temple. The great Temple at Jerusalem echoed some of these characteristics, and provides an important background to understanding more than just how Christian churches evolved. The Dome of the Rock stands on the site of the original Temple in Jerusalem.

The Lion Companion to Church Architecture

THE BIBLICAL BACKGROUND

The Mountain of Sacrifice

The Old Testament begins with a description of an ideal harmony, a paradise in which humankind and God enjoyed a creative partnership in caring for the world. Soon that ideal partnership is shattered, and the human beings, created to care for the world, find themselves competing for God's attention. Abel's sacrifice of a lamb is acceptable, as is that of Melchisedek, the priest 'who brought out bread and wine' (Genesis 14:18); but Cain's cereal offering is not, and he kills his brother in a fit of jealousy. This breakdown of relationships between God and his creation, between man and his brother, and indeed between the whole human race and the natural environment we were charged with caring for, signals a dislocation that only a sacrifice can bridge. It is this terrifying sacrifice – the sacrifice of his only son – that is demanded of Abraham as he journeys to Mount Moriah, and is only averted when God accepts Abraham's faith and the angel directs Abraham to a ram caught in a bush nearby.

The Place of a Dream

Not long after in the story comes another encounter with the hidden world, this time in a dream. Jacob is on the run from his elder brother Esau, from whom – aided and abetted by his mother – he has stolen his father's blessing. Exhausted, he falls asleep and dreams of a ladder linking earth and heaven, and 'the angels of God were ascending and descending on it' (Genesis 28:12). When he wakes, Jacob takes the stone he had used as a pillow and sets it up as a pillar, anointing it with oil, saying, 'Surely the Lord is in this place and I did not know it… how awesome is this place! This is none other than the house of God, and this is the gate of heaven' (Genesis 28:16–17). This pillar marked a characteristic 'thin place', where a life-changing encounter had occurred, even if only in a dream.

Moses Meets God

When God meets Moses in the burning bush, the ground around it is designated as holy space, and Moses is instructed to take his shoes off. Today,

when you enter the great courtyard of a mosque, that sense of reverence remains: you will be asked to take off your shoes, and worshippers wash at the fountain.

Later, when the people of Israel, wandering in the wilderness after their escape from slavery in Egypt, are given the law engraved on tablets of stone (offered by God as guidance for his people on Mount Sinai), Moses receives instructions about providing an *ark, a wooden box, elaborately decorated with carved angels, in which these tablets are to be kept.

To provide a shrine for the ark containing the tablets of the law, the rod with which Aaron performed signs before Pharaoh and a jar of the manna that God gave as food for his people in the wilderness, Moses is instructed to make the *tabernacle – the tent of meeting that the Israelites re-pitch as they journey through the wilderness in those nomadic forty years. The tabernacle is essentially portable, but the Holy of Holies is separated from the tent of meeting by a veil. This

tent and the ark are the focus of God's presence with his people but do not contain him: when the people move forward, the ark goes with them, and the tabernacle is put up when they camp. Only Moses can go in behind the veil and converse with God 'face to face, as a man speaks to his friend' (Exodus 33:11), while Aaron and the priestly tribe of Levi are ordained to administer the sacrificial system. The tradition of a teaching ministry as distinct from a priestly ministry is established in Jewish worship at this early stage, and elements of that survive into the Christian era. When the sacrificial system comes to an end with the final destruction of the Temple in the year 70, the meeting place of the Jewish communities, led by a rabbi, continues to be the synagogue, with its emphasis on meeting and teaching. The home is the place where the festivals are celebrated, and the head of the household leads the celebration.

Solomon's Temple

When the people became settled in the Promised Land and began to build houses, the demand for a temple became overwhelming. King David's successor, Solomon, recognized this, and set about building a magnificent structure that would be a permanent home for the ark of the presence, and establish Jerusalem as the place in which God had chosen to dwell among his people. Solomon's prayer at its dedication draws attention to the ambivalence of a temple rather than a tent: 'But will God indeed dwell on the earth? Behold heaven and the heaven of heavens cannot contain thee; how much less this house which I have built!' (1 Kings 8:27).

This ambivalence resurfaces in Stephen's speech in response to the accusation that he too spoke against the Temple. Stephen was one of the deacons ordained to assist the apostles, whose claims that 'the Most High does not dwell in houses made with hands; as the prophet says, "Heaven is my throne, and earth my footstool"' so irritated his Jewish hearers that they stoned him to death (Acts 7:48–49).

Both these passages illuminate Jesus' dialogue with the Jews in chapter 2 of John's Gospel. There, in response to being challenged for cleansing the Temple, Jesus makes the provocative challenge: 'Destroy this temple, and in three days I will raise it up' (John 2:19). This challenge to the Jewish claim that the Temple in some literal way embodied the presence of God among his people was clearly a strand in Jesus' teaching. It was a memory of this claim that surfaced in his trial before the high priest. But, more significantly

for our purposes, this prediction that the Temple would be destroyed led to John's gloss on the Jews' amazement: 'It has taken forty-six years to build this temple, and will you raise it up in three days?' (John 2:20). But, says John, Jesus 'spoke of the temple of his body' (John 2:21). John's understanding of Jesus is that he himself is the new Temple, the place where God and humanity are one. This too is the theological significance of the veil of the Temple, which divided the Holy of Holies from the outer sanctuary, being rent in two at the moment of Jesus' death in the Gospels of Mark, Matthew and Luke (Matthew 27:51; Mark 15:38; Luke 23:45). In Jesus' teaching, the old Temple, the replacement of the tabernacle in the wilderness, has outlived its usefulness. The place where God and the human race meet is not a place but a person – Jesus himself.

At the start of the Gospel John spoke of the word of God being made flesh and dwelling among us: the Greek phrase of John 1:14 translates literally to 'pitched his tent in our midst'. He has grasped that the tabernacle with the ark of the presence, the meeting place between the human and the divine, is now replaced by the person of Jesus in whom the human and divine are seamlessly one. Nor should we be surprised: at the

Mosaic at Tabgha, on the shore of the Sea of Galilee, Palestine, showing loaves and a fish – symbols of Christ feeding his people (John 6:1–14).

end of chapter 1 in John's Gospel and before the dialogue about the Temple, Jesus recalls Jacob's dream of a ladder linking earth and heaven as he answers a question from an enquiring bystander, who calls him the Son of God and the King of Israel. This dream, says John, becomes reality in Christ: 'You shall see greater things than these; truly, truly, I say to you, you will see heaven opened and the angels of God ascending and descending upon the Son of man' (John 1:50–51). For John, this essential human longing is no longer a dream: Jesus himself is the ladder that links earth to heaven; he is the place where the Lord is present; he is the house of God, and his purpose of drawing people up from earth to heaven will be fulfilled as he is crucified. 'I, when I am lifted up from the earth, will draw all people to myself,' he says, when looking ahead to his being lifted up on the cross (John 12:32).

THE APOSTOLIC PERIOD

The New Testament Picture

The picture of the church we gain from the letters of Paul and the Acts of the Apostles shows groups of believers drawn from a wide range across the social spectrum meeting for worship in private houses. They were the *ekklesia*, those 'called out' from the unbelievers, whose life was marked out by the liturgical celebrations of baptism and Eucharist, and by a strong and cohesive pattern of social care and hospitality. Originally a purely Jewish development, in which believers attended the Jewish temple or synagogue service and then met in their homes for the breaking of the bread (Acts 2:42), under the insight of Paul it became a group that transcended the common boundaries of the first century. Gentile and Jew, slave and free, male and female, young and old, all had a place in the new religion; and this made it potentially subversive of the hierarchical structures and divisions that helped keep the subjects of the Roman empire in order.

Sometimes we glimpse the ideal of the church through Paul's attempts to correct abuses. The church in Corinth was plainly a vigorous and lively assembly, in which speaking in tongues – a form of ecstatic praying – reflected the apostles' experience on the Day of Pentecost, when the Holy Spirit descended on the assembled company, giving them fluency in many languages and courage to go and declare that God had raised Jesus from the dead. This is a potentially divisive practice, as the church found: did this ability mean spiritual superiority? Such practices tended to divide rather than unite, as did claims of social superiority. Such assemblies sound as though they are already outgrowing the hospitality of the wealthier Christians in whose large houses they appear to have met. Distinguishing the Lord's Supper from the common meal, in which the rich and leisured were able to get down to their own supper before all the assembly had arrived, was clearly important; failure to do so was an abuse of the common table.

The letters of Paul are the source for much of what we know in this early period. Writing to the church in Corinth, Paul concludes, 'The churches of Asia send greetings. Aquila and Prisca, together with the church in their house, send you hearty greetings in the Lord' (1 Corinthians 16:19). Not only does the church meet in their house, but its leadership also seems to include women. In the earlier letters, the images used to describe the church are more organic: the church is 'the body of Christ' (1 Corinthians 12:27); or the bride of Christ (Ephesians 5:25–33). By the time of the letter to the Ephesians, the members of the church are 'fellow citizens with the saints and members of the household of God', a much more social construct, and indeed they 'built upon the foundation of the apostles and prophets, Christ Jesus himself being the cornerstone, in whom the whole structure is joined together and grows into a holy temple in the Lord' (Ephesians 2:19–21); a building metaphor has taken over from the organic image.

Along with the shift in images of the church, we begin to discern signs of structural

IORDANES

BVS MEDICIS POPVLO SPES CER
SALRO CREVIT HONO

organization. The church has ministers – a bishop or overseer, deacons, and elders or presbyters (1 Timothy 3:1; 3:8; 5:17). In other places there are apostles and prophets, evangelists, pastors and teachers – according to the letter to the Ephesians (4:11); even here structural images of 'building up the body' are to the fore (Ephesians 4:12).

Other glimpses of the church in the early centuries are tantalizingly few. In the 'upper room' in which Paul preached at Troas to the Sunday assembly there were many lamps lit (Acts 20:7–8). Baptisms appear to have been celebrated in running water if possible, which implies an outdoor site by a river. The spring-fed pool in the crypt at Abu Gosh, a possible site for Emmaus and now a Benedictine monastery about 7 miles (11 km) from Jerusalem, is a fine example of a natural baptismal pool. A small *mosaic on the floor of a church in Tabgha, on the shore of the Sea of Galilee in the Holy Land, shows loaves and fishes. Paintings in the catacombs outside Rome represent Christ as young and beardless – like a Greek hero – often as the Good Shepherd, and show figures praying with their hands raised. A company who may be celebrating the Eucharist are reclining round a table in a very domestic setting. The Good Shepherd who gathers his sheep and feeds them is a frequent image in mosaics, as is Christ as the sacrificial lamb himself.

In the past, it was believed that when Christianity was a forbidden religion, worshippers met in the catacombs outside Rome. We now know that the *chapels in the catacombs are later than the early centuries, and were probably constructed for worship at the shrines of martyrs who were buried in them. Catacombs were originally constructed as burial places. When Justin Martyr (around 150) was asked by the Roman prefect where the Christians usually met for worship, he got an evasive answer, hinting that they gathered in an assembly that met in one or another house. In this context, when the assembly met in the larger houses of wealthier members, people from outlying districts would come in to the town: Christianity was essentially urban in its style. The meal setting would have taken place in the dining room, or *triclinium*, but no special architectural arrangements were made. A hundred years later, St Cyprian, writing in Carthage, specifically mentions the *ambo (raised platform) as the place from which the word was proclaimed: this means that the room in which it stood must have been pretty large.

Early Archaeology: The House Church

The first real archaeological evidence of a house adapted specifically for Christian worship is in

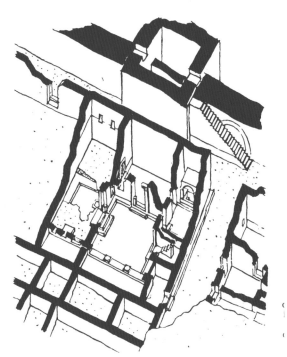

Syria at Dura Europus. Christianity had been introduced there by the Romans during their occupation around 163. There was a synagogue close by, and also a temple of Mithras, and then in the 240s a house was adapted by the Christian community for worship. Built typically around a courtyard, the Christians removed one partition wall to create a large space for the assembly – more than 200 square feet (18.5 square metres) in area – with a raised platform at one end, presumably for the person who presided at the *Eucharist, though no trace of a table has been found. The *baptistery, the place in which the sacrament of baptism is administered, is clearly identified by a raised pool standing under an arch decorated with stars. On the baptistery walls are paintings of the Good Shepherd and his sheep, the fall of Adam and Eve, the women bringing spices to the tomb of Jesus to anoint his body, the healing of the paralysed man, David and Goliath, the Samaritan woman at the well, and Peter saved from drowning when he tried to walk on the water. Grapes, wheat and pomegranates – symbols of refreshment in a desert place – also decorate the space to remind the newly baptized of the nourishment they would receive in their Eucharistic life. From the outside, it would have remained just like any other large house; but once

you were into the courtyard, the character and purpose of the rooms would have been visible to the initiated.

In these house churches, the primary emphasis was on the assembly: they were spaces for Christian celebration, and it was the celebrating community that gave them their character. Baptism required a bath, but the Eucharist was celebrated on a wooden table. There might be a chair for the person presiding, but that, along with a *lectern for the scriptures, would have been moveable. The places where the community assembled depended on the presence of the community for their character. These assemblies, linked in communion with one another, never inherited the sense of shrines, nor were they akin to the Jewish temple – a sacred space, unique and static. The liturgy of the church was designed to emphasize the unity of the community gathered into one in Christ, the new and living temple, by the one Spirit, and so each baptized Christian became a temple of the Holy Spirit (1 Corinthians 3:16).

All this provides a contrast with the Jewish cult, with its professional priesthood and central temple. However, over the early centuries, the new faith found itself almost unconsciously adopting the ideas and imagery of its parent body. It is not only that the scriptures remained the same; there

The steps descending into the baptismal font in the centre of the circular cathedral at Zvarnots, Armenia.

The font, shaped like a church with an apsidal end, at Le Dorat, France.

also was no agreement as to which of the writings of the apostles and Gospel accounts of Jesus should make up what we now call the New Testament until the end of the second century. Before that date, the early church's scriptures were what we would refer to as the Old Testament, which is why the images and vocabulary of the Old Testament remained so formative for Christian discourse. The Old Testament was full of the stories of deliverance and release appropriate to Christians in a period of uncertainty and oppression; and many of these were read during the night-long vigil as Christians waited to celebrate the resurrection in the dawn of Easter day. These are the stories that are often shown on early Christian *sarcophagi (carved tomb chests used for Christian burials) or on paintings associated with burials.

The Community Focused on Sacraments: Baptism in the Early Church

The new Christians found the dream of intimacy becoming reality as they stepped out of their old persona and entered into Christ. Their old nature stripped off and their past life sluiced away is the essential baptismal experience. Some churches – notably those built primarily as baptisteries – convey that focused sense of personal change. Whether the movement is down into the waters

(with overtones of the tomb) or through them (with echoes of the exodus); whether much is made of stripping off and re-clothing in the white robes of the new Christian (Colossians 3:9–10) or being anointed as you come up from the waters (Mark 1:10–11): all these images speak of personal encounter and transformation.

Architecturally, this was expressed in a circular or centred form. Baptisteries were constructed over *fonts, which gave expression to the sense of descending into the waters and being raised up from them. The tomb-like construction of early baptismal basins or the reuse as fonts of actual sarcophagi identified the believer who went down into the dark waters of death closely with Christ's dying and rising.

There are baptismal fonts with descending steps, such as that in the centre of the church at Zvarnots in Armenia; later, they might be great basins, shaped like churches, complete with nave and apse as in Le Dorat, France. The natural pool below the abbey church at Abu Gosh in Israel offers an alternative model of descent into a cave where a living spring bubbles up.

The Movement from Font to Altar

As the newly baptized Christian steps 'out of darkness into his marvellous light', the procession

much sense. The experience of those disciples who accompanied Jesus up the mountain and saw him transfigured would have built on that initial revelation and given them some insight into Jesus' ultimate destiny. It would have allowed them to understand, with John, that the moment of Jesus being lifted up was the moment when his glory was revealed. An essential part of the Christian experience was the movement upwards into light to be welcomed with the kiss of peace and anointed with the oil of blessing.

Many churches built on high points, such as the Abbey of Mont-Saint-Michel in Normandy, the basilica at Vezelay in Burgundy, or the monastery of St Martin de Canigou, set high in the Pyrenees, echo this movement upwards. In Greece, many mountain tops are crowned with a small church dedicated to the holy Elijah. But even without such height, a pilgrimage church – placed at a high point or destination of a pathway or vista – becomes a goal, long before you arrive at it.

Reaching the End of the Journey

In a longitudinal hall, the focus is at the end, and the aisled building itself invariably provides a processional approach to the place that the emperor's throne – or later, the bishop's chair – was set. The goal of the journey, such as that at

to join one's fellow believers offers the worshipper an experience of growth and change by holding out a vision, however distant, of transforming glory. The voice at Jesus' baptism by John in the River Jordan declared, 'Thou art my beloved Son; with Thee I am well pleased.' These words echoed Psalm 2, a coronation psalm, and a phrase from Isaiah 42, a servant song, and the hearers would have recognized the two very different allusions: how could Jesus be addressed both as a viceroy of God and at the same time as one who would bear the sins of the people? Such apparent contradictions would not have made

Porec (see chapter 2, pages 34–35) was heaven itself; but what gave the worshipper a sense that the space was inhabited, that the throne was an icon of the throne of heaven, was the decoration of the *apse, the semicircular east end of the church. It might be a Greek-style *Pantocrator* (Christ as ruler of all) as at Cefalu in Sicily; or a more abstract design, like the cross as the Tree of Life in San Clemente in Rome.

Various elements combine to give a more or less imperial feel to the experience of approaching the apsidal end: there is the conscious adoption of the Roman triumphal arch, with its figures bearing not the spoils of war, but gifts, to define the gateway to heaven. Sometimes the *altar is merely a sideboard before a great *reredos (a painted or sculpted backdrop to the altar), in which case the liturgical action of the offering of the Eucharist can easily be dwarfed, as it is in the Sistine Chapel or at Coventry Cathedral; sometimes the altar stands beneath a canopy known as a *ciborium, which indicates that it is – or stands over – the tomb of a martyr or saint at the goal of the pilgrimage, as at San Niccolo at Bari, Italy.

Later, in the Medieval period, when pilgrimage became a major way of expressing the longing for the transforming vision, the focal point of a major church often became the shrine of the

Top left: The *Pantocrator* in the apse of the cathedral, Cefalu, Sicily.

Above: The ciborium over an altar in the cathedral at Molfetta, in Apulia, Italy.

miracle-working saint, rather than the altar of Christ's sacrifice. But in each case, the development of the east ends of churches as circulatory spaces, with provision for a multitude of subsidiary altars clustering round the shrine, becomes as fascinating as the development of baptismal spaces.

The Place and Purpose of the Altar
If the bishop's throne in the apse reminds the newly baptized of the throne of God, as it is described in the Revelation to John (the last book of the New Testament), then the goal of the journey is the altar, the table that offers a foretaste

of that heavenly banquet at our journey's end.

In the early centuries, the Eucharist was understood primarily as a sharing in one perfect offering to the Father that Christ had made. Worshippers, baptized into his dying and rising, were caught up in the sense of movement that the ascension describes, and so found themselves not only united in Christ with all other worshippers, but also transported to heaven. The essential movement from darkness to light, from the drab life of the street to the splendours of the apse, with its altar surrounded by lights and incense and the offering of the bread of heaven and the cup of salvation, was a foretaste of eternal life – the Christian belief that one day you would come to the heavenly banquet where the host was God himself. Later, the emphasis on the sacrificial nature of Christ's offering would become more central, and even in the early centuries there was little doubt that discipleship was a costly business. But the cross was not as dominant an image as it was to become later, and indeed there are very few surviving representations of the cross in early paintings.

Through these early centuries, as the church grew as a community with a distinct voice, there were few recognizable church buildings. When they

Sacred Space

Top left: Christ, dressed as a pilgrim, leads his disciples to Emmaus; from the cloisters at San Domingo de Silos, Spain.

Top right: The triumphal arch in Santa Prassede, Rome, showing the new Jerusalem, articulates the approach to the throne of God.

Above: Ciborium over the altar raised above the tomb of San Niccolo at Bari, Italy.

began to be built, this was not because the sacred or the divine was felt to be absent, but rather to provide a more visible and understandable focus of its presence. In the early years, when Christianity had a precarious existence, its adherents were bound as a body by their beliefs and the sacramental life they shared within the body of Christ. When the Christian faith became more visible in the wider community, church buildings that gave visible and public expression to this sacramental faith began to emerge.

The Throne Room of God:

From the Peace of the Church

When the Roman emperor Constantine won his victory over Maxentius at the Milvian Bridge in 312, the landscape of the Christian church changed. Inspired by the vision of the sign of the *chi-rho* (the first two letters in the Greek spelling of 'Christ'), the Labarum, in his dreams, Constantine embraced the cult of the God who had brought him victory.

No longer were Christians a persecuted minority: following the Edict of Milan, which proclaimed religious freedom, they were walking in the light of day. It was Constantine's policy to forge close bonds between the church and the state. Deferring his own baptism until shortly before his death in 337, Constantine none the less made Sunday a public holiday in 321 and endowed the spate of church building that followed.

Two things of great significance emerge from his reign. First, after becoming sole emperor of both East and West, he fixed his capital at Byzantium, now renamed Constantinople, in 330. This had the consequence of bringing the patriarchs of the

Piero della Francesca, *The Dream of Constantine*; fresco in the Franciscan church of Santa Croce, Arezzo, Italy.

Eastern church under closer imperial supervision and making the sole patriarch in the West at Rome a more significant figure: it is from the fourth century that the Papacy begins to assume its modern form. Second, in 326 Constantine's mother Helena made a pilgrimage to the Holy Land in her old age. Under her influence, Constantine endowed the building of the great basilicas in Jerusalem and Bethlehem, which were hugely influential on Christian building in both East and West. For the first time in Christian thinking, Constantine's building programme in the Holy Land highlighted the idea that the church building was itself significant because of the site it enclosed and the events it marked.

A NEW SETTING FOR A PUBLIC LITURGY

By the fourth century, the shape of the liturgy in the Roman empire had become more or less standard. It fell into two parts: a service centred on the word, like the synagogue services of readings – psalmody, sermon and prayer; together with the distinctively Christian breaking of the bread. This was celebrated by the community as a body and required an apse, with a platform and an altar; a baptistery; an ambo, for the readings; and a nave, where the assembly gathered. The experience of the liturgy would have been of a community on the move, and there were frequent processions from one part of the building to another. The distinctive role of the bishop and his presbyters in presiding, together with the deacons' ministry of enabling, was becoming clearer, and the community's experience of worship would have been shaped by where the altar was placed in relation to the community, and how the liturgical action was interpreted by the mosaics on the floor or the paintings on the walls. Buildings had begun to have a distinctive character and atmosphere.

SITING CHURCHES OVER THE TOMBS OF THE MARTYRS

Although there had been some churches in Rome constructed specifically for Christian worship before 312, those built afterwards were mostly constructed outside the old city. This is not only because there was more space than in the crowded city and new sites were readily available; it is also because the custom had grown up in the age of the martyrs (those who had imitated Christ by dying for their faith) of celebrating the martyrs' heavenly birthday or anniversary of their death by a memorial Eucharist, followed by a picnic at their tomb. Tombs began to acquire canopies to keep the elements off, and from these canopies derived the ciboria, which were raised over their tombs when Constantine had brought peace to the

Canopies in the cemetery of the monastery at Khor Virab, Armenia, today echoing those over the tombs of the early martyrs.

Facing east towards Jerusalem and the rising sun became the characteristic position for the presiding celebrant, whether the altar was at the west or east end – as became the norm later. But when an altar was raised high over a martyr's tomb, with steps down from the nave immediately in front of it as is still the case in the majority of old churches in Rome, there would be no place for the presiding celebrant to stand on the people's side. In these basilicas the presiding celebrant has always stood facing the people over a free-standing altar in the apse.

DISCOVERING THE HOLY PLACES

What gave this whole movement towards siting churches over the tombs of the martyrs its major impetus was the discovery of Golgotha, the supposed site of the crucifixion, and the Holy Sepulchre in Jerusalem. Helena's persistence in searching for the remains of the cross on which Jesus had been crucified seemed to be rewarded by the discoveries made in 326, which led to the building of Constantine's great Basilica of the Anastasis. These events and the devotions that surrounded them are recorded by Egeria, the Spanish nun who was the first to record the celebrations of the Jerusalem liturgy when she went on pilgrimage there around 381. They are the subject of the fine series of *frescos painted by Piero della Francesca (c. 1412–92) in the Franciscan church of Santa Croce in Arezzo, Italy (see page 26).

Top: Ciborium over the altar in Santa Maria, Sovana, Italy.

Right: The rotunda of the Anastasis, Jerusalem.

church. An example of a church with a complex history of rebuilding on the same site is San Clemente in Rome, which was built over a second-century house where there was a third- or early fourth-century *mithraeum*, a temple to the sun god Mithras. San Lorenzo in Rome is a good example of a church built over or alongside a cemetery, but the key example of that is St Peter's. There a series of churches has been raised over what is believed to be the tomb of St Peter. What may surprise the visitor to St Peter's is that the apse of the church, as in many of the early Christian basilicas in Rome, lies not at the east end, but at the west. The altar was raised over the tomb, and the bishop presiding at the Eucharist faced east – that is, facing the people and the great doors through which the rising sun would stream.

Left: Reconstruction of the *confessio* beneath St Peter's, Rome.

Centre: Altar with ciborium above the *confessio* at San Clemente, Rome.

Right: The rotunda of the Anastasis, Jerusalem.

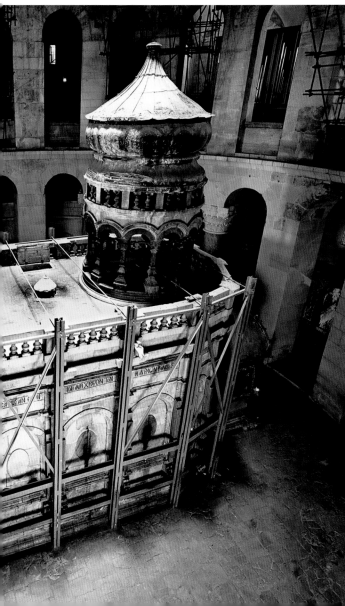

CIRCULAR MARTYRIA AND THE LINK WITH BAPTISM

The Anastasis in Jerusalem is one of the most remarkable buildings of the Constantinian period. Although much altered, we know that a circular building stood at the western end of a large complex of buildings and courtyards on Golgotha, and was believed to have been built directly over the tomb of Christ, which stood at the centre, surrounded by twelve columns to represent the twelve apostles – the twelve disciples of Jesus who were the original witnesses of the resurrection. The inspiration for this type of building was undoubtedly the tradition of Roman mausoleums, such as the circular church of Santa Costanza in Rome. The pagan tradition of royal mausoleums was transferred to the tombs of the martyrs; and then in turn to places of baptism, where the tomb-like construction of early baptismal basins identified the believer who went down into the dark waters of death closely with Christ's dying and rising.

Architecturally, this conjunction of tomb and baptism has given us the centred form, whether circular, octagonal or cross-shaped, and its transference from the *martyria (canopies over the tombs of the martyrs) to baptisteries has ensured

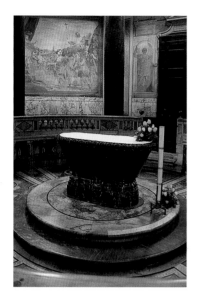

The Lion Companion to Church Architecture

that centrally planned structures continue to have a place in the Christian architectural vocabulary.

In Italy, baptismal fonts of this period were usually large structures, about 6½ feet (2 metres) across; they were set into the floor in the centre of the baptistery and raised about 2½ feet (0.7 metre) at the sides, so that candidates standing in the water would have been up to their thighs, or chests if they knelt. Fonts were sometimes hexagonal, as at Grado at the head of the Adriatic, or more frequently octagonal, such as that at Porec on the Istrian peninsula, signifying the eighth day and so the fresh start of the new creation. The octagonal baptistery at the Cathedral of St John Lateran in Rome uses an antique porphyry bath for its basin, as does the Duomo in Milan. The reuse of Classical materials is characteristic, and these fonts are normally set in detached circular or octagonal buildings, as in Frejus in Provence, and in the baptisteries of Ravenna near the mouth of the River Po, dating from the first half of the fifth century. It is a tradition that continues to the Romanesque baptisteries of Parma in Lombardy, and in Florence, Tuscany and beyond.

In the cathedral in Paros, Greece, known as the Ekatondapiliani (the church of the 100 doors) there is an early cross-shaped font. In North Africa, fonts were sometimes sunk into the ground in a quadrilobe (having four lobes, or rounded projections) or cruciform shape. Steps down into the waters enabled the candidate to sense the movement down and up into the dying and rising

Below: Hexagonal font at Grado, Italy.

of Christ, and that passing through the waters into freedom that had characterized the experience of the children of Israel crossing the Red Sea. All through the season of Lent the candidates would have been preparing intensely for the moment of their baptism at Easter, and the mysteries of the faith would have been revealed progressively, accompanied by a series of exorcisms. Christians were conscious of inhabiting a world that was a battleground between the forces of good and evil, and the struggle was real and sometimes costly, even after the peace of Constantine.

Most baptisms took place in the dawn of Easter day after a night spent in prayer and vigil. The immersion in water after professing the faith was frequently accompanied by anointing: before baptism this prepared the candidate to resist the clutch of evil so that, like a wrestler or athlete, their body would be slippery and supple; and after emerging from the water this was a sign of incorporation into the royal, priestly people of God, paralleling the descent of God's spirit on Jesus in his baptism in the River Jordan. Candidates were accompanied down into the waters by deacons of their own sex, and then brought into the basilica to have hands laid on them and receive the kiss of peace from the bishop. As they were led up the basilica to take their place with their fellow Christians, they could have been in no doubt that they were entering the presence of God, and after receiving the sacrament for the first time, they also received a chalice of milk and honey to show that they had entered the Promised Land.

Much of the early Christians' experience of worship was shaped by their knowledge of the Old Testament, and their understanding that it was fulfilled in Christ. This is especially true of baptism. They understood baptism to have been prefigured in the experience of the people of Israel, whom God brought out of slavery in Egypt and then tested in their wanderings in the wilderness for forty years before they entered the Promised Land. The forty days of Lent in the church's

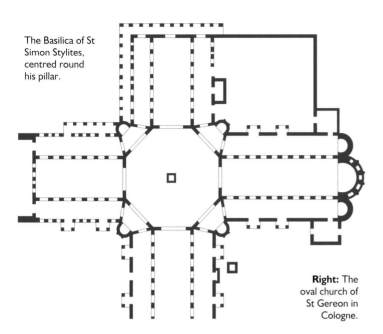

The Basilica of St Simon Stylites, centred round his pillar.

Right: The oval church of St Gereon in Cologne.

annual observance was a period of testing originally shaped by the intense preparation for those who were to be candidates for baptism at Easter. The processional liturgy of baptism itself conveyed an experience of journey, and the iconography of the circular baptistery and the longitudinal basilica reinforced the experience of personal encounter in the waters and the journey to the Promised Land that followed.

CONTINUING THE ROYAL CONNECTION

As well as the circular or octagonal martyria over the tombs or the other sites, there is evidence of cross-shaped buildings in this early period. The first Church of the Holy Apostles in Constantinople, according to the historian Eusebius, stood in the centre of a large courtyard framed by other buildings and was cross-shaped and lined with marble. At the *crossing rose a drum pierced with windows surmounted by a conical roof. In the centre of the crossing stood the sarcophagus of the emperor Constantine, surrounded by twelve *piers inscribed to the twelve apostles, which also embraced the altar. So the building was both the mausoleum of the emperor and at the same time suggested a

martyrium, implying that Constantine, who had conquered under the sign of the Labarum, was the centre of attention, if not devotion, and perhaps a kind of thirteenth apostle.

This church was widely imitated, as in the cross-shaped shrine erected over the tomb of St Babylas at Antioch. In Syria, a number of cross-shaped churches were built as shrines, such as the famous basilica enclosing at its crossing the pillar of the hermit Simon Stylites. But the other shape that evolved was the octagon, such as the Golden Octagon that was begun by Constantine near the Royal Palace of Antioch in 327 and completed by his son Constantius in 341, dedicated – rather like an old pagan temple – not to a saint but to Harmony, with a sense that it was still the emperor who had brought these blessings rather than the Almighty! The octagonal core was enveloped in

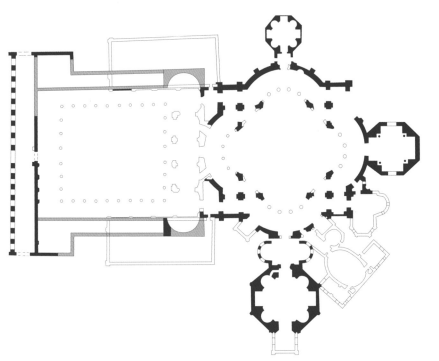

The Basilica of San Lorenzo, Milan.

aisles and galleries and provided the model for buildings such as San Vitale in Ravenna and St Sergius and St Bacchus in Constantinople nearly 200 years later. These centrally planned structures certainly carried a royal connotation and appear to be linked with the imperial throne room at Diocletian's palace at Spalato, or Split in modern Croatia, where the emperor appeared as a god.

In the West, Milan emerged as an imperial and – from the time of St Ambrose's election as bishop in 373 – a religious centre. His cross-shaped Church of the Holy Apostles, with the altar and its relics of the apostles in the centre of the crossing, has been incorporated into the Romanesque Church of San Nazaro. Close to the Imperial Palace was built the Church of San Lorenzo, a *tetraconch within a squared outer shell. More than any other church of its date in the West, San Lorenzo, with its centred design, feels like an imperial building, creating the wide vaulted space that was to be the hallmark of Justinian's great Agia Sophia in Constantinople and even Charlemagne's Imperial Chapel at Aachen in Germany, described in Chapter 3 (pages 70–71).

When the emperor Gratian made Trier in the Rhineland his residence around 380, he rebuilt the cathedral there, which survives in essence within the present Romanesque frame, adding a centrally

planned square structure to the end of the old nave in place of the *chancel (the part of the church near the altar that is marked out or railed off). This may well have been a martyrium, as a circular cavity surrounded by twelve *niches has been found below ground. In Cologne, the oval church of St Gereon, dating from the 870s, with its semicircular vaulted niches jutting out from the long sides, has a later chancel and an apse framed by twin towers to the east and a *colonnaded portico with semicircular ends to the west. This unusual building has strong links both with the martyria of the East and the imperial court, and provides an essay in how to create an open floor plan with a sense of directional movement that is also true of Agia Sophia.

THE BASILICA

While circular or centred buildings other than baptisteries are found in the West, such as San Lorenzo, the principal building style adopted by Christians in the wake of Constantine's new dispensation was modelled on the old Roman basilicas, which, since the early days of the Roman republic, had been the typical public buildings. They were large halls, used for public gatherings and official business, including the administration

THE BASILICA AT POREC

The evolution from the house church to the series of spaces grouped within or around a public basilica can be seen best at Porec on the Istrian peninsula (c. 550). There a passageway leads off an unassuming doorway in the main street to arrive at a colonnaded atrium (1). As you look from the atrium you can see the tower of the *campanile* rising to the west (2) and below it the lower, octagonal roof of the baptistery (3), with its octagonal basin partly sunk into the floor (4). The other side of the atrium leads directly into the basilica (5), with the marble columns of its aisles guiding the worshipper up to the chancel where, behind a triumphal arch, encrusted with mosaics, is the altar surmounted by a ciborium (6). Behind, on the walls of the apse, mosaics depict scenes of offering (7), while in the centre is the host of this heavenly banquet, Christ himself, on the knees of his mother. Added to the north aisle is a tiny triconch martyrium, and to the north of the atrium an episcopal reception area, a place where bishops could receive people. The whole is richly decorated with mosaics, marble and mother of pearl inlays.

Certain features in Porec reflect early practice: the access to the atrium is still relatively domestic and low-key, and the baptistery is a quite separate building the other side of the atrium from the main basilica. Other features are later: the explicit iconography of the mosaics, the elaborate ciborium and the lofty *campanile*, which proclaims the presence of this hidden place of worship.

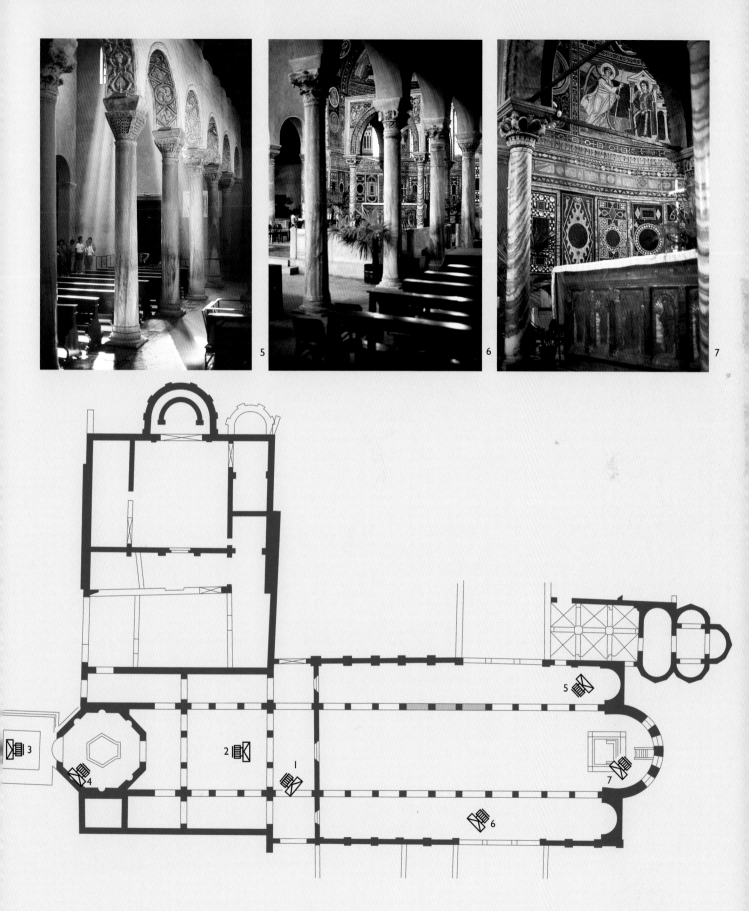

5

6

7

3

2

1

4

5

6

7

of justice. Typically a basilica had a longitudinal nave, with colonnaded aisles covered by lower roofs, so that windows in the *clerestory (the upper stage of the central walls of the nave) could light the main space. At one end was a raised apse, sometimes with a T-shaped *transept (the north and south 'arms' of the church protruding from the nave) before it. Unlike the house churches, which had little exterior sign that they were anything other than private houses, these buildings were essentially public, frequently with a colonnaded porch or entrance that proclaimed their accessibility. When used as law courts, the judge (who acted in the emperor's name) with his assessors sat on the bench that ran round the apse at one end of the building, which was separated from the body of the hall by steps and a railing. Before them stood a table for the depositions and a bust of the emperor with an incense burner, on which a few grains were offered to show loyalty to the emperor as the divine guarantor of justice.

The church adopted this basilica style for the majority of its religious buildings, preferring the basilica with a single apsidal end and the principal entrance on the short side opposite it to the model of the pagan temple, which was largely a house for the image of the god. The liturgy soon adapted itself to these buildings, and in some ways there was an obvious continuity with the worship of the synagogue. A seat for the leader of the worship and an ambo were common to both. In other ways they were distinct. There was a *synthronon, or bench, for the presbyters (the elders of the church) around the apse flanking the bishop's chair, sitting where the presiding judge and his assessors sat when a basilica was used as a court. At the head of the nave there came to be a railed area enclosed by low screens or *cancelli, from which our word 'chancel' ultimately derives, within which the various ministers of the liturgy, the deacons, the readers and the acolytes gathered. The ambo, sometimes an elaborate and lofty pulpit-like structure with a canopy and sometimes a raised platform with a reading desk, varied in position. In the Syrian church, it was usually a raised platform or *bema in the middle of the nave, where several ministers might assemble to read the scriptures with people gathered round. Later, in the West, the ambo was placed on one side or the other of the cancelli, or, as in the case of San Clemente in Rome, there was one on each side. From their place within the cancelli, the readers, cantor and deacon could have ready access to these places, from which the scriptures could be easily heard. Most distinctive of all the interior features was the altar, and although there is some

Opposite page: Basilica of San Clemente in Rome, showing the ambos in the *coro*.

Left: The atrium with its fountain before the Basilica of San Clemente, Rome.

Below: Basilica of Sant' Agnese, Rome.

evidence to suggest that at first a wooden table was brought forward for the celebration of the sacrament only when it was needed, very soon a stone altar became the norm, frequently housed under a stone or wooden canopy or ciborium, derived from the canopies built over the shrines of the martyrs.

Outside, there was frequently an *atrium or forecourt with a fountain for a ritual washing, which was sometimes linked with the baptistery. This baptistery was more than just a font: it continued to be a separate room for some centuries, as the majority of candidates for baptism were either adults, or adults with their households, and they went down into the waters of baptism naked, emerging to put on the white robe of their new life in Christ.

In a basilica like that at Porec, or at Aquileia or Grado at the head of the Adriatic, it is easier to picture the processional liturgy of Easter than in some of the major basilicas of Rome, like Santa Maria Maggiore, Santa Sabina, or Santa Maria in Cosmedin, where the relation of the subsidiary spaces to the main basilicas is less evident today.

Behind this sense of processional movement up a longitudinally planned basilica lies a vision of our relationship to God that was to prove dominant for some 800 years or more. This basilica

functioned like a gigantic throne-room, with little to impede the progress of the worshipper towards the apsidal end. The worshipper is drawn into the procession – St Augustine called the whole of Eucharistic worship 'making the offering' – of the saints and martyrs of the Christian faith. In the Basilica of St Apollinare Nuovo in Ravenna (c. 490) the procession is led by the three magi in short tunics and close-fitting tights, dancing along on the tips of their toes, who are depicted in mosaic on the walls making their way towards the throne at the apse, where God sits in majesty. If the vision is one of being summoned to attend the heavenly banquet, then the reality here and now is to join in the procession of those 'making the offering' and to take part in the foretaste of that banquet, the Holy Eucharist. Below the figure of Christ in the apse sits his earthly representative, the bishop, surrounded by his elders as Christ is surrounded by the apostles of the church and the twenty-four elders of the apocalypse. As the bishop moves from his throne in the apse to the altar, he is accompanied, as he takes the gifts, by deacons, some of whom hold fans.

The approach to the apse was sometimes heightened by the creation of a decorated archway, almost like a Roman triumphal arch. The *arch at Santa Prassede in Rome has the

major prophets announcing Christ on either side, opening the doors into Jerusalem, an obvious reference to the entry of the believer into the heavenly places, as described in the letter to the Hebrews (Hebrews 7–10). In some basilicas, a lateral transept separates the apse from the nave, giving the basilica an essentially cruciform plan, though that rarely appears very pronounced. One writer suggests that this T-cross shape is the hallmark of basilicas dedicated to the apostles, who were the first to obey their Lord's command to take up their cross and follow him. Originally, the people would have crowded into the space in front of the altar, but as the altar was raised over the tomb of a saint and the distinctive transept and its arch obtruded, let alone the *cancelli* which kept an area reserved for the clergy, they became more distanced from the heart of the celebration. And it was not just physical distance from the altar: in the post-Constantinian period of the fourth century, when clergy began to adopt the marks of secular rank and public office (as the purple we associate with bishops still does today), the church changed radically from being primarily a spirit-filled body of worshippers, gathered around the Lord's table to celebrate Christ's presence in their midst, into a hierarchical organization, modelled on the imperial court, in

Right: The substantial ambo in the centre of the nave of the cathedral at Kalambaka in northern Greece, illustrating the presence of God among his people in the word made flesh.

which lay worshippers were made conscious of their place as they approached the throne of God, or of his vice-regent on earth, the bishop seated on his throne.

The liturgy in these large public spaces was equally impressive. Everything was sung; even the readings were chanted, a tradition that Christianity continued from the synagogue practice. This meant that to be a lector or reader was a distinct office for which suitable candidates were selected and trained. The singers and the readers of the scriptures had a designated place in the church, the ambo; this was a pulpit-like structure, sometimes situated to one side or the other of the *cancelli*, or sometimes placed centrally in the middle of the nave, with steps up and down from west to east, and surmounted by a canopy.

An ambo of this type is preserved in the church of Alba Fucens in the Abruzzi in central Italy, though now placed under the north *arcade of the nave. A better example, still in place and entirely occupying the centre of the nave, is the ambo of the cathedral at Kalambaka in northern Greece, the town at the foot of the group of monasteries on rocky pinnacles known as the Meteora.

Proclaiming the gospel from such an ambo gives vivid expression to the concept of the incarnation expressed in John's Gospel (1:14): the word was made flesh, and pitched his tent in our midst.

Along with the provision of an ambo for the proclamation of the gospel goes respect for the Book of the Gospels itself. Written on vellum or parchment, not the more ephemeral papyrus, the *Gospel Books were provided with illustrations or illumination from at least the beginning of the sixth century, and frequently with rich bindings incorporating metalwork, jewels and carved ivory panels. The Gospel Books embodied what they proclaimed: they were a treasury of the words of life. After the gospel had been read, it was reverenced by the clergy much in the manner that the devout in a synagogue still reach out with their prayer-shawls to touch the scrolls of the Torah as it is carried by.

When not in use these Gospel Books were kept in the sacristies either side of the apse in special cupboards called *armaria, which can be seen illustrated in the mosaics in the Mausoleum of Galla Placidia at Ravenna (c. 450). These armaria are reminiscent of the cupboards called arks in which the *tabots, or altar tabletops, are kept in the churches of Ethiopia.

The Throne Room of God

Left: The interior of a church at Gondor, Ethiopia, showing the Holy Trinity – depicted as the three persons who appeared to Abraham – above the crucifix.

A page of a Coptic Gospel Book illustrating the judgement of Solomon.

THE CHURCH IN ETHIOPIA

When the reforming emperor Zar'a Ya'kub (r. 1434–65) sought to consolidate the foundations of Ethiopia, he reinforced its ties with Jerusalem. The royal house was said to have sprung from the liaison between the Queen of Sheba and King Solomon, and the divine authenticity of the royal house to have been guaranteed by the transference to Axum of the ark of the covenant and the tables of the law by their son, Menelik. This gives a very Judaic feel to this Coptic version of the Christian faith, where, for example, all the Jewish dietary laws are kept and the principal apostle is held to be Matthew. Deriving from the Church of the Holy Sepulchre in Jerusalem, where Ethiopian monks have a jealously guarded place on the roof of the great basilica, a large number of churches in Ethiopia are circular, with an exterior colonnade. In the centre is a cubical *cella, with three doors, surmounted by a drum. This is the Holy of Holies, entered only by the priests, and houses the ark containing the tabot – the sacred wood representing the tables of the law, the two tablets of stone given to Moses on Mount Sinai. These tablets are brought out of the ark within the Holy of Holies and form the altar top, so each Eucharistic celebration recreates

The Bishop of Lalibella and his deacons prepare to bless the waters on the Feast of Timkat.

Tabots are wrapped in cloths and carried under umbrellas to be washed in fresh water.

Below: A circular Ethiopian church with a square cella in the centre.

in that place the centre of the world, hidden from the eyes of the faithful. Once a year, on *Timkat, the Feast of the Baptism of the Lord, the tabots are wrapped in cloths and carried on the heads of the priests in procession down to the source of water to be washed and re-hallowed.

The other distinctive feature of Ethiopian churches, especially the dozen or so in and around the mountain vastness of Lallibella, is that like the rock-cut churches of Cappodocia they are entirely carved out of stone rather than built from it. The most striking example is the Church of St George, but the other churches in Lallibella and in the caves in the mountains that surround it are equally impressive. Many of these churches have retained their treasures, including illuminated Gospel Books and elaborate metal crosses, with which the priests will bless the visitor. These crosses continue to be made in much the same way and to the same designs as they have been for centuries. The primitive feel of much of the worship is reinforced by the distinctive style of Ethiopian painting. This is seen not only in the painting with which the cella, and sometimes the whole interior of the churches, is adorned, but also in the style of icon painting with which the pages of the Gospel and service books that many of the monasteries still use are illustrated. This is reinforced by the style of chanting, accompanied by drums and a metal rattle called the sistrum, which together with the slow and rhythmic body movements produces a hypnotic effect.

DEVELOPMENTS IN THE EAST

While the basilica and the baptistery or martyrium largely remained two distinct forms in the West, and the welding of the circular to the longitudinal had to wait until developments in the Romanesque age found a new way of expressing the significance of the shrine or reliquary of a saint as a point of contact with the divine life, Christian architecture in the East developed in a different direction. In the East, a more centralized plan began to emerge, and already it is possible to see in the

The cross-shaped Church of St George, Lalibella, cut out of the living rock.

death and resurrection. Around the altar itself stand the fathers of the church, witnessing to the continuity of the timeless sacrifice that is offered. The whole effect is of a continuous present, where the marriage of earth and heaven offers a still moment of eternity in the ever-shifting sands of time. The fully worked out iconographical schemes of churches, such as the Peribleptos or Pantanassa at Mystra in Greece, the last stronghold to hold out against the Turkish forces on the foothills of Mount Taygetos, date from the fourteenth and fifteenth century. Like those in the monastery churches of Osios Loukas (c. 1020 and c. 1040) and Daphne (c. 1080), they date from much later than this period in the fifth century; however, the unchanging nature of the Orthodox liturgy and the architectural expression of that theology have essentially remained the same, so they give a good sense of what Greek churches have always conveyed.

In Greek language and conceptual thought as well as in architecture, there is much less dependence on the linear, logical development of cause and effect, and much greater emphasis on the eternal present of the events of the past. The

incorporation of domes into a compact cross-in-square plan the essential difference between East and West along with a different pattern of iconography for the building.

Instead of a linear processional route to the apse with a mosaic of Christ in the conch, the Eastern pattern was to develop a vertical dimension, placing the icon of Christ in the centre of the dome. Against a background of gold *tesserae the figures seem to float in the timeless space between heaven and earth. Below the figure of Christ comes the hierarchical order of the heavenly host and then the prophets, pointing on the scrolls they hold to the incarnation, the Son of God made flesh. The Virgin Mary, the Theotokos or God-bearer, is set in the semi-dome of the apse, the evangelists in the four curved, V-shaped surfaces known as *pendentives, which support the dome – supporting quite literally the edifice of faith – then the apostles, until on the vaults and semi-domes over the apse and transepts the worshipper is surrounded by events of Jesus' incarnate life: his birth and baptism, his miracles and acts of power, and the events of his passion,

THE LITURGICAL FAN

The earliest surviving liturgical fans are silver, dating from 577, and are decorated with seraphim and cherubim. The Apostolic Constitutions says, as the bread and wine is set out on the altar, 'Let two of the deacons, on each side of the altar, each hold a fan made of fine membranes, or the feathers of a peacock, or thin stuff and let them silently drive away the flying insects so that they do not come near the cups.' Originally a purely practical device, they soon came to symbolize the six-winged cherubim and seraphim of Isaiah's vision (Isaiah 6:1–6) and are still used in the Orthodox tradition today.

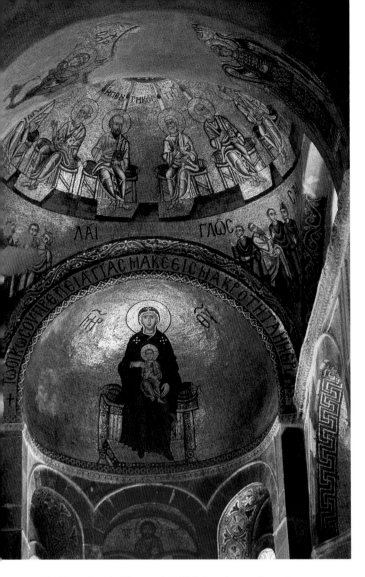

The *Theotokos*, the Virgin and Child, below the apostles in the semi-dome of the apse of the large monastery church at Osias Loukas, Greece.

The *Pantocrator*, or figure of Christ, judge of the world, in the monastery church of Daphne, outside Athens.

Orthodox liturgy is a making alive of that eternal action of God in Christ, so that the worshipper is drawn up into the ever-present continuity of the divine life; in the West, the sense of making the memorial, of the celebration of the Eucharist being a sequential series of recollections building towards a moment of revelation, gives a far more linear sense. The languages and the consequent ways of thinking in the East and West gradually diverged, and with them the styles of architectural expression. To simplify, Greek is the language of timeless, abstract reflection; Latin is the language of engineers and leverage, and this distinction shows in their buildings.

The essential building unit in the Eastern church is a cube surmounted by a dome, expressing the welding of heaven to earth. To stand under the dome in an Eastern church is to sense that you are in the place where heaven and earth are fused together, and this – emphasized by the lofty nature of Greek churches in relation to their length – gives a different dimension to the experience of worship. In a typical Greek church, the dome rises over a solid cross-shaped building, with a series of smaller domes over the apsidal ends of the aisles or the corners of the Greek cross plan. Although the eastern ends of the aisles may terminate with apses, the nave is hardly longer than the transepts or chancel, and is extended west by an arcaded *narthex or porch. East of the central dome is the *templon, or *cancelli* in Italian, the screens with a solid latticework base and pillars supporting a rail or beam like that which can be seen in the Greek-inspired churches in the West, such as Grado or Torcello at the northern end of the Adriatic, to distinguish the *presbytery. In time, this screen began to be hung with icons, and so developed into the solid structure with three doors that is familiar to us today in Orthodox churches as the *iconostasis. In the transepts or wings of the central space are the lecterns for the cantors; at the head of the nave,

among his people, is the bishop's throne, placed
centrally in the Georgian tradition; and while the
priest who celebrates the liturgy is often behind
the iconostasis, only opening the royal doors to
emerge and bless the congregation, the deacon
is frequently among the people, not only for the
proclamation of the gospel, but to offer their prayer
in one of the many litanies that he sings.

JUSTINIAN'S BUILDING PROGRAMME

Constantine's Basilica of Agia Eirene in
Constantinople is a longitudinal building with
an apsidal end that has a *synthronon* or tiered
benches for the presbyters, even if its *bays are
constructed as a series of vaulted cubes. But the
shape of Eastern architecture was changed for ever
by the substantial building programme developed
under the emperor Justinian (r. 527–65). It was
Justinian's builders, who were not experienced
architects, who dared to build the great Church
of the Holy Wisdom (Agia Sophia) close by.
Their astonishing achievement was to create an
enormous open space, uncluttered by columns,
over which the golden roof seems to hang in
space, as if suspended from heaven. It has always
taken peoples' breath away, and when he saw it,

Justinian is said to have cried out, 'Glory to God.
Solomon, I have outdone thee!' Only twenty years
or so after its completion, Procopius wrote:
> 'So the church has become a spectacle of great
> beauty, overwhelming to those who see it and
> altogether incredible to those who only hear
> of it. For it soars to a height to match the sky
> and… looks down upon the rest of the city…
> It exults in an indescribable beauty, for it subtly
> combines mass with harmony of proportion…
> and abounds exceedingly in sunlight and
> gleaming reflections. Indeed, one might say
> that its interior is lit not by the sun from
> without but by a radiance generated within,
> such is the abundance of light that bathes this
> shrine all round.'
> *De Aedificiis I.i.27–30*

What they created was an enormous central dome,
based on a square. This square was supported
by walls north and south, pierced by arches
and windows, and two great arches east and
west buttressed by semi-domes raised on two
*exhedrae, so that a curved assembly of pillars
gives an oval appearance to both ends of the
central space. The ambo was set centrally under
the eastern semi-dome, in a way that surprisingly

Top: The bishop's throne at the head of nave in the Metropolitical Church at Mtskheta, Georgia.

Bottom: Early *cancelli*, or sanctuary screens, in the church at Alba Fucens, Abruzzi, Italy.

anticipates the position of many centrally placed three-decker *pulpits in churches in England in the late seventeenth and eighteenth centuries (see Chapter 8). To the east of this extended rectangle with its curved corners was an altar in the apse, with a throne for the bishop and benches for his presbyters, like that in Agia Eirene. Buttressing the semi-dome to the west was a substantial narthex, running north/south. Always a daring concept, the dome has partially collapsed a number of times, but from that moment on, the dome became the trademark of the Eastern church.

It was the culmination of an ideal. Agia Sophia celebrated a partnership between the emperor and the church, and when the emperor and the patriarch were both present, the liturgy clearly and visibly embodied the spiritual partnership between the human and the divine that this incarnational theology demanded.

This relationship between the divine and the human transfixed Prince Vladimir's emissaries when they experienced the liturgy in Agia Sophia. After Vladimir's conversion in 988, they had been sent from Kiev to find the best form of the Christian faith for Russia to adopt, and their famous verdict on the great Church of the Holy Wisdom in Constantinople is recorded in the Russian Primary Chronicle:

> 'We knew not whether we were in heaven or on earth. For on earth there is no such splendour or such beauty, and we are at a loss how to describe it. We know only that God dwells there among men, and their service is fairer than the ceremonies of other nations. For we cannot forget that beauty.'

Around the same time, the nearby church of St Sergius and St Bacchus was built, an elegant and miniature version of Agia Sophia, which itself may have influenced other churches, such as St Gereon in Cologne in the West.

BRIDGING EAST AND WEST

After Constantine founded a new Rome at Constantinople, centres of power in the West rose and declined with the repeated assaults on the frontiers and even the sack of Rome itself in 410. As Germanic tribes flexed their muscles, so the Western capitals shifted. Milan was a major centre in the last third of the fourth century; and Trier boasts a brick basilica as well as the much rebuilt cathedral. Cologne was a major Roman outpost, and there are traces of early churches and monastic settlements at Vienne and Lyons in France. But the most significant buildings that bridge the widening gap between East and West are around the head of the Adriatic, in Ravenna, Grado, Aquileia and Venice.

The emperor Honorius transferred the Western capital from Milan to Ravenna, and its first group of buildings, erected between 402 and 425, drew on the architecture of Milan and the Aegean coastlands. Under Galla Placidia, the emperor's sister, a cross-shaped basilica in the Milanese style was laid out, of which only the nave survives. To the end of the long colonnaded narthex was added what is known as the Mausoleum of Galla Placidia, a smaller cross-shaped building with the sarcophagi of Honorius, his sister and her husband together with the relics of the martyrs – a dual purpose building like the original Holy Apostles in Constantinople. Built of an elegant brick, the interior has grey marble facing the walls and vivid mosaics on a blue ground, with very refined detail.

By 490, Ravenna was the capital under the Ostrogothic king, Theodoric, who was responsible for San Apollinare Nuovo. The *capitals feel Byzantine, the buttress pilasters Syrian, the polygonal (several-sided) end of the apse Aegean. The aisle windows are larger in proportion to the clerestory ones, giving a more even spread of light. Above all, the basilica is remarkable for the great mosaic processions – on the south of the male saints, who stream out of Theodoric's palace towards Christ, and on the north of the female saints, who move from the city of Ravenna to the Virgin Mary.

The basilicas and baptisteries of Ravenna with their mosaics would be remarkable anywhere, and San Apollinare in Classe (532–49) continues the tradition, but Ravenna's history is crowned by the Imperial Church of San Vitale (546–49), built after the Byzantine reconquest by Justinian's army, when a Byzantine viceroy was established there. This octagonal building, with an apsidal projection to the east and a portico to the west, set akimbo to the western entrance, is a refined and elegant imperial statement. Its rich marble decorations and the abundance of high-quality mosaics make it an important link between the buildings of the Eastern empire and the West. It was to San Vitale in Ravenna that Charlemagne's architects looked

Opposite page: The basilica of San Apollinare in Classe, Ravenna.

Above: The procession of saints above the arcade of San Apollinare Nuovo, Ravenna.

Left: The golden interior of St Mark's, Venice.

Below: Interior of Agia Sophia, Istanbul.

is St Mark's in Venice. Begun in 1063, this great five-domed church is another private chapel on a grand scale. Though now the Cathedral of the Patriarchs of Venice, it was built for the doge and was the city's civic church. Its Greek cross of domes, looking like a metalwork shrine on a grand scale, was consciously based on the Holy Apostles in Constantinople, a church already 500 years old at the time, to give it an antique authenticity as it received the remains and became the shrine of

Above: The Basilica of Torcello, in the Venetian lagoon.

Right: San Vitale, the Imperial Chapel of Ravenna, was the model for Charlemagne's chapel at Aachen.

when they began to conceive the Imperial Chapel in Charlemagne's new capital in Aachen several centuries later, and looked to legitimize his reign within the continuing tradition of the Roman empire.

A later basilica in a Venetian lagoon that combines the richest mosaic and marble decorations with a more basilical plan is the cathedral on the island of Torcello (639). But the final triumph in this bridging of East and West

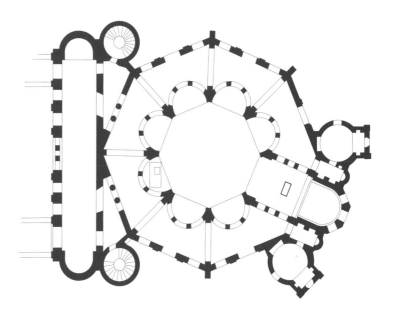

St Mark. Inside, the domes – including the smaller domes of the narthex – are entirely covered in mosaics, even if a number of these have been reworked later. This and the Pala d'Oro, the great golden altar front, give it a rich and exotic quality which hardly another church in the West can match.

Above: Plan of San Vitale, Ravenna.

Above left: A golden dome in St Mark's, Venice.

Below: St Mark's, Venice.

Beacons of Light

CHAPTER 3

The Competing Lure of the Monastery and the Imperial Court in the Dark Ages

Alongside the more urban patterns of the church's life that developed in the fourth and fifth centuries grew another and more radical expression of the gospel. Early in the fourth century a movement gained momentum in the deserts of Egypt that we associate with the name of St Antony. Following in the tradition of Jewish groups, such as those who produced the Dead Sea Scrolls, there began to gather in the desert first individuals in the mould of John the Baptist and then groups seeking the purity of a strict observance of gospel values. Under the leadership of an abbot – the *abuna* or father of the community – the first monks began to explore a form of the Christian life based on a very literal reading of the demands for perfection in Jesus' Sermon on the Mount. They saw their life as a calling to withdraw from the temptations of the world, and Antony is most frequently shown battling against various lurid demons who try to entice him to sin. Rather than engage with the world and seek to convert it, monastic life sought to withdraw in order to explore the interior life. By analogy with the time of testing that formed the people of Israel in their journey through the wilderness to the Promised Land and Jesus' own period of testing by Satan after his baptism, there were those who claimed

that the monastic vocation was the only path to true holiness. Others found it admirable if eccentric, and felt called to take on the world and work to transform it. There began to be played out in this divergence the difference between seeing the world as irredeemably fallen, in which the flesh and the devil would lead you into sin, and as created by God, with every potential for growth and redemption. Had not God himself taken our human nature and entered this world to redeem it, and should we not be continuing his work?

Some of these early monks were hermits, living in caves or inaccessible holes in the cliffs. Some, like Simon Stylites, lived on pillars or crags. Their ascetic practices drew the curious, and others copied them. Sometimes each monk lived an independent or *idiorhythmic life; others joined together and led a *coenobitic life, which evolved into a community under a rule, or code of practice. The most influential and formative of these rules in the West came to be that of St Benedict. In France, a community gathered around St Martin at Liguge, near Poitiers. When he finally acceded to popular demand and became the Bishop of Tours, he established a monastery just the other side of the Loire from his cathedral city.

The monastic movement is important for three reasons: first, for the influence that the monasteries with their patterns of regular prayer had on the development of worship; second, for the power they came to wield through their influence on education, and so on communication; and third, because many monks, having received a monastic education, became bishops and found themselves pastorally engaged in the apostolic role of leading the church, such as Martin, Caesarius of Arles and Gregory the Great.

DISTINCTIVE PATTERNS OF MONASTIC WORSHIP

If baptism and the Eucharist are the principal liturgies of the bishop's church, where the bishop presided at the sacraments and taught in the Sunday homily, then we should not forget the importance of daily prayer. The Eucharist was rarely celebrated on weekdays in the early centuries; praise and prayer at the dawn of the day and at the lighting of the lamps at sundown formed the heart of the community's daily offering. These services included the singing of psalms and canticles, many of them repeated each day and so learnt by heart, with extensive intercessions for the needs of God's people, and concluding with the Lord's Prayer and 'a coming to the Bishop's hand' for an individual blessing – a more prayerful way of ending a service than the shaking of the priest's hand in the porch at the end of a service that many are accustomed to in churches today. The influence of the synagogue was still strong, and the singing of the psalms and the reading of scripture seems to have been led among the congregation.

Coming to the Bishop's hand at the end of the liturgy in Armenia.

The monastery of Khor Virab, Armenia, built over the dungeon where St Gregory the Illuminator was imprisoned before the year 301.

Surviving traditions from different churches reveal various ways in which this was done. In the Syriac tradition as it developed in Armenia, for example, the bema was in the heart of the assembly.

This so-called 'Cathedral' prayer, with its small number of psalms repeated frequently, was a largely urban pattern. In the desert communities – what came to be monasteries – the whole Psalter was prayed as the chief means of living a life focused on God. In the monasteries of the West this led to the psalms being divided up and sung over the course of a week. The chanting of so many psalms became the work of a small number of experts – the members of the community – rather than the congregation. Indeed, there was no 'congregation' in that sense: the solitary monk in his cave or cell or the group who formed the community was the entire worshipping community. Individually guided meditation and an increasingly personal style of praying were the results of this pattern, as we can see from the psalm prayers in the Celtic tradition, which frequently reflect a very individualistic concern for the protection for every part of the body from the assaults of the evil one.

Egypt and the Desert Monasteries of the Middle East

The Coptic monasteries of Egypt give the best picture of these small desert communities, which have survived to this day. Wadi el Natrun in the Western Desert is a monastic city, within which four monasteries survive, including the Syrian one in which the English traveller, Robert Curzon, discovered in 1833 a number of early manuscripts which are now in the British Museum. Under the

Above: A monastery in the Judean Desert.

foot of Mount Ararat is Khor Virab monastery, in which St Gregory the Illuminator was imprisoned before curing King Trdat, which led to the conversion of Armenia as the first Christian nation in 301. More remote, and even more evocative, is the Monastery of St Catherine at the foot of Mount Sinai, built between 548 and 565. This retains its defensive walls, and its monastic buildings huddle round the central church, though interestingly leave the burning bush in which God appeared to Moses, the chief focus of the monastery, unenclosed behind the apse of the basilica.

Although clefts and caves continued to provide shelter for hermits and solitaries in countries such as Ethiopia and around Jerusalem, in other parts monks sought refuge from the world on peaks and mountain tops, and on cliff-top sites. In their spiritual warfare against the demons, monks invoked the angels under their leader, Michael the Archangel, and the dedications of many mountain-top churches and oratories reflect this spiritual conflict. The Church of St Michel tops a basalt pinnacle in Le Puy (see illustration page 8), and Mont-St-Michel on its crag in the bay off the Normandy coast is echoed by St Michael's Mount near Penzance in Cornwall, the Sacra di San Michele, a monastery perched west of Turin, and, perhaps most isolated of all, Skellig Michael – a precipitous rock in the Atlantic off the south-west coast of Ireland.

Cappodocia and Syria

Of the early monasteries and cave dwellings, little survives, as many were built of wood. But in the East the rock-cut churches of Cappodocia, now in the part of Turkey round Kayseri, give the most evocative picture. There, where whole cities were built by hollowing out the rock underground, the eroded cliffs and peaks of Goreme are full of small churches with fine wall paintings. The deep valleys in which some are set are highly fertile, and it was a wise choice to establish a monastic

Wall painting in the churches of Goreme, cut out of the rock.

Above left: The ambo in the cathedral at Kalambaka for the proclamation of the gospel.

Above right: A characteristic bema in the centre of the nave in a church in Georgia for the readings.

Right: The Episcopal Church at Mtskheta, north of Tiblisi, with its characteristic tall, round arched openings and pointed roof capping the central drum.

culture in a place where communities could support themselves off the land. For the most part, the churches are small and irregularly shaped, as they are essentially caves; but much labour was expended in giving them vertical walls and domed or barrel-vaulted ceilings. The quality of the air has meant that many wall paintings in and around the monasteries where the Cappodocian fathers – St Gregory Nazianzus, St Basil the Great and St Gregory of Nyssa – lived and wrote have survived. They are remarkably well preserved, and the visitor can gain from these womb-like spaces, peopled with frescos, some sense of living in community with the saints and fathers of the church. It is also possible to experience here something of the provisional nature of the religious life. Cappadocia is now in Turkey, and these monasteries have been in a predominantly Islamic country for more than 1,300 years. In many of the frescos, the eyes of the saints have been gouged out, and the human figures sometimes obliterated.

This is even more evident in Syria, where there are still the remains of numerous monasteries, including the remarkable Qualat Simeon, the open-air octagonal courtyard round the pillar on which Simon Stylites spent the last forty years of his life. Branching out from this central octagon are four arms, each a small-scale

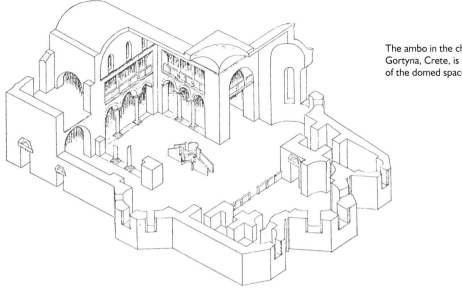

The ambo in the church of St Titus, Gortyna, Crete, is set in the centre of the domed space.

basilica, so that the effect was rather like a Victorian star-shaped prison, where a single viewpoint could command the whole, or – in this case – each arm could have an unfettered view of the central space. Even at this stage, the holy man on his pillar was a sign of a life utterly consecrated to God.

Syrian churches are notable for the survival of the bema. The Gospel Book is displayed on a stand before the screen, called the *Golgotha, in a place analogous to the ark in the synagogue. The bema survives in some churches in Georgia and Armenia, where the Orthodox Church is the inheritor of the Syrian tradition. These churches are characterized by central octagonal drums raised over the crossing of the nave and transepts, tall vertical windows framed by round-headed exterior arcading, and – even when there is no bema remaining – they have the bishop's *cathedra*, or teaching chair, set centrally at the head of the nave, facing east. An example of such a tall drum, surmounted by a conical cap, is the Episcopal Church at Mtskheta, north of Tiblisi. The significance of the bema, as a place around which to gather to hear the scriptures, is paralleled in the great ambo in the cathedral at Kalambaka in Thessaly, a unique survival in Greece in a cathedral that betrays its early origin by a basilical plan. Such a prominent ambo was clearly a feature of

churches in the East: an ambo was placed in the centre of the eastern hemi-dome in Justinian's Agia Sophia in Constantinople, and a reconstruction of St Titus, Gortyna, in Crete, based on an archaeological survey of the ruined church, shows a large central ambo in the nave.

The Greek Monastic Tradition

In Greece, the monastic tradition is still a major force in the life of the church. The Greek Church, like the Orthodox Church in other countries, chooses its bishops only from its unmarried clergy. The village clergy – the familiar Pappas at the Greek café, riding his donkey in from his rural parish – are married, and have traditionally made their living as subsistence farmers like their parishioners. The monks are better educated and live together in a community; from them come the theologians and the bishops. In Greece new monasteries are being built today in large numbers, and many of the monastic communities have been constantly rebuilt over the centuries. Some are in inaccessible caves in the mountains, but the two most famous groups are the monasteries of the Holy Mountain, as Mount Athos is known, and the monasteries of the Meteora. The withdrawal symbolized by monasticism has been a necessary feature of Greek life: as a result of the sack of

Left: The Meteora in northern Greece is a collection of basalt pinnacles on which hermits sought solitude. Later, they became small monasteries.

Right: Originally, the only access to these pinnacles was by being winched up in a basket.

Constantinople by the diverted fourth crusade in 1204, large parts of Greece came under foreign occupation and were to remain so until the liberation of Greece from the Ottoman Turks in the early nineteenth century. Mainland Greece is full of what older guidebooks dismissively call 'Frankish Castles', and while the maritime powers of Venice and Genoa controlled many seaports, the feudal lordship of the West provided some of the most settled governance of the Middle Ages.

Mount Athos is the easternmost of the three promontories of the Chersonese in Thrace, and a wall across the isthmus defends the monasteries from any unauthorized visitors. No women are allowed on the mountain – nor the females of any species – and a visitor will need a signed recommendation from his bishop. Founded in 963, the twenty monasteries include one Russian, one Serbian and one Bulgarian foundation, while the remainder are Greek. Mount Athos is self-governing under a chrysobull (edict) of 1312, and the earliest monastery, the Great Lavra, remains the only one not to have been rebuilt after a catastrophic fire. As well as the *katholicon*, or community church, the Great Lavra is famous for its *trapeza*, or refectory, where the marble tables offer seating for several hundred monks. In Vatopedi, early mosaics survive.

The Meteora is a group of basalt pinnacles, rising out of the plain near Kalambaka in Thessaly. The smooth rock face makes these pillars, whose heads are often in the clouds, entirely inaccessible, and until recent times the only way to gain entrance to many of them was by being winched up perilously in a net or basket. Given the age of many of the monks whose duty it was to man the winches, and the voracious appetite of the beetles that live on ancient baskets, it is a miracle that not more travellers plummeted to their deaths. These days stairways have been carved out of the rock, and it is possible to visit these crags relatively easily. Even so, the small amount of soil and the even smaller amount of water that can be collected and retained in crevices make you wonder how the monks sustained life at all. I remember seeing three tomato plants, four chickpea shrubs and one hen, which were the sole apparent source of sustenance for an ancient solitary monk in 1967. And while none of these monasteries is outstanding architecturally, the jockeying for living space in the cramped area around the *katholicon* is remarkable, as is the exposure to the extremes of heat in summer and cold in winter.

Among the more significant monasteries architecturally are the monasteries of Osios Loukas, not far from Delphi, and Daphni, outside

Above:
Deposition from
the Cross: a rock
carving from
Exernsteine, a
curious natural
rock formation
in northern
Germany, where
small chapels on
the pinnacles form
a pilgrimage site
like the Meteora.

Left: At the centre
of the tiny space
on a pinnacle
in the Meteora
stands the
katholicon, round
which the other
buildings huddle.

Athens. With these can be linked the fine churches at Arta and Monemvasia, and the sequence comes to an end with that remarkable cultural centre in the Peloponese that linked the Classical world with the neo-Platonists of the Florentine Renaissance: Mystra. In the fifteenth century, Greece was under constant threat from Turkish – and so Moslem – invasion. After the fall of Constantinople in 1453, the fall of Mystra in 1460 marked the end of Greek freedom for three and a half centuries.

THE DEVELOPMENT OF ARCHITECTURAL FORMS IN GREECE

In common with the rest of the early Christian world, Greece developed the basilica as its earliest pattern for church building, a pattern that was reinforced by the adaptation of Classical Greek temples such as the Parthenon in Athens. There are fine examples in Thessalonika: the Basilica of the Acheiropoietos ('made without hands') was begun in 447, and still conveys the sense of an early Christian basilica of the kind described in Chapter 2. Even larger is the Basilica of Agios Demetrios, which has suffered both fire – most disastrously in 1917 – and earthquake. It has double aisles and an eastern transept, and the outer aisles continue round an apsidal east end. The lamp-lit, silver-clad shrine of St Demetrios stood in the centre of the transept over his tomb.

Even more remarkable is the enormous rotunda of Agios Giorgios. This was built soon after 300, and may have been intended as an imperial mausoleum. Essentially a huge drum capped by a shallow *cupola, it became a church either late in the fourth or early in the fifth century. An apse was constructed from an opening on the east side, and later a circular aisle was added to give access to the central space. Mosaic figures of the saints and martyrs ringed the outer stage of the cupola, standing in an architectural frame to give the effect of a lower drum. Here, not far from Constantinople, was a circular building with imperial associations being used as a church from

Above: A small hermit's church in the southern Peloponese grows out of the cliff above the sea.

Opposite: Domed church on Cape Malea, south-eastern end of the Peloponese, Greece.

the turn of the fifth century. Did the interplay between circular and basilica forms prepare the way for Justinian's great Agia Sophia, though we know his architects came from Asia Minor? It is certainly not long before the larger basilicas begin to have a central cupola over the nave, as at Philippi. And while the basilica form survived in Greece, especially for a bishop's church such as the Mitropolis at Mystra, the dome soon became the defining feature of a Greek church.

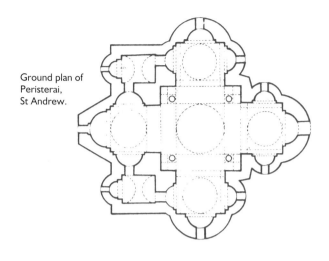

Ground plan of
Peristerai,
St Andrew.

Right: Osias Loukas, Greece.

To support a dome over a square means either bridging corners of the square to make an octagon – carrying this up to the dome or transferring the octagon to a circular drum – or else taking the weight of the dome and its drum down through pendentives, or frequently a combination of the two. By the eleventh century, it had become common to support the dome over the central space of the *naos on four columns, or frequently on two columns and two wall sections either side of the main apse. The central space was often enlarged to the north, to the south and to the west by lateral barrel vaults. Frequently the western section might be extended until it met the narthex, a large porch-like structure that ran laterally and frequently communicated with the main naos by three doors. The narthex, with its own decorative scheme of Old Testament and even pagan worthies, was the place for the catechumens. East of the dome, two subsidiary vaulted spaces were added to the north and south, each with a small apse to complement the principal apse at the east end. That to the north is called the *prothesis, and is used for preparing the Eucharistic gifts before the Great Entrance – a procession with the unconsecrated elements at the Offertory that leaves the prothesis and enters the *sanctuary by

the Great Doors, symbolizing Christ's triumphal entry into Jerusalem before his passion. The space to the south is called the *diakonion, the place of the deacon – the liturgical minister who assists the priest who celebrates and who, in the Orthodox rite, has a substantial task both in receiving and preparing the gifts as well as in instructing the assembly in what is going on behind the iconostasis.

The tall, thin, round-headed arches of St Donat in Zadar link the Balkans with Georgia.

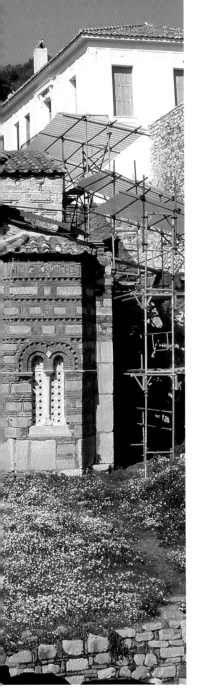

This pattern becomes known as the inscribed cross or cross-in-square design: on the plan, the dome and its supporting vaults appear inscribed within what appears as a square outer space. However, there are many variations on the theme: the four corner spaces might be roofed by subsidiary domes, or the *naos* extended not by barrel vaults, but by supporting semi-domes to the east and west. There were sometimes galleries in the larger churches, especially over the narthex, and a second storey to the north and south of the central dome increased the sense of height. Occasionally, the northern and southern arms of the cross-in-square terminated in apsidal projections, giving an overall *trefoil (three interlocking circles) or even *quatrefoil (four interlocking circles) shape, as in the remarkable Church of St Donat in Zadar.

Bands of brick or carved stone ornament sometimes articulate the exterior with blind *arcading or window mouldings, and occasionally you find majolica dishes – decorated pottery, with Arabic or geometric decoration – set in the stucco. Inside, churches follow to this day a prescribed pattern of decoration that reflects the unchanging nature of the Orthodox liturgy.

Osios Loukas and Daphni

The *katholicon* at Osios Loukas, a monastery founded to commemorate a local hermit who died in 953, is possibly the finest church in Greece. The church is raised on a *crypt with shallow groin *vaulting (see box, page 98), containing the tomb of Holy Luke among others. Frescos cover the walls with a series of paintings related to the Passion of Christ, and the groin vaults carry groups of four roundels of apostles, martyrs and holy men. The church above them was built around 1040, and is a sumptuous structure. The lower walls are clad in marble, and the upper walls, vaults, galleries, lunettes and *squinches are covered in mosaics. Architecturally, the structure is elaborate. The central dome, which has lost its

Below: The Baptism of Christ spreads over a squinch in the main dome of the large *katholicon* at Osias Loukas, Greece.

Right: Sheets of marble panel the walls and mosaics fill the domes and vaults of the large *katholicon* at Osios Loukas, Greece.

The Lion Companion to Church Architecture

mosaic of the *Pantocrator*, is carried on an octagon. Pendentives, which use the curved form to display the movement in the scenes depicted, such as the presentation of the Christ-child to Simeon in the Temple by his mother or the baptism of Christ in the River Jordan, carry the thrust onto square clusters of piers that act like pierced buttresses. Arched galleries span the north and south sides of the central *naos*, and carry over the spacious narthex, where the mosaics of the crucifixion and Anastasis are visible at close range. A second dome, east of the main dome, carries mosaics of Pentecost, with the *Theotokos* in the conch of the apse. Everywhere there are cross vaults, giving glimpses of the icons of saints, and the proportions of the building make this large church grand without dwarfing the liturgical action it enshrines.

This *katholicon* is built into the earlier church of the *Theotokos*, which lies to the north. Dating from shortly after the middle of the tenth century, it is a simpler form of inscribed cross plan with a double-width narthex with central columns and a deep east end. The quality of the marble carving in the capitals and the templon, and even the flooring itself, is splendid. Nor is the carving confined to the interior: the *pilasters of the exterior of the drum of the cupola are carefully worked.

The monastery complex at Daphni, not far west of Athens, dates originally from the sixth century, but the rebuilding of the *katholicon* and its mosaics dates from around 1080. The plan is simpler than at Osios Loukas, with no galleries or pierced passageways, and the drum of the cupola resting directly on walls to the north and south. Inhabited by Burgundian Cistercian monks from 1207, the pointed arches of the narthex porch witness to the Western influence. Happily, none of this altered or destroyed the mosaics. The great *Pantocrator* in the centre of the dome is supported by a drum containing the sixteen prophets in between the sixteen windows. Below them on the pendentives come the annunciation, the nativity, the baptism and the transfiguration, with the cave of the nativity receding into the cleft behind the

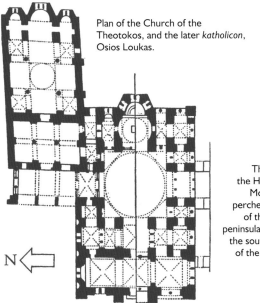

Plan of the Church of the Theotokos, and the later *katholicon*, Osios Loukas.

N ⇐

The Church of the Holy Wisdom, Monemvasia, is perched on the top of the cliff of this peninsular fortress off the south-east coast of the Peloponese, Greece.

manger and the angel calling to the Virgin over the void. Here you can see a complete scheme of mosaic decoration of the finest quality.

Arta and Monemvasia

The Church of the Panagia Parigoritissa in Arta in northern Epiros may have been the despots' church. Looking from the outside like some Italian palazzo, with several storeys of domestic-looking double-arcaded windows, the interior gives a quite different feel. Entering through a lofty narthex hardly prepares you for the way the central dome towers over the nave. It is raised on an octagon, supported on three superimposed storeys of columns and lit by sixteen windows. In spite of losing much of its marble cladding, there are mosaics in the central dome and there are finely carved details. It is a rich man's church on which no expense was spared.

Different is the remarkable church perched on the summit of a cliff on Monemvasia ('single entrance'), a mass of rock off the south-east of the Peloponese. This natural fortress was frequently in Venetian hands, and its lower town, near the single entrance – hence its name – was never taken by Sultan Mehemet. The lower town has twenty-four churches, but Agia Sophia, the Holy Wisdom, clings to the cliff edge at the top of the fortress-like upper town. Another grand church of imperial scale, the very short arms of the cross-in-square are absorbed by the adjacent vaults, giving maximum emphasis to the large dome that rests on a sixteen-sided drum, carried on an octagon of squinches and vaults. There are the marble remains of the templon, and some frescos survive, but above all, its position is what is so breathtaking.

Mystra

The last great group of churches on mainland Greece is at Mystra, on a steep east-facing slope of Mount Taygetos above Sparta. The seat of the despots of Morea since 1348, Mystra became the cultural and administrative centre of the whole of the Peloponese under the Cantacuzene and later Palaiologue dynasties.

The *Pantocrator* in the weather-beaten dome
of the Holy Wisdom, Monemvasia.

The Presentation in the Temple, from the
convent of the Pantanassa, Mystra.

Mystra: *Pantocrator* surrounded by angels.

The Mitropolis was originally a purely
basilical church, but later domed; a double-
headed eagle set in the floor commemorates the
coronation of Constantine XI here on the Feast
of the Epiphany in 1449. To the west lie the two
oldest churches. Agioi Theodoroi was built in
the 1290s and has a large dome resting on an
octagon, with fine exterior decoration. Nearby is
the Asfentiko, built between 1310 and 1322. Like
Arta, it has two storeys, but the central dome is
surrounded by four smaller domes, and is carried
over the colonnade of the basilical nave, so that
the weight of the dome is taken by the gallery
piers, which are themselves supported by the
colonnade. This makes the interior feel lighter and
more spacious than if the dome had been carried
only over the central piers of the *naos*. A fifth dome
is built over the gallery above the narthex, before
which stands a *campanile* (tower).

The other two major churches are the
convent of the Pantanassa, dedicated in 1428,
and the monastery of the Peribleptos, dating from
the late fourteenth century. The design of the
Pantanassa derives from the Asfentiko, with the
upper storey forming a cross-in-square with five
domes over what is essentially a basilical nave.
There is a fine *campanile* and an open exterior
arcade with splendid views over the plain of Sparta.

The Church of the Asfentiko, Mystra.

Above: Convent of the Pantanassa, Mystra, exterior arcades.

Below: Bominaco: apse and throne.

In the interior, four small cupolas cover the gallery level each side, while further cupolas and barrel vaults are covered with well-preserved paintings contemporary with the church.

The monastery of the Peribleptos, near the south-eastern edge of the walls, is wedged against a cliff, and so the conventional domed structure supported by two columns to the west and two walls to the east has a curious additional space to the south-west. Again, there is a fine series of wall paintings, with vivid landscape backgrounds, including some less usual subjects, including the denial of Peter.

MONASTICISM IN THE WEST

The origins of organized monasticism in the West are associated with Lerins, an island off the coast of Provence. But the influential leader, through his editing of the Rule of the Master, was St Benedict. While his remains now rest in the crypt of the Abbey of Fleury at St Benoit-sur-Loire, his cave-monastery at Subiaco remains a place of pilgrimage. His famous foundation at Monte Cassino was heavily damaged in the Second World War, and little of the former abbey survives: the rebuilding disappointingly echoes the Baroque makeover of the interior rather than the early basilica that underlay it. The isolated – and therefore better preserved – churches of the Abruzzi, like the pair at Bominaco, give a better sense of the early Italian monastic foundations, as do some of the abbeys round Lake Como in the north. The smaller church at Bominaco, a simple barrel-vaulted nave covered entirely with Romanesque frescos, is set into the hillside; the larger church, complete with an apse with a throne, a ciborium over the altar and a fine barley-sugar *paschal candlestick, is a light and spacious interior, and, together with its neighbouring Abbey of San Clemente in Causuria, shows what many early abbey churches looked like before later eighteenth-century 'improvements'.

THE GREEK LANDSCAPE

Above: Agios Stephanos, a town church in Kastoria, a lakeside town in northern Greece, showing the influence of Thessalonika.

Right: Agios Achilleos, a grand basilica on a peninsula in Lake Prespa, the summer residence of the kings of Bulgaria.

In Greece, churches cover the landscape, but there are remarkable concentrations in certain places: twelve small Byzantine churches survive in the lakeside town of Kastoria in northern Greece. Surprisingly, only one is domed, and most are so small that they must have been more like private chapels. Agios Stephanos, with its tall, barrel-vaulted nave, is probably the earliest and may date from c. 900, as does the church of the Taxiarchs by the Mitropolis. Most of them have fine early frescos, but it is the Panagia Mavriotissa down by the lakeside that has the most remarkable paintings, outside as well as in. Not far from Kastoria in modern Macedonia are the fine churches on and around Lake Ochrid. Between the two are the significant ruins of the major basilica of Agios Achilleos on a peninsula in Lake Prespa, the summer residence of the kings of Bulgaria.

A similar concentration of small churches, many in ruins, is in the Mani, the middle peninsula of the southern Peloponese. Many of these churches are difficult to find, and some have been robbed of their paintings within the last generation, but sufficient numbers survive to give an unrivalled picture of church building in Greece, where churches are as common as wayside shrines, and are built to mark a place or event by a wealthy patron rather than to serve the needs of a community.

Left: A small country church at Nomitsa on the Mani.

66

But earlier than that, St Martin was establishing a community at Liguge near Poitiers in Gaul. Like St Hilary at Poitiers, Martin found himself pressed into becoming Bishop of Tours in 372, and transferred his monastery to Marmoutier. After his death, the story of his life provided a bishop saint who could rival Antony of Egypt in the West, even if his biographer Sulpicius Severus had to disguise the fact that he had been a soldier. That was because in the fragile world of the late fourth and early fifth centuries, the old Roman aristocracy, who had come increasingly to rely on the barbarian soldiers they conscripted to defend the straggling boundaries of the empire, found themselves no longer in control. Visigoths, Vandals and Ostrogoths swept down through western Europe, culminating in the sack of Rome by Alaric in 410 and the capture of Carthage in 439. Worse, these barbarians were not just successful settlers; they were Arians, the followers of Arius, who denied the divinity of Christ.

This was the basis on which a surprising alliance was formed between the Franks, who from their centre of gravity in northern Gaul posed little threat to the old Mediterranean culture, and the world of senators and bishops. Clovis may have been little more than a local warlord, but he was a Catholic and distant, so he could be hailed as 'a new Constantine'. In this new world of smaller local kingdoms, communications became less certain; at the same time, there is a sense of the Catholic Church and its bishops emerging as the only trans-national identity. In the Gallo-Roman Church, these bishops were becoming the local leaders, as they alone could weld together the noble families and their dependants in a sub-Latin culture relating to the legitimizing authority of the Papacy.

Out of these confused shadows emerge three strands that take the Christian faith forward into the next phases of architectural expression. One is the self-consciously backward-looking alliance of senators and clergy in Rome, re-inventing themselves under the romantic banner of 'eternal Rome', of whom Pope Gregory (r. 589–603) was

Bede's Wearmouth-Jarrow, an early Northumbrian monastery.

Beacons of Light

the personal embodiment. This was not quite what the emperor Justinian imagined when he re-entered the western Mediterranean to secure what he thought of as his Western empire; and with the rise of Islam in the East and the iconoclast controversy brewing, the two halves of the empire with their by now quite different strands of the Christian faith were already parting. This left the Papacy and the network of bishops in the West as the only effective instrument of European unity. Second, in northern Europe a new confidence was building in the Frankish kingdoms, in which the competent rule of the kings and the desire for stability among older and newer landowners alike would eventually lead to the revival of the Roman empire under Charlemagne. And third, in the Insular world, including Galicia in Spain and Brittany in France as well as Cornwall, Wales, Ireland and Scotland, a pattern of monastic life grew strong in the soil of the far west. The preaching of a series of Celtic saints, including

Left: The Ruthwell Cross. Monks preached from the scenes carved on such crosses, which were the 'Bibles' of their hearers.

Right: A very early church in northern England, with characteristically tall narrow openings: Escomb in County Durham.

Patrick, Ninian, Columba and Aidan, nurtured the seeds of an artistic and passionate faith. From their ministry a strand of worship and witness was re-introduced into continental Europe by missionary figures such as Boniface in the eighth century.

It is the monasteries of St Gall in Switzerland and Bobbio in Italy that offer the evidence of just how powerful and far-reaching this missionary movement came to be. On the mainland of Great Britain, the ministries of Aidan and Cuthbert in Northumberland, of Columba on Iona and Ninian at Whithorn in Scotland explain the survival of Insular remains. Very few buildings remain, though the ruins of the monastery at Bede's Wearmouth-Jarrow, including the chancel of St Paul's Jarrow, and an early church at Escomb in County Durham give us some idea of the tall, narrow buildings with small windows that are characteristic of this period. Coming from Northumberland, and probably betraying continental influence, are the Ruthwell Cross and the Lindisfarne Gospels, both products of the Anglo-Saxon rather than the Insular world.

ROYAL PATRONAGE IN THE WEST

Royal patronage had become important as the Roman world crumbled. The baptism by Remigius of Clovis, the Frankish king, in the closing years of the fifth century was a great event. In Northumberland, the partnership of Aidan and King Oswald was fruitful. But the most significant bridge between the Anglo-Saxon world, which had been close to the Papacy since the time of Gregory I, and the continent was the ministry of Boniface, a missionary to the German tribes from Crediton in Devon, who was made archbishop by the Pope in 732 and martyred at Dokkum in 754.

Anglo-Saxon zeal and scholarship – Bede's scholarship was widely respected – was the context that gave birth to Charlemagne's dreams of the re-establishment of the Roman empire, with

IRISH MONASTICISM

The most extreme example of a local church that was almost entirely monastic was that in Ireland. Ireland's links with the other Celtic communities in Brittany, Cornwall, Wales and Scotland form a network along the western fringe. During these so-called Dark Ages, which extended from the end of the fifth century to the beginning of the eleventh century, it is amazing to think of the Christian faith being kept alive in such inhospitable places as Skellig Michael, a rocky cone of an island with a few terraces on which an oratory and several beehive huts capped the crag, with not enough

A cross at Clonmacnoise on the Shannon, Ireland.

sophisticated version of these churches, such as the 'house of St Columcille' at Kells dates from considerably later. Irish monastic settlements were often very basic, but some – such as the extensive group of buildings at Clonmacnoise on the Shannon or around the so-called St Kevin's Kitchen at Glendalough – were laid out with a series of churches, round towers and carved crosses. The best preserved cross is the Cross of Muirdach at Monasterboice. Around the churches were grouped a number of smaller cells and domestic quarters.

This is the culture from which remarkably intricate stone carving, highly sophisticated metalwork in the form of bell reliquaries, Gospel Book covers, crosier heads and chalices, and the equally striking 'carpet pages' of the famous illuminated books, such as the Book of Kells and the Lindisfarne Gospels, come. The contrast between the rugged architectural context and the intricate decoration of seemingly woven strips (whether of colours or metalwork) inhabited by small foliage motifs or tiny animal forms is quite extraordinary. This was the cult of saints who lived close to the natural world, and who understood the processes of creation and the new creation. Their architectural forms may be basic, but the imaginative interplay is considerable and cross-fertilizes with the arts of Scandinavia.

Gallarus Oratory, a boat-shaped, single cell church on the Dingle peninsula in the west of Ireland.

soil to cultivate more than a few vegetables. Monasteries in Ireland were mostly a collection of small churches and living quarters, serving different needs: one church for men; another for women; and a part of the monastery enclosure reserved for anchorites or virgins. Most of the early Irish churches were built with wood, so little survives. In some of the more exposed sites, simple rectangular dry-stone walled oratories were built with sloping walls eventually meeting like an upturned boat, such as the Gallarus Oratory on the Dingle peninsula in County Kerry, which may date from the eighth century. The more

Charlemagne's octagonal Palace
Chapel in Aachen.

The interior of Charlemagne's chapel,
showing the arches and columns at the first-
floor level from behind the throne.

himself as emperor. Instrumental in this was another
Englishman, Alcuin of York, whom Charlemagne had
appointed head of his Palace School. It was Alcuin
who helped integrate the overly papal Gregorian
*sacramentary with the more practical strands of
the Gallican liturgy to provide the unifying liturgical
framework Charlemagne desired. Royal patronage
of building as well as learning re-established an
ordered society, spreading from the German/Frankish
kingdom, the most significant feature of which was
the partnership in education between the royal
courts and the monastic schools. This united the two
potentially life-giving strands in a common enterprise
that brought a renewed energy to Christendom.

Charlemagne's Imperial Chapel

To celebrate this vision, Charlemagne built a
chapel attached to his palace in Aachen, using the
Classical vocabulary of royal mausoleums, derived
more immediately from the Church of San Vitale at
Ravenna. In unifying the empire, Charlemagne set

out to establish a permanent presence in Aachen;
work on the palace had begun in 788, but the
crowning achievement is the chapel. Modelled on
the proportions of the heavenly Jerusalem described
in the Revelation to John as descending to earth,
this lofty octagon was richly decorated in marble
and mosaics, and length, breadth and height were
all equal, making a perfect cube 144 feet square
(13 metres square). The chapel was entered at first
floor, or *triforium, level, directly from the emperor's
apartments. Here at the western end Charlemagne
had a simple throne set on six steps, like Solomon's
throne in the temple, with a view down into what
was then a short eastern projection housing the
principal altar. Ringing the octagon at the emperor's
level is a series of wonderful cast bronze latticework
screens. Inside each of the eight double-height
arches on this level are set two antique marble
columns supporting three arches. On top of these
runs an *entablature supporting two further, shorter
columns, which support the three upper arches,

Below: Detail from the gilded shrine-reliquary, showing Charlemagne.

Above: Barbarossa's chandelier, fashioned to represent the heavenly city, the new Jerusalem, descending with blessings (Revelation 21:1–7), hangs in the centre of the octagon.

The Glass House of Aachen, the Gothic choir added to the east of the octagon to house the relics.

Aachen, the imperial throne, commanding a view down onto the altar in the chapel and up to the *Pantocrator* in the centre of the dome.

and then the pierced walls leading to the cupola, so the mosaics in the dome appear even higher than they are. Two turrets flank the *westwerk, which extends out to the west to provide a narthex or porch on the ground floor. Beyond this, and still clearly visible in the layout of the courtyard, was a rectangular atrium. Towering over this, the two parts of the building – one for God and one for the emperor – sit side by side. This dual building is shown clearly in Charlemagne's hand, in the golden statue on the gabled end of the gilded shrine *reliquary, which now houses his remains in the eastern arm of the building.

In 1156 the emperor Frederick I Barbarossa gave the immense wheel-shaped chandelier, with its lantern turrets and hoop-shaped bands of candle sconces, which hangs in the centre of the octagon. Its inscription again recalls the heavenly Jerusalem, descending in splendour: a heavenly blessing on the earthly king was the essential gift for a successful ruler, and underlines the importance of

Charlemagne's coronation by the Pope on Christmas day in Rome in 800.

Originally, it seems that Charlemagne was buried in the centre of the narthex, below the throne in the gallery. Barbarossa was also responsible for getting Charlemagne canonized, and had the large shrine, an oak chest covered with gold and silver plating and reliefs, made to house his remains. In 1355 the decision was made to add a great Gothic choir to the east of the centralized building, a slender reliquary shrine modelled on the Sainte-Chapelle in Paris, where the tall glazed windows and spindly ribs of the structure give architectural expression to Jesus' crown of thorns, which the chapel was built to contain. Eventually, Charlemagne's remains were translated to this 'Glass House of Aachen', as the eastern chapel came to be called, where they stand alongside an equally magnificent reliquary shrine containing relics of the blessed Virgin Mary. As in the octagon, the reference to the heavenly Jerusalem is reinforced this time not only by the 'sea of glass' as the Revelation to John describes before the throne of God, but also by the addition of statues of the twelve apostles to the columns, those foundations of the church whose names are written on the cornerstones of the celestial city.

A forest of columns forms the narthex, or lower stage, of the westwerk at the abbey of Corvey, Germany.

Below: The crown of towers makes the cathedral at Tournai in Belgium appear like a heavenly castle.

Above the narthex in Corvey's westwerk is a spacious two-storey chapel, the principal space in this 'royal' part of the monastery.

Right: The westwerk of the monastery at Corvey.

The Development of the Westwerk

The model of partnership between the king of heaven and his viceroy on earth, the emperor, to which Charlemagne's chapel at Aachen bore witness was echoed in the developed westwerks of other churches, particularly in Germany and its neighbouring countries.

The model for such westwerks was the abbey at Centula or St Riquier on the Somme, around 799, where the Bishop had secured a major royal contribution to the foundation of this influential monastic school. Although little of the eighth-century building survives, there exists a plan and a description of how the church was used, which makes it clear that the Chapel of St Michael, in the upper stage of the westwerk, had a significant place in the daily celebration of the life of the monastery. It was here that the early morning *Office was celebrated. The whole layout of the monastery and its church reflected an ordered pattern of living – an earthly reflection of the heavenly city – in which different parts of the church were used for different liturgical celebrations.

Parallel to Centula in the east of the empire was the monastery at Corvey on the River Weser.

Although the monastery was substantially rebuilt in the Late Medieval and Baroque periods, the westwerk (873–85) survives complete, forming a low vaulted narthex on a cluster of piers on the ground floor, with a substantial two-storey chapel on the first floor over it containing the remains of frescos showing scenes from the Orpheus myth. As the 'keep' at the heart of the monastery's life, this fortified strong-room could be easily defended, and gave commanding views into the abbey church.

It was not only the westwerks like that at Soest that gave the impression of the church as a fortified citadel, standing against the flux of daily life. The forest of towers around the central tower of the cathedral at Tournai in Belgium still offers a powerful statement of the temporal power of the church. In Kalundberg in Zealand (Denmark), the ring of brick turrets around the central tower makes the church appear like a castle.

The royal association is visible in another notable survival from this period – the oratory of St Theodulph at St Germigny-des-Pres, east of Orleans (806). This building was originally a tetraconch, with four equal apses gathered round a central *lantern. Though much rebuilt according to nineteenth-century archaeological theory, and enlarged to the west by the addition of a conventional nave, the church preserves its essential Carolingian character and retains a fine mosaic in the eastern apse, showing the cherubim hovering over the ark of the covenant, where in a Romanesque church you might expect to find

a figure of Christ in Majesty. Instead a more subtle image of the presence of God tabernacling with his people is depicted (see illustration page 17).

Left: The oratory of St Theodulph at St Germigny-des-Pres.

Right: The painted interior of St Georg at Oberzell, the monastic settlement at Reichenau, a peninsula on Lake Constance.

MONASTIC FOUNDATIONS ON THE CONTINENT

The closest parallel in central Europe to the Irish monastic settlements is the series of churches on Reichenau, a peninsula projecting from the northern shore of Lake Constance on what is now the border between Germany and Switzerland. Tradition says that a Franco-Irish monk, St Pirmin, founded the monastery in 724. Of the three groups of buildings, the Minster Church at Mittelzell is the largest, with a developed westwerk and a free-standing shrine. In the Church of St Georg at Oberzell is a series of frescos showing miracles from the Gospel stories. Like many Carolingian churches, a very high clerestory (a gallery on columns) leaves a large wall space suitable for painted decoration above the low

The tribunes over the south aisle of St Cyriacus at Gernrode, where the Easter sepulchre stands.

St Michael's, Fulda: a rotunda raised over a crypt.

arcade to the nave aisles below this gallery. Like other churches of the period, a high presbytery, mounted on a crypt at the east end, is balanced by a large, porch-style westwerk.

Fulda in central Germany is the site of the burial of St Boniface. The Church of St Michael there is raised over a Carolingian crypt, and is an early ninth-century rotunda with a stout, square tower to the south and a later nave to the west. A church in a similar tradition to that of St Georg at Oberzell on Reichenau is St Cyriacus at Gernrode in eastern Saxony (c. 961). This wonderful church has apses at both ends. The western apse is now the pre-baptismal crypt, surmounted by a choir gallery, while the eastern apse, heavily repainted, remains as the presbytery, raised over an eastern crypt. The gallery apertures give glimpses of the ceilings of the

*tribunes and the triforia (low arcades) over the side aisles. In the south aisle, occupying two bays, is a substantial Easter sepulchre, with carvings of Christ and Mary Magdalen. Not far away is the pair of churches at Hildersheim: St Michael, a double-ended Ottonian church with a fine painted ceiling; and nearby the reconstructed cathedral with its great chandelier, eleventh-century bronze pillar, Bishop Bernward's bronze doors, with their cast panels, and the attractive metalwork font.

In Cologne, the ancient Roman city with the remarkable oval Church of St Gereon, the Church of St Pantaleon (966–80), though much altered later in the Romanesque period with Baroque decoration at the east end, retains a splendid westwerk (see illustration p. 263). The trefoiled east end of Santa Maria in Capital offers a link between the extended rotunda of San Lorenzo in Milan and the churches of the east.

The original plan of the monastery at Corvey, showing the substantial westwerk.

SAXON CHURCHES IN ENGLAND

Few churches of this period survive in England. Major Saxon churches, such as Wing in Buckinghamshire or Repton in Derby, remain only in part. Among smaller buildings, the Saxon chapel at Bradford-on-Avon (c. 975) owes its preservation to being used as a barn. The extreme height, tall narrow arches and small windows give the interior a distinctive Insular feel, as at Escomb: blind arcading runs all round the outside, and two carved angels high above the chancel arch give it a sculptural presence. The tall proportions and the small amount of natural lighting bear a close resemblance to some of the Irish churches. Of the larger churches, Brixworth and Earls Barton in Northampton, and Breamore in the New Forest remain, even if altered. While the lonely chapel of St Cedd at Bradwell-juxta-Mare in Essex is a bare survival, Bede's church at Wearmouth-Jarrow retains some of its original features, with a heavy central tower dividing the chancel from the nave, and the tower of St Peter's at Barton-on-Humber may date from the time of St Chad in the mid-seventh century.

An interesting link is visible with the carved wooden churches in Norway, such as Bogrund. The pattern of entwined serpents has echoes in the early carved fonts of Herefordshire, such as at Eardisly, and the small Romanesque church at

An apse at the west end as well as the east, whether or not surmounted by a westwerk, as at the shrine church of St Gertrude at Nivelles in Belgium or at the Abbey of Maria Laach in Germany, introduces another way of giving architectural expression to the partnership between the king of heaven and his earthly counterpart. The twin apses of the Palatinate churches of the Rhine, such as the cathedrals at Mainz and Worms, continue this pattern which began in Carolingian and Ottonian buildings, such as Gernrode and Hildesheim.

Breamore in the New Forest, England: a substantial Saxon church.

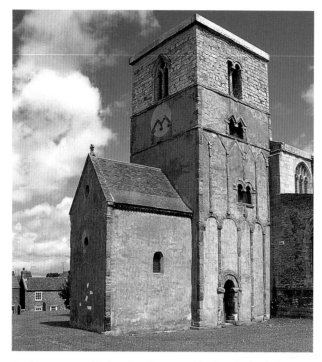

The Saxon tower of St Peter's at Barton-on-Humber, England, shows typical blind arcading and windows.

Above: The font at Eardisly, Herefordshire, England.

Left: Carving reminiscent of Scandinavia at Kilpeck, Herefordshire, England.

Below: Gamala Uppsala, Sweden. The original wooden-framed structure of the old cathedral.

Kilpeck. Such intricate interlacing belongs to the same tradition as the so-called carpet pages in the Lindisfarne Gospels, the Book of Kells and other manuscripts of the period and may be derived from Scandinavian woodcarving, with its origins in pagan rather than Christian mythology. In Sweden, the ancient cathedral at Gamala Uppsala retains a primitive form, related to the Saxon churches in England. Early Medieval churches in Sweden, such as Sigtuna, retain a sense of their Medieval integrity, with carved crucifixes, substantial painted ceilings and even, in some cases, Medieval vestments. In Scandinavia the Lutheran Reformation brought little change in the externals of worship, unlike in Elizabethan England, where the Reformation and the later Puritan assault on images and painting resulted in much destruction.

MUSLIM INFLUENCE IN SPAIN: THE MOZARABIC TRADITION

One other interpenetration in this period is worth noting: the interface between the Islamic culture of northern Africa, which had penetrated Spain by 711, and the Christian world of the

Borgund: a characteristic wooden church in Norway.

late Roman empire. The most striking and visible example is the Great Mosque at Cordoba, dating from 784 to 786, which became the cathedral in 1236 and into whose pillared hall of double horseshoe arches a great Late Medieval cruciform cathedral was raised in 1523 (see illustration page 12). Examples of this kind of reuse of buildings of the Islamic tradition by Christians are not common, though of course the great Agia Sophia in Constantinople, along with many other Christian churches there, became mosques with little alteration other than the whitewashing over of mosaics and wall paintings. In Spain, Visigothic structures such as Santa Maria de Naranco near Oviedo, with its pillared porticos on the upper level, are a rare survival, but the legacy is most clearly traced in the widespread adoption of the horseshoe arch in the Mozarabic churches of the ninth to tenth centuries, such as San Miguel de la Escalada, near Leon (c. 912), and in the fortress-like tower of the brick church of San Tirso at Sahagun.

Perhaps more than in any other age, the complex interpenetration of cultures and styles that is reflected in the buildings of this period provides both surprises and challenges. The similarities as well as the differences between Mount Athos and Skellig Michael, between Charlemagne's Palatine Chapel at Aachen and San Vitale at Ravenna, show the enduring interplay between a faith that renounces the world and seeks for solitude, and the determination to create heaven on earth, with an earthly monarch attempting to mirror the king of heaven.

Left: Santa Maria de Naranco near Oviedo, Spain.

Overleaf: The fortress-like brick tower of San Tirso at Sahagun, Spain.

Romanesque: The Language of Kings

Earthed Presence, Richly Decorated

The buildings we know as Romanesque date from the beginning of the second millennium onwards for some 200 years. While the date of 1000 may seem somewhat arbitrary, the outbreak of church building that began then is at least partly due to the fact that the world had not ended with the arrival of the millennium, as had been expected. Raoul Glaber, an eleventh-century monk, described the rash of church building as the world being clothed in a 'white mantle of churches'; certainly an enormous creative energy was unleashed, providing the first group of churches in the Christian West to have survived in a style that is easily recognizable whether you are in Italy or Spain, France or Germany, Scandinavia or England.

Several factors combine to provide this sense of universality, comparable to that which had already been achieved in the Christian East.

THE KINGSHIP OF CHRIST

First is the belief in the kingship of Christ and the reality of his presence. The dominant image of this period is not the sacrificial death of Christ on the cross, but of Christ as victor in the fight over the powers of darkness. Christ may be portrayed on the cross, but he wears the robes and crown of a king, and he looks out in triumph over the world

he has saved. More often than not, and especially on the richly jewelled Gospel Book covers or the mosaics or painting in the apse, Christ is seated on his throne in heaven from where he rules the world. He may have an orb or sceptre in his hands, but frequently, while his right is raised in blessing, his left holds the scriptures – the rule of life. Right living and the just ordering of the world go hand in hand, and it is Christ who is not only king but also judge. Frequently the ascended Christ sitting in judgement is what is sculpted in the tympanum (the semicircular carved panel between the lintel over the main door of the church and the semicircular arch above it that relieves the weight). In time these sculpted tympana become a main

feature of Romanesque portals, and most commonly display the last judgement. God in Christ has come among his people to share their life, and calls them into his presence, with all

Christ is King seated in a mandora surrounded by the symbols of the evangelists; from the east face of the tomb of St-Junien in the Limousin, France.

Tympanum over the west portal of the cathedral at Autun, France, showing Christ in Majesty.

the consequences that brings for how they should conduct themselves. Within the church itself there are signs of his majesty and his life: paintings cover the walls, and the altar is richly adorned to express the presence of Christ among his people.

No one entering one of these churches could be in any doubt that Christ rules over all things: his majesty outdoes the temporal power of the feudal ruler. This sense of pervasive kingship is evidenced in a number of ways: the rites for the coronation of a king, which confer divine

Even though he feels the weight of our sin, Christ reigns from the cross as king of all; pre-Romanesque sculpture *Il Volto Santo* from Sansepolcro, Italy.

approval as well as acknowledge human legitimacy, are developed, and the anointing and conferring of the symbols of office and authority come to resemble in several ways the consecration rite of churches. Kings are vested, and the robes and crown that the victorious Christ wears in sculpture and painting are decidedly regal. The celebration of the Eucharist is presented as the coronation feast of the king, and the acclamations *Christus vincit* – Christ has conquered – are a signal of that regal confidence.

Another distinctive feature of this period is the extensive use of gold, with its royal connotations. The covers of the Gospel Books were frequently of precious metals, studded with gems. These books were carried in the entrance procession by the deacon, who would later read the gospel from them. Lifted high above the shoulders of the ministers, they were a visible sign of what they embodied – Christ himself, coming among his people to save and redeem. Not only were the manuscripts embellished with paintings and

illuminated initials, but much attention was also given to the bindings. Gold was the preferred metal for the altar and its vessels as well. The Pala d'Oro or gold altar front in St Mark's, Venice, and the gold altar front in the Palatine Chapel in Aachen are two of a large number of such surviving. The inventories of great churches record the gifts of large numbers of *chalices and patens (dishes on which the *host is laid), many of which were fashioned from gold. And although the altar and its vessels and the Gospel Book were the chief recipients of such splendour, elaborate decoration was applied elsewhere. The rich pulpits of the Romanesque cathedrals of Apulia such as Bitonto, the tessellated decorations of paschal candlesticks, and the patterned sanctuary floors use precious marbles – often from antique sources – for their inlays in a style we associate generically with the *Cosmati family.

But the chief recipient of such decoration was the reliquary or image of the saint. In this period, reliquaries are predominantly in one of two main forms: those that are made in the shape of the body part they contain, and those that are in the shape of a sarcophagus with

THE TRIUMPH OF THE CROSS

We are so used to seeing the crucifix that it is difficult to remember that for a large part of the first millennium, there are very few representations of Christ's suffering. The small ivory panels of the passion in the British Museum show the crucified Christ as victor; the large polychrome wooden cross in Volterra and the Santa Volta in Sansepolcro in Tuscany echo the same style, as do many of the carved wooden figures in Catalonia. Seeing the cross as a sign of triumph is how John presents the passion of Christ, with the cry 'It is finished' (John 19:30), or completed, referring to the achievement of the new creation, and it is this Gospel that is always read in the Good Friday liturgy.

a pitched or roof-shaped lid. We shall return to the questions about where the shrine was placed later.

The use of gold is nowhere more visible than in Sicily, where

St Mark's, Venice.

the Norman dynasty allied with Greek skills established a powerful kingdom. The exterior of the cathedral at Cefalu, with its twin towers and steps leading up to the western portal, hardly prepare you for the spectacular interior, dominated by an enormous, Byzantine-style Christ (1131), rising in his golden apse above tiers of angels and archangels. In the cathedral at Monreale is a similar Christ in the apse, and there the walls of both the nave aisles and the nave itself are entirely covered in mosaic, dating from 1174. More Greek in feel is the Palatine Chapel in Palermo (1132–89), built by Roger II, and the smaller church known as La Martorana or Santa Maria dell'Ammiraglio from its dedication by the admiral George of Antioch (1143), in which Byzantine influence in the mosaics is strong. The only comparable building of the period on mainland western Europe is the remarkable domed church of St Mark's in Venice (begun in 1063), betraying Venice's dominance of the Adriatic. St Mark's was built as the state chapel of the doges of Venice and has since become the cathedral. As in the Palatine Chapel in the Norman Palace in Palermo, every square inch is covered in decorative mosaic, though some of the originals have been replaced by florid recreations in the styles of the seventeenth and eighteenth centuries.

Right: The cupola and dome of Santa Maria dell'Ammiraglio, Palermo, Sicily, showing the gold background to the mosaic work.

POLITICAL STABILITY

The second factor in shaping this period is the relative stability of the social and political order in much of Europe. Behind this lies the achievement of Charlemagne's Frankish empire, in which allegiance to a feudal lord locally mirrored the allegiance those rulers had to the emperor. And this pattern of allegiance was not just true of the secular order: in this period the allegiance of local bishops to the Bishop of Rome begins to develop in a way that makes the reign of a great reforming pope such as Gregory VII (r. 1073–85) possible. Under the kingship of Christ, the feudal order in both church and state developed in tandem. By 937 the emperors had claimed authority over the selection of bishops and abbots in their realm, conferring the crozier on their appointee as a sign of the imperial authority. Henry III (r. 1039–56) deposed three popes and placed a German bishop on the throne of Peter. Yet only two decades later, his son, Henry IV, travelled cap in hand to Canossa in 1077 to petition Gregory VII to lift his excommunication, and the Divine Right of the Emperor to invest bishops was challenged. A reformed and better organized church was again an international power to be reckoned with. This balance of power between pope and emperor was a reminder of the reality of the dominion of Christ over all things.

MONASTIC LIFE AND CULTURE

Third, the monastic life, which in an earlier period had been a counter-cultural force, setting up an ordered life as an alternative to the chaotic disorder of much of the secular world in which family feuds and local struggles between competing interests predominated, now became a major force in the political scene. This was partly because monasteries had come to have the major hold on education, but also because the different monastic orders that were developing were beginning to provide an international network with a powerful economic pull. In the Western world, monasteries were organized into tighter families than their more independent foundations in the Eastern church, and they provided not only the scholars and teachers, but also the clerks and administrators. These monastic families – and this was especially true in the case of the new orders that sprung up in the wake of the great reforming movements – provided a network that crossed boundaries of both ecclesiastical and secular jurisdiction.

The remains of the south transept of the abbey at Cluny, the greatest Benedictine abbey of the eleventh century.

The nave of the Cistercian abbey at Fontenay, showing simple lines, clear light and squared piers.

Cluny

It would be impossible to grasp the development of Romanesque architecture – especially in France – without understanding the significance of the great monastery at Cluny, rebuilt three times and almost entirely destroyed in the French Revolution. But its influence was enormous, as was the influence of Bernard of Clairvaux (1090–1153), a reforming abbot who recalled monastic life to simpler ways and was the effective founder of the Cistercian Order.

It was at Cluny in Burgundy in the tenth century that a new style of monastic life took root. Successive abbots built up numbers of monks and assured the abbey's security in times when a rich monastery might easily fall prey to marauding bands by making connections with rich and powerful protectors. At the height of its eminence, when Abbot Hugh of Semur began the building of the third abbey church in 1088–89, and a Cluniac monk became pope as Urban II, saying of the community, 'they are the light of the world', Cluny had some 300 monks at Cluny itself, not counting the abbeys, priories and nunneries they had founded. Of this great church, only a part of one of the south transepts survives.

Partly in reaction to such obvious power and success, a group of monks left what had

The clear space and even light of the nave at Pontigny.

Pontigny nave aisle.

The *chevet* of the Cistercian abbey at Pontigny.

already become a very austere monastery at Molesme in 1098 to found a new community at Cistercium (Citeaux), near Chalons-sur-Saone. Citeaux flourished, and began to found other communities at Pontigny, Morimond and Clairvaux. It was here that an ardent new monk, Bernard, became abbot and began writing. Pugnacious and critical of what he perceived to be the lax ways of Cluny, Bernard established the Cistercian Order as counterbalance to the great Benedictine tradition. The churches built by the Cistercians were significantly plainer than other Romanesque buildings: Bernard was suspicious of decoration, preferring his monks to build their own imaginative landscapes out of their biblical and patristic reading, so Cistercian churches rely for their effect on their proportions and the quality of light that floods the interior through their large windows, filled with *grisaille, textured or patterned glass in shades of sepia and grey.

The abbeys at Pontigny and Fontenay (founded in 1118) in Burgundy display these principles, as do Senanque, Silvercane and Le Thoronet in Provence. At Fontenay, the simple towerless façade gives onto a plain nave with two aisles, ending in an aisleless transept with two square-ended chapels each side of a short, square-ended presbytery. At Pontigny, the low structure

seems to hug the ground. Acquiring, almost by accident, the shrine of Edmund of Abingdon – a thirteenth-century archbishop of Canterbury who died there – its simple *chevet (semicircular eastern end of the church) with a ring of apsidal chapels, its plain glass and limewashed interior (in spite of the elaborate eighteenth-century screen, choir stalls and organ) still marks it as a Cistercian abbey designed for an austere liturgy. The nave has square piers with engaged semi-columns supporting pointed arches at two levels: mounted on pilasters in the main nave to carry the central nave vault, and half-height to span the transverse barrel vaults of the side aisles and give a large window into the side aisles. There is no triforium, sculpture or painting, but a great sense of simple harmony and increasing light as you move to the east end.

It was not only monks who began to travel frequently; in the relative stability of post-millennial Europe, a merchant class also began to form, and traders opened up new markets as artists, sculptors and metalworkers brought new styles and new skills. Perhaps the most important factor was the rise in pilgrimages to the shrines of the saints, and especially to that of St James in Compostela. With the holy places in Jerusalem in the hands of the Muslims, pilgrimage to this shrine

The east end of the abbey at Conques, in south-west France on the pilgrimage route to Compostela, showing the cluster of chapels around the apse.

PRINCIPAL ARCHITECTURAL INFLUENCES ON THE FORM OF ROMANESQUE CHURCHES

The development of the cult of the saints had a significant effect on the placing, shape and material of the altar. This led to the development of the characteristic apsidal east end or *chevet*.

In the early basilicas, the Eucharist had been celebrated on a wooden table that stood in the apse. By the sixth century, stone was already mandated for altars, and this had become universal in the time of Charlemagne. At the same time, the rites for consecrating an altar had become more developed, and as altars either had the bodies – or more usually just a relic – of a saint sealed in them, or else were built vertically over the tomb in a crypt below, they came to look less like tables and more like sarcophagi. Formerly the focal point of a large church or cathedral had been the bishop in his *cathedra*, seated in the apse of the church under the mosaic or painting of Christ whom he represented, and the focus of the worship over which he presided was an interactive celebration. But gradually the altar, with its relic of a martyr or other saint who had in some sense participated tangibly in Christ's sacrifice, displaced the throne of the bishop from the centre of the apse to the side of the sanctuary. This change indicates the shift in the perceived source of power to the relic of the saint who is close to God, and through whom (rather than through the bishop) worshippers felt they had access to spiritual authority. A theology of tangible realities replaces a theology of relationships and grace. The altar and the re-presentation of the sacrifice of Christ in the Eucharist that was celebrated on it became a more significant feature in the church building than the apostolic figure of the bishop surrounded by his community.

of the apostle provided a sufficiently arduous and dangerous alternative. Travel on the routes to Compostela not only spread a family likeness in architectural styles, but also meant that returning pilgrims brought new cults home with them.

THE DEVELOPING PLAN OF THE CHURCH BUILDING

This essential link between the altar and the tomb or shrine provides a major feature of the east end

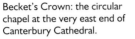
The crypt of St Benigne, Dijon: all that survives of the three-storey rotunda.

Becket's Crown: the circular chapel at the very east end of Canterbury Cathedral.

we regard as typical of a Romanesque church. In the Church of the Anastasis in Jerusalem, the circular tomb structure and the basilical hall were distinct, though joined. The most explicit example of this dual focus in the Romanesque period is the church – later the cathedral – of St Benigne in Dijon. Here, a great three-storey rotunda – almost a lantern, like the lantern reliquaries so favoured in the twelfth century – was built to house the relics of the apostle to Burgundy. It was constructed to the east of the apse of an immensely solid, double-aisled basilica in the classic style (1001–18). There are a few other circular, almost separate, eastern lantern-style buildings in France: the ruined abbey at Charroux south of the Loire has a substantial polygonal east end; Neuvy-St-Sepulcre, like the Templar's churches, was built to model the Holy Sepulchre directly; and the abbey at Ferrières-en-Gâtinais has an octagonal structure in the centre of the crossing. Becket's Crown in Canterbury Cathedral is a later English example.

But in practice, this pattern of a sequence of separate spaces at the east end such as St Benigne at Dijon was rarely followed. The distinct rotunda attached to the east end became just a hemisphere of an apse, with a substantial ambulatory (semicircular walkway) with its radiating chapels providing that characteristic *chevet* that we

associate especially with those churches on the pilgrim route to Compostela in north-western Spain, such as Conques.

The first ambulatory with radiating chapels in what was to become the definitive form was constructed at Tours to give access to the tomb of St Martin. The water level there was high, so what might have been contained within the crypt – the tomb in the apse with access from a passageway or corridor ringing it, as in the cathedral at Auxerre, for example – became the prototype of what we regard as the typical French Romanesque east end, with

The octagonal structure in the centre of the abbey at Ferrières-en-Gâtinais echoes the central octagonal structures of churches like St Simon Stylites in Syria.

The tomb of St-Junien, with a locked cupboard door for access to the relics.

Right: The Church of the Holy Apostles, Cologne, where the central space is flanked by towers and turrets.

The tomb of St-Junien, with a locked cupboard door for access to the relics.

The Lion Companion to Church Architecture

the radiating apsidal chapels visible from within the sanctuary.

One of the consequences was that church buildings themselves begin to look like shrines, with a central lantern or dome surrounded by a forest of towers or pinnacles.

Churches such as the Holy Apostles in Cologne or the cathedral at Tournai in Belgium look like splendid stone reliquaries. Reliquaries came in different shapes. Some were a long rectangular shape with a pitched roof, like the carved shrine of St-Junien in the Limousin or the metalwork Charlemagne shrine in the Palatine Chapel at Aachen. Others echoed the more centralized domed shape, as in the reliquary in the treasury at St Mark's in Venice; or the lantern or turret style shrine, as in the Lantern of Begon in the treasury at Conques. Stone carving, metalwork and architecture had a fruitful interrelationship.

What welded the circular shrine to the longitudinal basilica was bringing the shrine and the altar into the closest possible relationship. The raising of the apse over the tomb of St Peter, so that the altar in the apse could stand directly over the tomb of the martyr – a practice followed in many of the early Roman basilicas – was a key factor in bringing the altar and the tomb together. When there was a crypt, this practice was still frequently the case, as at

St Benoit-sur-Loire. But as altars themselves became more like tomb chests and less like tables, under the influence of a liturgy that had come to emphasize the sacrificial aspect of the Eucharist rather than the communal meal; and as the regulations for the consecration of an altar demanded that it contain at least some relic of a saint, the high altar and the tomb-shrine were drawn closer together. This can be seen at St Menoux, south-west of Bourges in the Bourbonnais in France, where they were joined, or at St-Junien, south of St Menoux, or in Westminster Abbey, where they were separated. What appears to have driven the development of the ambulatory round the apse was the demand for continuous access to the shrine, even when the liturgy was being celebrated. The more revered the saint and his miracle-working properties, the closer the pilgrims wished to draw, thrusting the affected part of their bodies into the holes in the

Top left: The crypt shrine at La Celle-Conde, France.

Top right: The tomb-shrine of St Menoux, backing onto the altar.

Bottom left: A silver and guilt reliquary of Greek workmanship dating from the end of the twelfth century, possibly intended to hold the bread of the Eucharist.

Arles, and moved via St-Gilles-du-Gard and Agde to Toulouse, crossing the Pyrenees to Jaca. The next gathered at Le Puy, and travelled over the Aubrac via Conques and Moissac to Roncevalles. A more northerly route gathered at Vezeley, and travelled by La Charite-sur-Loire, Neuvy-St-Sepulcre and Perigueux to the same crossing at Roncevalles, while the Parisian route travelled via Orleans, Tours, Poitiers, Saintes and Bordeaux to join the others.

The churches along these routes display a distinct family likeness, and whether they had a great shrine, such as that at Conques or Toulouse, or not, the sense of the church being focused in the centre of the *chevet* is a strong feature.

Among the principal churches along the routes are Ste Foi, Conques (c. 1050–1130), St Sernin, Toulouse (c. 1080) and the great Santiago de Compostela (c.1075–1150). Iconic of the pilgrim way is the figure of Christ with his disciples on the way to Emmaus, dressed in the garb of a pilgrim to Compostela, in the cloister of San Domingo de Silos (c. 1085–1100) (illustrated on page 25). And when you arrive in Compostela, there is the minstrel king David, perched to the side of the pilgrim's door (see illustration page 90), waiting to soothe your sore feet.

*ferramenta, or base, of the shrine. Even today, at the shrine of St James at Compostela, a one-way system operates for pilgrims who have completed the pilgrimage to embrace the image of the saint regardless of whether the liturgy is being celebrated or not.

THE ROUTE TO COMPOSTELA

All along this route, which had several starting points in France that converged once they had crossed the Pyrenees, is a series of great Romanesque churches. The southern route gathered at St Trophime at

Left: The westwerk of St Gertrude, Nivelles, Belgium.

Right: Pilgrims gathering in the narthex pass John the Baptist, who announces the coming of Christ, sculpted on the *trumeau* that supports the tympanum as they enter the basilica at Vezelay.

Below: The minstrel King David on the south transept portal of the Cathedral of St James, Compostela, Spain.

THE IMPERIAL LEGACY: THE WESTWERK

If the *chevet* was a particularly French contribution to the development of the apsidal end of a basilica, then the most significant contribution from Germany was the westwerk (see Chapter 3, page 72).

From the Palatine Chapel at Aachen onwards, with its imperial throne at gallery level on the western side of the octagon, there developed in the Carolingian and Ottonian periods a style of building in which an equally imposing place – almost a palace in its own right – was built for the emperor at the west end. A central tower or tower block, flanked by a pair of turrets containing staircases, provided an extended porch or narthex on the entrance level and a 'royal box' as it were on the first-floor level – which at Aachen could be entered directly from the royal apartments – from where the emperor could enjoy a commanding view of the altars at both levels, the dome and the ambo.

St Gertrude, Nivelles, in Belgium (1046) is one example of this, and the westwerk at St Pantaleon in

Cologne is another (see page 263). A series of great imperial cathedrals down the Rhine – Speyer, Worms and Mainz (1181+) – continue the tradition. With a lantern tower over the crossing, and additional towers or turrets attached to the transepts (as at Canterbury or Exeter in England) or either side of the apse (as at St Benoit-sur-Loire) an equally imposing feature at the west end signalled the partnership between the human and divine kings. The porch was a place where kings were welcomed, and it was a small step from there to developing an iconography of kingship at the western portal. Pilgrims arriving at the basilica at Vezelay met in the narthex, surrounded by the symbols of the kingship of Christ, with John the Baptist displaying the *Agnus Dei* (Lamb of God) on a salver on the **trumeau*, the central sculpted pier supporting the **lintel* of the tympanum (c. 1120), like some heavenly butler.

Variations on this theme in France include the large tower porch at St Benoit-sur-Loire, where a forest of columns with carved capitals provides a tunnelled narthex and supports an elegant vaulted chamber at first-floor level, and Moissac, where a richly sculpted southern porch has a *trumeau* that supports one of the finest sculpted tympana of Christ in Majesty. At his feet, the twenty-four elders of Revelation hold their rebecs (stringed instruments) in a remarkably nonchalant series of poses as they crane

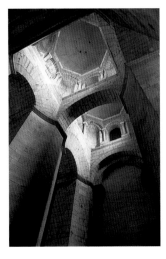

Below: The west towers of St Front, Perigueux, rising over the site of the shrine.

Top left: The elongated, almost Chinese-looking figure of a prophet on the *trumeau* at the Abbey of Moissac, France.

Above: The massive narthex of the Abbey of Moissac, France.

their necks upwards. The *trumeau* supporting the lintel is perhaps the most remarkable of all: on the sides of the pillar, two elongated figures of prophets, with strangely oriental features (surprising in a time before there was much travel between East and West) provide the support for the revelation of the majesty of God. Behind this portal is a square narthex with a central ribbed vault, and again a chamber above. Different, though equally imposing, is the narthex at Tournus, where three bays of low groin vaulting with a chapel of St Michael above lead to a lofty nave as you pass from darkness to light.

Of a different character altogether is the remarkable westwerk of St Front, now the cathedral, at Perigueux. Here a tall, many-storeyed tower with decidedly Classical details in its pilasters rises east of an early atrium, and leads to an unusual Greek-cross church with five domes. The tower was not simply a grand entrance: it rose over the shrine of St Front. The *quincunx of domes to the east held the main body of worshippers who faced westwards, towards the shrine: pilgrims who were only interested in the shrine could gather in the western atrium and have free access to the tomb without entering the main worship space, though none of this is visible from the existing twentieth-century liturgical layout, which – although there is an altar under the central dome – perpetuates the later eastern orientation.

To be greeted by the figure of Christ in Majesty as you approached the church was to be confronted by the fact that Christ is the door; he is the gateway from this life to heaven, as the Gospel of John makes plain. In the same way, the westwerk where you encounter the king becomes the west porch with the tympanum of Christ in Majesty. The gates of heaven are open wide to receive the king as he enters; and – as in any triumphant procession – the victor takes with him those he has ransomed. The portal at Autun (c. 1120–32) may point the way; the west portal at St Trophime, Arles (c. 1170–80), modelled on a Roman arch, turns judgement into triumph (see illustration page 173).

FONTS, ALTARS AND AMBOS

It is not only their construction and iconography that make Romanesque churches speak of the reign of God; their liturgical furnishings and fittings also do the same. Romanesque fonts are substantial and may speak of the struggle against the forces of evil, as does the font at Eardisley in Herefordshire, or of the new creation, as do the Tournai marble fonts of East Meon and Winchester; or they may be in the shape of a church with an apse, such as Le Dorat, or represent entering the heavenly city. Even when they are large metal tubs, such as that at Hildersheim, with its cast reliefs, they are substantial presences: you cannot ignore them or mistake them for a holy water basin, known as a *stoup.

The same is true of altars: a particularly fine altar, with carved panels on the sides and architectural arcading and strapwork on the front, is hidden in the first-floor chapel dedicated to St Michael in the westwerk of the church at Bessejouls, near Espallion in south-west France. In Catalonia there survive a number of painted altar fronts as well.

The ambos, or paschal pulpits, together with the great paschal candlesticks, are a particular delight in the Abruzzi, in central Italy. The paschal ambo at Santa Maria del Lago at Moscufo is particularly fine, but there are good ambos at – among others – San Clemente in Causuria, Santa Maria in Porclaneta and Alba Fucens.

As well as the carved stone and metalwork shrines that survive, there is some impressive Romanesque metalwork. There are the great candelabra and the seven-branched candlesticks that are a feature of the choir in north Germany and Scandinavia; there are Gospel Book covers and gilt altar fronts. There are reliquaries – especially the bell reliquaries of the Celtic tradition – and the cast crosier heads.

Opposite page:
Left: The cast metal font at Hildersheim, Germany.

Top: The westwerk of the tower at Bessejouls, in south-west France on the pilgrimage route to Compostela.

Bottom: The Romanesque altar in the first-floor chapel of the westwerk at Bessejouls.

This page:
Right: The paschal ambo at Santa Maria del Lago, Moscufo, Italy.

ARCHITECTURE OF THE ROMANESQUE

Architecturally, the language of Romanesque is one of solid, earth-bound, sculpted mass. Walls and masses are pierced with openings, raised on crypts and surrounded by towers. The arcade begins as a wall, pierced with a series of arched openings, as in many simpler churches. The vocabulary is squares (cubes) and circles (domes).

Italy

The great atrium before the Basilica of San Ambrogio in Milan is a conscious echo of the early Roman basilicas, and the church there had an almost continuous development from the late fourth century onwards. You gather in the atrium, and – as on Palm Sunday, when the whole company processes into the basilica as if they are accompanying Christ entering Jerusalem on a donkey in triumph – this forecourt tips you forward into the basilica. The abbey church at Pomposa in the Po delta, with its decorative brickwork and detached *campanile* – the number of apertures increasing in each successive storey – is characteristic of Italian plans, with its three colonnaded aisles ending in apses without any transept, and a rich scheme of wall decoration as in the basilicas in Ravenna nearby. San Zeno in Verona is

Above: Simple pierced rubble walls form the arcade of this Swiss church.

renowned for its remarkable bronze doors, and also has that characteristic Italian raised choir over a colonnaded semi-crypt, as in the cathedral in Modena or the Pieve di Santa Maria in Arezzo, so that the worshipper in the nave can see both the liturgical action in the raised choir and into the cavernous crypt that houses the shrine below.

In Apulia, the abundance of white limestone set against the azure of the Adriatic Sea and sky makes for a wonderful series of churches. The cathedrals at Trani, Molfetta, Bitonto and the shrine church of San Niccolo at Bari, to name but a few, have tall arcaded exteriors with a T-shaped

Right: The atrium, or forecourt, provides gathering space before the Basilica of San Ambrogio, Milan, Italy.

Below: A cast bronze panel from the doors of the Basilica of San Zeno, Verona.

Below right: The west front and *campanile* of the cathedral at Trani, Aquileia.

Clemente in Causuria, not far from Popoli, and two churches at Bominaco in the hills above. The larger church in Bominaco has a finely proportioned layout, with a tall barley-sugar twist paschal candlestick, a ciborium over a solid altar block, and a carved throne in the apse; while the smaller church, set into the hillside, is entirely covered in frescos, including a remarkably late-feeling deposition from the cross. Another fine church with a large number of its frescos surviving in a decorative scheme dating from 1072 to 1089, which at one stage covered the entire interior, is San Angelo in Formis, not far from Naples, which came under the aegis of the abbey at Montecassino. Here the paintings are partly influenced by Byzantine

transept at the east end from which projects a shallow apse, like some of the very early basilicas. Some of the central naves are roofed with a series of domes, but the light, finely worked ciboria over the principal altars, the remarkable Cosmati work in the pavements of the sanctuary, the episcopal thrones, the pulpits and the paschal candelbra make for a scale and clarity that is quite unlike anything in the east and owes more to the Lombard style of northern Italy.

In central Italy, there is a remarkable set of churches in the Abruzzi. They include San

Above: The paschal candlestick, ciborium and altar in Santa Maria Assunta, Bominaco, illustrate the liturgical ensemble. The throne in the apse is shown on page 65.

Right: The story of Jonah from the steps to the paschal ambo, Santa Maria del Lago, Moscufo, Abruzzi.

del Lago at Moscufo, where the steps up to the ambo are carved with the story of Jonah, who was cast overboard and swallowed by a great fish only to be spewed up three days later. This Old Testament story was told by the early church as prefiguring the resurrection of Christ.

In some Italian churches, the early font survives as a pool fitted into the floor in a separate building set aside as a baptistery. Such a succession of spaces can be seen at the cathedral in Porec in the Istrian peninsula (see Chapter 2, pages 34–35), now in Croatia, or in Grado, at the head of the Adriatic, and near the early basilica at Aquileia, where the pulpit appears to have a closer association with the proclamation of the gospel, as it has the symbols of the evangelists carved on all four sides of its quadrilobe form.

In other churches, the font is a sizeable basin, sometimes with florid sculpture, such as that in the Church of San Frediano in Lucca, where the paschal associations of baptism and its

style, though the iconographic scheme is decidedly Western.

The church at Alba Fucens, converted from a pagan temple, stands above an upland plain and is chiefly remarkable for its Cosmati screens and double-sided ambo (see Chapter 2, page 39), which may once have stood centrally in the nave, like that at the Cathedral of Kalambaka (see Chapter 2, page 39) in central Greece at the foot of the Meteora. At the foot of Monte Velino stands Santa Maria in Porclaneta, with its exterior decoration round the apse and a lacy ciborium over the altar. The chief marvel here is the carved ambo, with scenes from the paschal readings, as at Santa Maria

Romanesque: The Language of Kings

95

PASCHAL CANDLES AND THE EXULTET

The placing of pulpits with a strong paschal reference in their sculpture and decoration opposite paschal candlesticks makes it clear that the chief function of such pulpits was not the preaching of sermons so much as the proclamation of the *Exultet, or solemn blessing of the paschal candle, which was a key feature of the Easter liturgy. The pulpit in the cathedral at Ravello has a sculpted angel with a pricket for a small candle, inscribed with the words of the deacon's acclamation: 'Lumen Christi' – the light of Christ. After the lighting of the great paschal candle, the deacon mounted the pulpit and sang the praises of God for the victory of the light from a text inscribed on a great roll. As the roll was unwound over the edge of the pulpit's desk, the worshippers below were able to see illustrations of the story of God's deliverance, from the fall through the exodus to the resurrection, as it unfolded, since the illustrations of the stories were painted upside down to the deacon who sang from the text. Several of these exultet rolls survive, and they stand in the tradition of Jewish Passover scrolls, which frequently had vivid illustrations of the exodus, primarily for the benefit of the children present.

Top right: The ambo, with the symbols of the evangelists carved on its quadrilobe projections, in the basilica at Grado.

Right: The font at San Frediano, Lucca, with the escape of the children of Israel through the Red Sea carved in great detail on the basin.

antetype in the events of the exodus are splendidly illustrated in the carvings of the passage of the children of Israel through the Red Sea. Rising out of the waters in the font is a central column in the shape of a flame, and on the canopy sits Christ the Good Shepherd: baptism is not only about being saved from the waters of death and being transferred into the kingdom of light; it is also about being made a member of Christ's flock.

Perhaps the most remarkable group of Romanesque buildings in Italy is that at Pisa, where the cathedral, its *campanile* – the famous leaning tower – and the baptistery are set on the edge of the city. The cathedral was designed by a Greek architect, and the double aisles have echoes of early basilicas such as those in Thessalonika. Here the exterior arcading, especially on the west front, is typical of Tuscan Romanesque, in which

Above: The relationship of the duomo to the detached baptistery in the cathedral complex at Pisa.

Right: The Abbey of San Antimo, Montalcino, Tuscany, is almost Burgundian in its austerity.

Below right: The south transept and *campanile* at Pisa.

tiers of arcading became a hallmark of that region, as in San Michaele in Lucca. Equally remarkable is the vast baptistery, a successor to the early baptisteries at Ravenna, and paralleled by those at Florence and Pistoia, for example, set on the main axis west of the cathedral, replacing an earlier one to the north of the new cathedral. At that time the Archbishop of Pisa, together with Venice a prominent sea power, was also the patriarch of the newly founded jurisdiction of Jerusalem, and it may not be too fanciful to detect similarities with the Dome of the Rock.

Other fine Tuscan churches are San Miniato al Monte in Florence, which is entirely cased in marble inside, and the almost Burgundian-style Abbey of San Antimo, not far from Montalcino. For the most part, Italian Romanesque follows the classical basilical tradition of open wooden roofs, so the novel vaulted roof of the narthex at Casale Monferrato (c. 1200) is a rare exception. Here, ribs criss-cross the space in a manner reminiscent of the narthexes of some Armenian churches, perhaps

ROMANESQUE VAULTING

In northern Europe particularly, stone vaulting gradually replaced the low-pitched wooden roofs of the Romanesque churches. Stone was less vulnerable to fire and provided a better acoustic. But a simple barrel vault could only span a relatively narrow width, such as an aisle or the ambulatory of a crypt, without risking collapse. A series of cross vaults, like those in the nave of Tournus, was one solution, rarely followed. The alternative that in the end proved more promising was to raise a barrel vault on a clerestory, or even intrude the clerestory lighting into the barrel vault itself, leading to a criss-cross of tunnels at right angles. From this it was a short step to a basic pattern of groin vaults, with the stress distributed equally over the square.

Below: The unusual cross-vaulted roof of the narthex at Casale Monferrato.

an idea brought back from the East by returning crusaders.

The dome of Agia Sophia in Constantinople is the earliest example of an ambitious ribbed vault, and the use of ribbed vaulting was taken up later by Islamic architects, as in the *mihrab* (the niche in a mosque that faces towards Mecca) of the mosque at Cordoba. Vaults such as that at Torres del Rio in Spain (twelfth century) show Islamic influences working their way north. But it was the Armenians in terms of Christian architecture who first developed ribbed vaulting systematically. An Armenian architect worked on the vaults of Agia Sophia around 975, and a pattern of criss-cross vaults, from which Casale Monferrato may have been derived, was developed especially for the narthex.

Another distinctive feature of Italian Romanesque is the lofty and frequently detached *campanile*. Frequently the pierced openings increase in number and diminish in size the higher you go. This artificial trick of perspective makes your eye travel up, and so draws your vision up to heaven, as in the cathedral at Trani (see illustration page 94).

Right: The inspiration for the façade of the abbey church of St Gilles-en-Provence may have been the backdrop of a Roman theatre.

Below: Continuity with the Classical world: the west portal of St Gabriel, near Tarascon, Provence.

France: Provence

Three churches in Provence provide good examples of continuity with the Classical world that this Mediterranean part of France illustrates.

First, the small chapel of St Gabriel near Tarascon has a pediment mounted on two Classical columns within the arched recess of the west front. The round-headed archway over the door itself with its sculpted tympanum sits within this frame. It feels as if you are entering a Classical tomb set within the arched opening of the main church itself. Classical elements are used to emphasize the continuity between the Roman world and the Early Medieval, as the chapel dates from around 1200.

The recently conserved west portal of the church of St Trophime in Arles has the same Classical feel (see illustraion page 173). A single triumphal arch, where Christ in Majesty sits in the centre of the tympanum surrounded by the symbols of the four evangelists, known as the tetramorph, projects from the plain façade under a pediment. The high-quality carving of the vertical figures of the apostles under the jambs, separated by Classical columns of a blueish marble, seems almost Early Medieval in style. Scenes of the last judgement with processions of the righteous and the damned continue the Classical tradition of the processions of

Right: The star vault at Torres del Rio, Spain, reveals Arabic influence.

Above: Processions of the righteous and the damned link the west portal of St Trophime, Arles, Provence, with Roman triumphal arches.

Romanesque: The Language of Kings

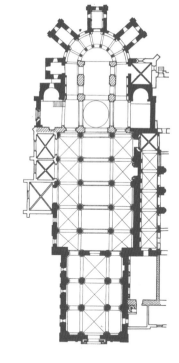

Above: The lateral cross vaults in the aisles of the abbey at Tournus, Burgundy.

Plan of St Philibert, Tournus.

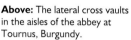

Right: Nave of the basilica at Vezelay.

captives, and space is found not only for the patron, St Trophime, but also for St Stephen, some of whose relics were here.

An even closer identification with Italy, and with Classical Rome, comes with the western façade of the abbey church at St-Gilles-du-Gard. Three arched openings, with sculpted tympana over each portal, are framed by two square

Christ in Majesty in the apse of Berze-la-Ville.

Autun: nave capital of the Annunciation.

towers. Over the central arch runs a *hood mould, embracing a narrative *frieze supported on Classical columns that shelter figures of the apostles and panels of richly flowing foliage carving. Either side of the main portal the columns stand on lions as in the cathedrals of Lombardy, such as Modena or Fidenza. Here the convention of the triumphal arch is linked to the backdrop of the Roman stage. The theatre at Orange, not far distant, may have provided a model, and the whole front is remarkable for its complete sequence of the passion narrative.

Tournus

The development of the abbey church of St Philibert at Tournus offers an insight into the liturgical development of the building and the successive attempts to solve the problems of vaulting in stone, which – in view of the large number of disastrous fires in churches with wooden ceilings – became highly desirable.

As it stands, the church has three clearly distinguishable building stages: the deep, apsidal east end; the lofty nave; and the heavy, two-storeyed western narthex. In 950, the monks of St Philibert-de-Grandlieu, who had been driven inland from the Atlantic coast, began the rebuilding of their church in Tournus after a fire, setting out the ground plan of the east end that survives today with five square-ended apsidal chapels over a crypt. At the west end a narthex, surmounted by a chapel of St Michael, survives from an earlier period, but the central nave and aisles were clearly rebuilt, with an interesting series of parallel tunnel vaults on diaphragm arches, around 1020 or later. The crossing probably dates from 1120. Virtually every possibility of vaulting in this period is shown here, as the monks tried to find solutions that were both robust and fireproof after a series of raids and sackings.

Because of the influence of Cluny, the Romanesque churches of Burgundy exhibit most of the characteristics of this style. The large church at La Charite-sur-Loire, though partially destroyed, offers a vision of the enormous scale

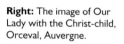

Right: The image of Our Lady with the Christ-child, Orceval, Auvergne.

Below: West front of Paray-la-Monial, Burgundy.

Top: The pyramidal roofs at Loches, near the Loire.

Bottom: Panels from the painted roof at Zills in Switzerland.

of these buildings; the perfectly shaped basilica at Paray-la-Monial illustrates the spatial geometry; the great basilica at Vezelay, renowned for its relics of Mary Magdalene and its hilltop site, has some of the finest sculpture, with its narthex in which the pilgrims gathered, its barrel-vaulted nave and the luminous, later, eastern end to draw the eye to the saint's shrine at the end of the pilgrimage; the small priory church of Berze-la-Ville, the retreat of the abbots of Cluny, still has an entirely painted interior; and the cathedral at Autun, as well as having the most stunning Romanesque sculpture in France, retains a strongly antique feel through the use of Classical-style pilasters on the piers in the nave, which carry some of the best-known capitals of the period.

Another group are the churches of the volcanic region of the Auvergne, such as St Michel at Le Puy; Ste Nectaire, with its polychromatic stonework and compact plan; Orceval, with its fine metal-covered image of Our Lady; and Issoire, where traces of the original polychrome painting inspired the nineteenth-century restorers to recreate something like the garish original.

The best example of a painted church in France outside Burgundy is St-Savin-sur-Gartemps, where the marbling effect on the columns on the nave is complemented by the most complete painted wooden roof in France. The other great painted roof of the period, much more rustic as well as alpine in style, is at Zills in Switzerland, where the figures look more like some modern coloured wood-cuts.

Notre Dame la Grand in Poitiers (c. 1130–45) preserves a fully decorated western façade, complete with its corner turrets, and on the Loire are some remarkable frescoed interiors at Lavardin, Montoire and St-Jacques-de-Guerets, and south of the Loire at Tavant and Le Liget in the Touraine.

In the west of France, and presumably influenced by Arab architecture emerging from Spain rather than by the Eastern church, is a remarkable series of domed churches, of which the former abbey at Souillac (c. 1130), the cathedrals at Cahors (1119) and Angouleme

The marbled columns and painted roof of St-Savin-sur-Gartemps.

(c. 1105) and St Front at Perigueux (c. 1120) are the most obvious examples. While Perigueux has a quincunx of domes in a cross-shape, giving it a more Eastern feel such as St Mark's, Venice, others have their domes in a straight row. This certainly provided one solution to vaulting over a wider nave than would have been possible with a simple barrel vault. Oddest of all is the church in Loches, perched on a limestone cliff south of the Loire, where the nave is vaulted with a sequence of pyramids.

England and Normandy

Different in style is the Romanesque of Normandy, more familiarly known in England as Norman, with its hallmarks of round-headed arches with a zig-zag design. Most famous in England are the great cathedrals of Durham, Southwell Minster, Peterborough, Ely (the nave and west end), Chichester and Gloucester, though all have later additions. St Cross at Winchester and Romsey Abbey are equally fine, but some of the best work is in the smaller churches such as Kilpeck in Herefordshire, Barfreston in Kent or the Chapel of St John in the Norman Tower of London, which are more characteristic of the English version of the style. At Barfreston, as on the west front of Iffley in Oxfordshire, strong mouldings over roundels and round-headed windows give a sense of local style, as does the rectangular east end. Kilpeck, with its apsidal east end and florid, interlaced carving on its doorway, feels closer to the continental – especially Nordic – style. In Scandinavia, the largest churches of this period are the cathedrals at Lund in Sweden and Trondheim in Norway, but more evocative of that old Norse world are the wooden stave-churches such as Borgund (see page 76).

Very distinctive of the English contribution are the deep tubs of fonts, frequently quite plain, but sometimes very elaborately carved, as at Eardisley (see page 76), Shobden (above) and Castle Frome in Herefordshire, or in the remarkably preserved – because the stone is very hard – fonts in Winchester Cathedral and East Meon in Hampshire (opposite), made out of Tournai marble. The font at Melbury Bubb in Dorset, like the projecting Viking-prow-style sculptures at Kilpeck, again feels distinctly Nordic. It comes from a strange, dark, pagan world of twisted serpents and suffocating vegetation from which baptism into Christ delivers the believer.

In its native Normandy, a characteristic of the style is a strong west front, frequently framed by twin towers, with an almost fortified feel. One of the finest churches, the former Abbey of Jumièges, has a pair of towers in this position,

Clockwise from top:
The Abbey of St Cross at Winchester; the west front of Iffley Church, near Oxford; the interior of Kilpeck, Herefordshire; the Romanesque font at Shobden, Herefordshire.

Above: Detail of the doorway at Kilpeck.

Left: The font at East Meon, Hampshire (top) and detail of the font (bottom).

Right: Tribune at the cathedral of Limburg-an-die-Lahn.

capped by octagons, making the central porch structure appear not unlike a German westwerk. But a classic church such as the former Abbey of St George at St-Martin-de-Boscheville or the Abbaye-aux-hommes at Caen, with their tall, thin spires is typical. Inside, the white Caen stone makes wonderful interiors, and the Abbaye-aux-hommes is characteristic in its developed *chevet* with radiating chapels, turrets on the eastern transepts and a substantial triforium over the solid side aisles. Alternate columns are carried right up to the level of the clerestory where the vaulting springs. The triforium is frequently – as at St-Cerisy-la-Foret – carried over the transepts, making open tribunes there and sometimes at the west end also. This development of a triforium or tribune level found its way to England, for example, in Southwell Minister, and to Germany, as at Limburg-an-die-Lahn.

Germany

The Romanesque in Germany is the close successor to the Ottonian. The best group of churches are those in and around Cologne, where St Pantaleon, with its

Above centre: St-Cerisy-la-Foret, Normandy.

Right: *Chevet* and towers of the Abbaye-aux-hommes, Caen.

developed westwerk, paves the way. The Church of the Holy Apostles, with its forest of towers, (see page 88) illustrates Germany's place in westernizing the centralized, imperial style that blossomed so differently in the East, and Santa Maria in Capital, with its fine wooden doors and its elaborate, trefoiled east end, its most developed phase. For a spacious setting with an atrium as well as a westwerk, the Abbey of Maria Laach (1093–1156) is the best example (see page 75); and the cathedral at Limburg-an-die-Lahn, perched on the top of its rock above the river, illustrates the transitional period between Romanesque and Gothic.

Spain

The Romanesque in Spain has many facets. There are the churches that line the pilgrimage route to Compostela, culminating in the cathedral there, including, most importantly, St Isidoro at Leon, St Martin at Fromista and St Tirso at Sahagun (see page 78); there are the successors to the Mozarabic churches in and around Oviedo; there is the domed lantern tower, the Torre del Gallo at Salamanca; there are the mountain churches of the Pyrenees both sides of the range – St Bertrand de Comminges, St Martin de Canigou, St Michel de Cuxa, the cathedral at Seo de Urgel and the finely

Top left: The elaborately carved rood screen at Serrabone in the Pyrenees.

Top right: St Martin, Fromista, Spain.

Above: The flight into Egypt, from the wooden doors of Santa Maria in Capital, Cologne.

decorated church of Serrabone with its elaborately carved *rood screen; and there are the churches of Catalonia, many of whose vivid and remarkable paintings have been gathered and conserved in the museum in Barcelona.

The Templars

Given the significance for Romanesque architecture of the welding of the rotunda to the linear, basilical church, it is worth noting the significance of the contribution made by the Templars. The Knights

Above: The circular church of Neuvy-St-Sepulcre.

Templar, originally founded to protect Jerusalem, became a powerful and wealthy order. Their churches were circular, in imitation of the Holy Sepulchre, and are paralleled by the Ethiopian circular churches with their external arcades and Holy of Holies in the middle. As well as in the Temple Church in London, with its additional Gothic hall-church choir, and Holy Sepulchre, Cambridge (c. 1130), there are Templars' Holy Sepulchre churches at Neuvy-St-Sepulcre (c. 1042), Torres del Rio (twelfth century), the Convento de Christo, Tomar (1162), Vera Cruz, Segovia (twelfth century) and Santo Sepolcro in Bologna.

A SEQUENCE OF SPACES

What developed from the basic atrium or gathering space before the church proper of an early Roman basilica, such as San Clemente, was the westwerk, a substantial building of several storeys that served as a towering portal or gateway to the church. Those that derived from Charlemagne's octagonal Palatine Chapel at Aachen often had a first-floor chapel with a throne for the ruler; others, such as at St Front in Perigueaux, had a tower over the saint's shrine, which was – unusually – between the atrium and the domed basilica; some, whether the tunnel-like vaults of Tournus or the narthex of the pilgrimage church at Vezelay, are shadowy gathering spaces from where the pilgrim is drawn into the church proper by a blaze of light.

What in the end served to break up the long interior vista of the basilica was the introduction – especially in monastic churches in which the singing of the Office seven times a day implied a space, often enclosed against the draughts, with *stalls for the community gathered round a great lectern for the chanters – of a *coro*, or choir, an extension of those low enclosures built at the eastern end of the early basilicas. England is not alone in having a number of cathedrals that had either Benedictine foundations or secular canons whose choir stalls were – or still are – enclosed by a substantial rood screen, surmounted by a great figure of the crucified Christ, and before which was a nave altar of the Holy Cross.

This developed succession of spaces can be seen clearly in the Basilica of St Benoit-sur-Loire.

Romanesque: The Language of Kings

The entrance is under a massive westwerk, a kind of covered gathering space with a first-floor chamber, a grand tower entrance-cum-gathering place for the same function – though very different in style – as the atrium or forecourt of early Roman basilicas such as San Clemente. A long nave leads to the crossing, under which are the stalls of the monastic *coro*. East of this choir is the presbytery, with the choir altar; and beyond that, raised over the crypt, is an apsidal high altar. This stands in an apse that is fuller than a semicircle, and immediately below this altar rises the massive central column of the crypt, which holds the reliquary of St Benedict at the very heart of the building.

Above: Daniel in the Lions' Den, a capital in the dark narthex of the Abbey St Benoit-sur-Loire.

Above right: The nave, monastic choir (with its stalls and choir altar) and the eastern altar in the apse, raised above the relics of St Benedict in the crypt, St Benoit-sur-Loire.

Right: The crypt built around a central pier containing the relics of St Benedict.

The Gothic Vision: Seizing Space

Pointing Us to the God Beyond Our Sight

Gothic was originally a pejorative word, coined by the humanists of the fifteenth-century Renaissance, who thought the architecture of the Middle Ages barbarous and essentially un-Christian because of its Germanic origin. Later definitions of Gothic are less precise, even if Gothic remains in most people's minds – in spite of what the humanists of the Italian Renaissance thought – the quintessential architecture of churches. Although the traditional trademark of Gothic is represented as the pointed arch, this had already been used in Romanesque vaulting. There is a more significant, though less visible, shift that defines the boundary between Romanesque and it architectural successor.

First, there was a growing awareness of the individual. Statues of kings and saints, like those of Christ, had taken an idealized form; the portals of Romanesque churches were full of them, and the emperor Frederick I Barbarossa (c. 1123–90)

Salisbury, Chapter House portrait.

had no difficulty in having his features represented on the statue of Charlemagne on his reliquary. But suddenly, from around 1150, the statues of the kings and saints on the portals of cathedrals such as Chartres and the portrait heads around the wall of the Chapter House of the cathedral at Salisbury were very clearly real people, and not just idealized types. There is a degree of individuality, of the infinite variety of the human character, and a sense of personal intimacy that is visible in the poetry as well as in the art of the period that takes us at once into the Modern Age. These are human persons, made in the image and likeness of God, as the famous carving of God creating Adam in the north transept portal of Chartres Cathedral illustrates so well. What made them different was that these were people whose individual characters shone out from within, rather than being moulded by external and prescribed roles.

A parallel shift took place in the way people came to think about the work of Christ. Whether set against the trailing serpents of Nordic carving or the clutches of demons pitch-forking sinners into the jaws of hell, Christ was presented in Romanesque sculpture as the victor in the conflict between good and evil. His triumph was everywhere displayed as the heavenly counterpart of successful earthly kings. In the new order of things, life did not seem so black and white. Christ was the person who had paid the price for the sins of the whole world himself. The cross was not victory in a cosmic struggle so much as an act of self-giving love, a redemptive act within a personal relationship. So the way Jesus is portrayed shifts from a regal figure arrayed in priestly garments, commanding the victory from the cross with his eyes fearlessly open, to a tortured human like one of us, bearing the penalty of human sinfulness, and expiring under the weight of our sins. Christ is no longer a stylized king, but a fellow human being.

In the church's worship, the service books reveal that there was a shift away from interest in the rites of baptism – that evangelistic rite that presupposes converts and forms a Christian nation. Baptismal fonts shrink in size and for the most part are less prominent; most people are now baptized in infancy as a guarantee of citizenship in heaven and as protection against the powers of evil, rather than as adults embracing the faith and taking the first step in the life of Christian discipleship. More emphasis was laid on those rites that restored sinful human beings to their right relationship with God – confession of sin and the Eucharist itself. It is in this period, when the transcendent is emphasized, that the language of transformation begins to emerge, focused on the host, the consecrated bread of the

Eucharist: as the host is elevated, so the celebrant genuflects, a sign that the world of heavenly light has penetrated the murk of our earthly doings. The emphasis in Eucharistic worship – now understood more as a participation in Christ's sacrificial self-offering to the Father than as a foretaste of the heavenly banquet – moved from the corporate to the personal, if not to the individual; from 'making the offering' to receiving God's grace. The same is true of penitential rites. Here too, the liturgy of the church began to be seen in transactional terms rather than as a celebration, and the priestly function became more focused on the exercise of the power given in ordination to confect the sacraments – to make them work – rather than to preside over a celebration of what God has done for us in Christ in a way that enables the worshipper to make it their own.

This tendency to interiorize, rather than to adopt an exterior form, is exactly what we find in Gothic architecture. A Gothic church does not appear to be carved out of a solid block, with its sculpture moulded to express the solidity of unshakeable conviction; a Gothic church grows from the inside; its columns, ribs and vaulting are like a skeletal frame waiting to be brought to life when clothed in the light from above. A Gothic building is essentially a network of interwoven lines, a spun web of ribs and vaults seizing heaven, rather than the shaping of a series of solid masses, bound to earth. Instead of the rounded forms, sitting comfortably on the ground to affirm the incarnational reality of God's kingly presence on earth, the pinnacles and spires of Gothic point away from this world towards a reality elsewhere, that heaven from which both judgement and deliverance will come.

Medieval grisaille in the Cistercian tradition: from the south-east transept, Salisbury Cathedral, England.

THE ABBE SUGER AND THE SEARCH FOR LIGHT

To some degree, St Bernard of Clairvaux's reforms of the monastic life that inaugurated the Cistercian Order paved the way for a new look at the essential aesthetic of architectural form (see Chapter 4, page 84). His stress on the interior life and the demand that each monk should develop a personal imaginative landscape made him suspicious of much of the decorative and sculptural elements of Romanesque architecture, and Cistercian abbeys are notably plain. They eschew the sculpted capitals and tympana of the Romanesque; their walls are limewashed and their windows are filled with grisaille. It is through the pure and abstract analogies of spatial geometry and the quality of light that floods a building that God can properly be conceived. So the visual aesthetic of the monastery, with its geometrical layout, and the harmonious shapes and forms of the abbey church and the cloister garden, was what was important in providing the architectural summons to the human soul to apprehend the divine transcendence.

The person credited with first giving this shift architectural expression is the Abbe Suger, of St Denis, north of Paris. Suger knew Bernard, and although they parted company to be reconciled only shortly before Suger's death in 1151, his writing reflects a move away from the incarnational realism of the Romanesque to a system of symbolic pointers that reveal a fundamentally transcendent vision. Over the main portal of the abbey he wrote this inscription: 'May this wonderfully bright work illuminate minds so that they may pass through its true lights to the one true light, where Christ is the true door... The dull mind rises to the truth through material things...' Suger's stress on illumination is telling. He wanted the building to point beyond its material self to the reality it embodied, the light of heaven. The Gothic architecture that developed from this vision was an architecture in which the building was made to look as light as possible. The pierced spires, the stone walls covered with tracery as if they were windows and the sculpted figures of the portals were as ethereal as they could be to maximize the large expanse of glass, with the stories of the saints set against the blue of heaven, so that the whole building felt as if it was being drawn upwards into the divine light.

BRIDGING BETWEEN ROMANESQUE AND GOTHIC

Although by no means the earliest Gothic architecture in England, the place where the contrast between Romanesque and Gothic can be most easily appreciated is Gloucester Cathedral. Formerly a Benedictine abbey, Gloucester was a typical example of 'Norman' Romanesque. The nave, with exceptionally large drums of circular columns and small windows, feels dark, low and very solid. This style continues across the transepts and provides an ambulatory with radiating chapels round the east end. Into this Romanesque envelope was inserted a Gothic choir, like some pinnacled shrine. The roof of the Romanesque choir was removed, and, east of a rebuilt central tower, a delicate *filigree of perpendicular *tracery, running up through a tall clerestory stage, was inserted to support a lofty vault, with carved and gilded angels playing musical instruments as the *bosses. It was indeed constructed to be a shrine: King Edward II had died nearby in 1327, and had been buried in a sumptuous tomb in the north ambulatory. The abbey hoped for his canonization, and gambled on the increased revenues that would have accompanied the possession of a wonder-working saint in his shrine. The contrast between the low, almost oppressive, nave and the soaring choir is tremendous as you step from the nave through the *pulpitum into this delicate construction, through

Top left: Early quadripartite vaults in the nave of Durham Cathedral, England.

Above: The pinnacled Neville screen forms a reredos to the high altar, and divides the presbytery from the shrine of St Cuthbert in Durham Cathedral.

Left: The lofty Gothic choir of Gloucester was inserted into the Romanesque abbey, and pierces the low ambulatory that circles it.

Below: Durham Cathedral from the east, showing the Chapel of the Nine Altars.

which the solid drums of the ambulatory columns that surround it are still visible.

A second example is Durham Cathedral, where again a substantially Romanesque building has a vault that is clearly Gothic in form, and equally remarkably – though quite differently from Gloucester – has a Gothic east end. Behind the delicate Neville screen, with its vertical tracery and pinnacles, which forms a reredos to the high altar, the apsidal end of the cathedral with the shrine has been entirely replaced by a lateral Gothic transept – the Chapel of the Nine Altars; this forms as remarkable an endstop to the east as the Romanesque Galilee Chapel is on the cliff edge to the west.

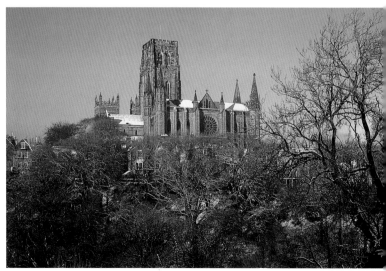

GEOMETRY AND DESIGN AT CHARTRES

Part of the Classical tradition that was being rediscovered was an awareness that carefully balanced proportion mirrored the reality of God. Often quoted are God's instructions to Solomon for building the Temple in Jerusalem (1 Kings 6 – 8:30), and scholars have discovered a carefully worked out system of mathematical proportions in the construction of the cathedral at Chartres. Earthly building should echo the harmonies of heaven. The harmonic proportions of the human figure, made according to Genesis in the image and likeness of God, were the basic unit of creation. Revealed in Christ as the word made flesh, the human form consciously formed the proportions of the ground plan. The altar was placed over the head, the crossing (the point at which the four arms of a cross-shaped church meet) at the heart, and the hands and feet determined the

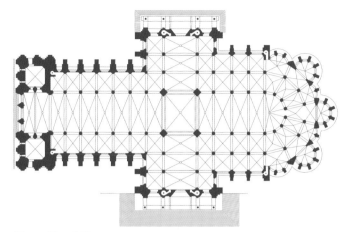

Above: Plan of Chartres.

Below: Chartres Cathedral, from the south-east.

portals. The cathedral was to be an image of the universe, whether vertically – in which the crypt represented the underworld, the floor level with its columns, the earth, and the vaults and clerestory, heaven itself, or horizontally – in which the nave represented the underworld, the crossing, earth, and the sanctuary, heaven. Integral to the design are the three great rose windows – the glorification of the Virgin Mary in the north transept, Christ in glory in the south transept and the last judgement in the west – and the plan is based on these three interlocking circles in each plane, where the

Left: The cloisters at Salisbury, providing a teaching space in the new cathedral.

Right: Salisbury Cathedral from the north-east: the only English cathedral built in a single phase.

vertical represents the heavenly and the horizontal the earthly dimension.

Few actual plans for cathedral buildings survive, but an exception is Strasbourg, France, for which designs from around 1250 are preserved. A notebook by Villard de Honnecourt dating from around 1225 gives the designs for a large church, but these are thought to be the work of an interested amateur rather than an architect's working drawings. In the nineteenth century, a drawing of 1482 was discovered and the spire of Ulm Cathedral in Germany was completed according to its original design, and it was only in the nineteenth century that the Medieval design of the great cathedral at Cologne was completed. For the most part, when a building was left unfinished, the next master builder produced his own designs according to the developing fashions and shifts in architectural practice and the changing patterns of liturgical use.

NOTRE DAME AS A MODEL FOR A UNIVERSITY CATHEDRAL

When the Bishop of Salisbury in the early thirteenth century, Richard Poore, wanted to escape from the constrained site on the hilltop chosen by the Norman conquerors for its defensive position, he went to Paris and saw in Notre Dame a different sort of cathedral. Poore's Norman cathedral at Old Sarum was a Benedictine abbey, with its monastic life and rhythms. In Paris he experienced a cathedral in which the bishop's teaching ministry was exercised in collaboration with a college of canons, and formed the nucleus of what we would today call a university. Bishop Poore chose a green-field site down on the water meadows, where the compacted gravel formed a secure foundation and, with the aid of a master builder, Elias of Dereham, began to build in 1220. Salisbury is almost the only Gothic cathedral in England to be built continuously in a single building phase from east to west, which accounts

Top: The nave of Salisbury Cathedral, showing a clear demarcation between the nave arcades and the upper region – the triforium and clerestory.

Bottom: The east end of Amiens Cathedral, showing the shallow triforium rather than the substantial tribune of a late Romanesque church like Limburg-an-die-Lahn (see illustration on p.105).

Opposite: The choir of Westminster Abbey, influenced by Amiens.

for its remarkable architectural unity. It has a cloister – unusual for a non-monastic foundation – which was clearly designed to be a teaching space, much like the *stoa of a Classical city like Athens. In effect, the bishop's vision was of a university cathedral, where from his *cathedra* he could exercise his apostolic ministry as a teacher.

THE DISTINCTIVE PATH OF ENGLISH GOTHIC

While Salisbury was being built in an Early Gothic plastic style, with sharply delineated horizontal elements – a nave arcade, on top of which stands a deep triforium, on top of which again rests a clerestory – what came to be called the *Rayonnant style was emerging in France, first in the choir of Troyes Cathedral and later in Amiens.

What happened in France was a systematic thinning out of the substantial members – the columns and piers, the mouldings and recesses – in favour of the thin lines of the window mullions (the vertical members dividing a window). The bay, or vertical division of the elevation, is seen not so much as a three- but a two-dimensional unit, in which the ribs, mouldings and shafts of the piers loose their volume and are clustered together to form the lightest of structures to support the vault and the enlarged windows, which are no longer deeply recessed. In addition, these piers and ribs are no longer static in themselves, set – like the pilasters and arches of the Romanesque nave at Vezelay, for example (see page 101) – at right angles to one another and the main axis of the building. In a Gothic building, the piers are set diagonally, turned through 45 degrees, and rise into the basic quadripartite ribs of the vaulting, so giving the whole building a twist, a sense of movement. Where a degree of thickness is needed, as in the shallow triforium passage – very different from the substantial tribune-type triforia of the Romanesque – the inner and outer walls are simply detached from one another while using the same pattern of apertures, giving the impression of a single thickness, and are read as a single surface with projections and recessions. Soon the filigree window tracery spills over onto the stonework, and indeed onto the woodwork of stalls and doors, providing a unified treatment of all surfaces. It is not long before the vestigial triforium, no longer functioning in any sense as a tribune but reduced to a high-level walkway, is subsumed into a passageway at the foot of the tall clerestory. In England, masons from Rheims and Amiens worked on Westminster Abbey, which Henry III began to rebuild in an international Gothic style in 1245. Started some twenty-five years after Salisbury, it remains consciously French in style, with a tall arcade, a high vault and a polygonal east end, containing the shrine of Edward the Confessor behind the high altar. Its nave was not completed for several centuries, but in substantially the same style, using white limestone from Caen to contrast with the columns and

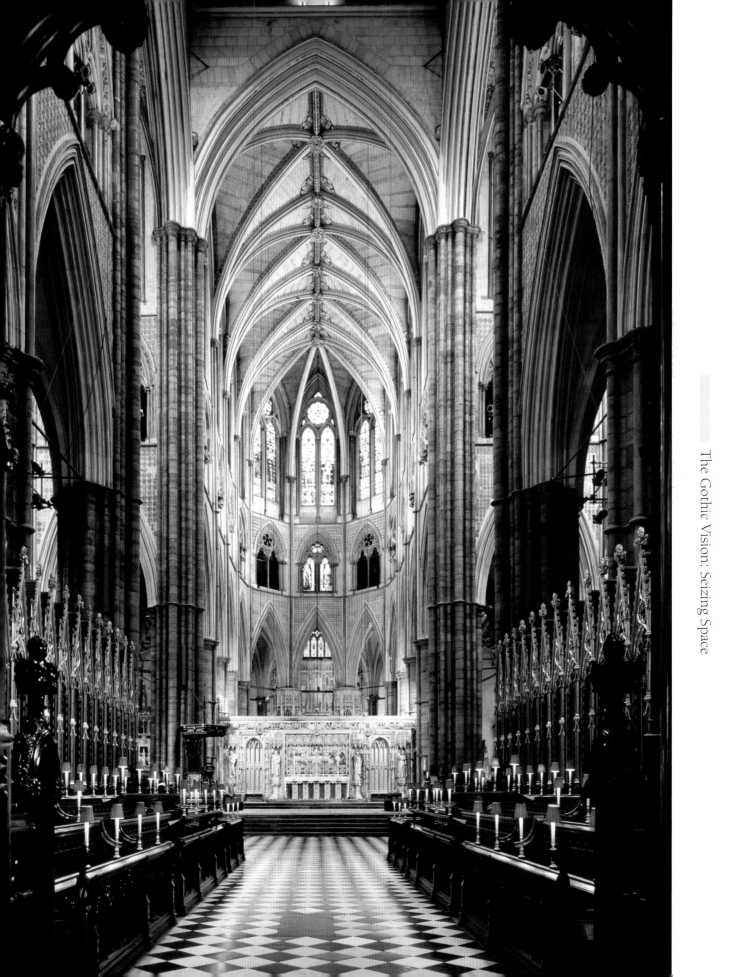

shafts of Purbeck marble from Dorset. Westminster Abbey remains the coronation church of the sovereigns of England, and after a brief period as a cathedral at the dissolution of the monasteries in the sixteenth century, became a Royal Peculiar, a private foundation directly under the authority of the sovereign.

The elements of the new, lighter window tracery were embraced in England, as in the chapter houses at Westminster and Salisbury, but for the most part these were isolated features that were used within a more plastic context. Even when the shafts of the piers ran from floor level to the springing of the vault, as in the nave of York Minster, the architecture remains more substantial, more plastic and less driven by the ethereal insubstantiality of the French Gothic. It was the new window style that caught the English builders' imagination, and it was soon adapted to windows of every size and location, including full-size windows at the east end or transept ends, so that very soon an elaborate geometry of forms, not merely the strictly geometric but also the curvilinear, filled the space.

In England, two elements fostered this different contribution. The first was the evolution of the *ogee arch. Derived from the East, possibly from India, the ogee arch was made up of pairs of reverse curves, and formed an ideal framework for a recess or

niche in which to frame a statue. Used on every surface, including the frames for embroidered figures of the saints on the famous silk *Opus Anglicanum* vestments, this arch made window tracery fluid rather than stiff. The second was a new freedom in handling interior space. Salisbury remains a narrowly confined space, but suddenly after 1280 large hall-church spaces began to emerge, such as the choir of the Temple Church or Bristol Cathedral choir (begun in 1298), in which the side aisles buttress the wide span, which ultimately led to the lofty, squared buildings and the flattened, four-centred arches we know as perpendicular.

SHAPING THE SKELETON

In Gothic churches the long hall in which the people gather is called the nave. This comes from the word *navis*, which is Latin for a ship. If you look at an upturned ship as it is being built you see the stem and the keel, then as the ribs are added you see the skeletal form taking shape. Walk down an avenue of trees, and it is hard not to be struck by how similar it feels to walking down the nave of a great Gothic cathedral: the columns and pillars fork diagonally into ribs and vaults that touch high overhead, while the windows let in shafts of oblique light in much the same way as the great trunks of the trees fork into branches that meet to form a tunnel, through which the light filters.

After the massive pierced walls of Romanesque, even Early Gothic, such as Laon

in northern France, feels a lighter, more natural construction. Pillars or clusters of columns carry shafts right up from the floor to the apex of the vault; by the thirteenth century, simple ring or coil mouldings at the tops of the columns – holding the bundle of shafts together, as it were – replaced the elaborately sculpted figured capitals. The highly stylized post-Classical foliage of Romanesque capitals gives way to more natural leaf carving, which is matched by the wood carving of stalls and pew ends, and the stone tracery in the windows begins to look like the pierced carving on screens and cupboard doors. Wood, not stone, looks like the medium in which the designs were conceived. Sometimes, faces peep out from the foliage as they do in the Angel Choir in Lincoln, and the Green Man – the pagan spirit of the natural world – never seems far away in this emerging style of architecture, which has its natural home in northern, rather than Mediterranean, Europe. The stiff-leaved curls on pinnacles, known as *crocketting, and the stylized ball-flower design are just two of the common forms of Gothic ornament that have a naturalistic origin.

Above all, what gives Gothic its height are the shafted columns that run from floor to roof. They give an immediate vertical thrust that is absent from the horizontal Romanesque arcade,

Above left: Crockets on a pinnacle at Bromham, Wiltshire.

Above centre: Ball flower decoration around a window inserted into the nave of Gloucester Cathedral.

Left: The Angel Choir, Lincoln Cathedral.

Above right: Bays of the nave at Laon Cathedral, showing a tribune set over the arcade, with a small triforium and clerestory above, linked by a shaft springing from the capital of the columns.

surmounted by a tribune, or gallery, above which may be a range of small apertures, each connected horizontally. In the new Gothic, even the Early Gothic of Laon, each bay reads vertically, with the nave arcade, the triforium and the clerestory seen as a unified composition, the spaces within the arched space being filled with the lightest amount of tracery that was compatible with structural stability.

The daring of the Gothic architects in replacing as much wall as possible by glass did not always succeed: if fire destroyed the wooden roofs and caused the collapse of many Romanesque structures, then it was structural instability that caused the collapse of some of the more daring Gothic buildings. The cathedral at Beauvais in northern France, begun in 1238, with a vault reaching the height of 157 feet (48 metres), remains incomplete after the collapse of its nave in 1284, and the weight of the unplanned-for spire on top of the crossing tower at Salisbury has caused the shafts

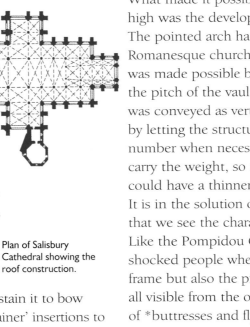

Plan of Salisbury Cathedral showing the roof construction.

The Development of Vaulting

What made it possible to lift the soaring roofs so high was the development of *ribs and vaulting. The pointed arch had already been used to vault Romanesque churches, but the new development was made possible by two factors: first, by raising the pitch of the vault, so that the structural thrust was conveyed as vertically as possible; and second, by letting the structural ribs – increasing their number when necessary to span wider spaces – carry the weight, so that the infilling *web of stone could have a thinner, and so lighter, construction. It is in the solution of these structural problems that we see the characteristic inside-out of Gothic. Like the Pompidou Centre in Paris, which shocked people when not only the structural frame but also the pipe-work of the services were all visible from the outside, the exterior system of *buttresses and flying buttresses, capped with a forest of pinnacles that supported the increasingly thin structural members that make the interiors so breathtakingly light and airy, was entirely visible. Indeed, this structural visibility is part of the attraction of Gothic; we marvel at the intricate construction of these buildings, with little in the way of architectural drawings and the most primitive of scaffolds, partly because we can see just how they work. For example, the tall pinnacles that form such a visible hallmark of

of the piers at the crossing that sustain it to bow noticeably in spite of the later 'strainer' insertions to north and south. When the Romanesque crossing tower of Ely in Cambridgeshire fell in 1322, the Gothic builders demolished what was left of the piers and built diagonally across the corners to create an octagon at the junction between the nave and transepts, continuing the Gothic style eastwards into a new choir. Over the new crossing space, they raised a much lighter glazed and pinnacled octagonal lantern in wood, like a princess's crown, a remarkable solution that unconsciously echoes the baptismal and royal references of the octagonal form.

The octagonal lantern of Ely Cathedral links the transepts at the crossing with a lightweight crown.

Ribs at Ourscamps, Oise, in northern France, provide the structure to transfer weight to the outer walls.

Above: The flying buttresses and pinnacles of the *chevet* at Le Mans.

Below: Gargoyles at Troyes Cathedral help throw rainwater clear of the building.

the exterior of Gothic churches were decorated as lavishly as any heavenward-pointing spire. But they were not merely decorative: substantial pinnacles were structurally necessary to exert the maximum downward pressure whenever a buttress was conveying a lateral thrust to earth. The flying buttresses that the pinnacles helped to stabilize were also the conduits for rainwater from the acres of roofs, which was frequently thrown clear of the building by great spouts carved with mythical creatures and the features of demons. These carved spouts or gargoyles provided wonderful opportunities for stonemasons to produce grotesque figures discharging the waste water, while in the interior the carved angels soared overhead, bearing the blessings of heaven.

The interior vistas of a vaulted Gothic nave are dramatic. Coming into the cathedral at night, lit only by exterior floodlighting, and

A series of vaults, increasing in complexity. Clockwise from bottom: Sens, Lincoln, Lichfield, Tewkesbury.

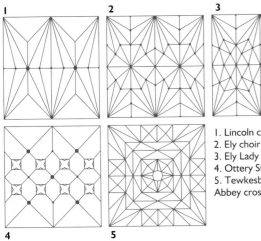

1. Lincoln choir
2. Ely choir
3. Ely Lady Chapel
4. Ottery St Mary
5. Tewkesbury Abbey crossing

hearing the story of Jonah in the belly of the great fish for three days (part of the sequence of Old Testament readings at the Easter Vigil preparing for the celebration of the resurrection) is to share something of Jonah's experience, as the ribs of the vault seem all too like the imprisoning ribs of a great beached whale.

To counteract this sense of imprisonment, over the centuries the vaults were raised higher and the web became thinner as the number of subsidiary ribs grew. To begin with, a basic quadripartite vault grew an additional member and became a sexpartite vault. The asymmetrical vault of Lincoln had few followers, but the extra members of the tierceron vault at Lichfield and Exeter soon led to the lierne vaults at Tewkesbury, which in turn blossomed in England into fan vaulting, as at Sherborne, where the early fan vaults of the choir were planned as early as 1437. The latest phase evolved into the lantern pendants of Christ Church Cathedral in Oxford, which seem to hang in mid-air, but those hanging vaults had a precursor in Peter Parler's work in the cathedral in Prague.

Above: A curvillinear window in East Anglia patterned by tracery.

Left: The east window, Gloucester Cathedral: a wall of glass.

Letting in Light: Enlarging the Windows

In parallel, the size of windows grew, and the increased space available for stained glass – the poor man's Bible – rather than the wall painting that was characteristic of the Romanesque period brings a lighter interior and a more vivid portrayal of the events of the Gospels and the stories of the saints. By the late Middle Ages, whole walls could be glazed, as in the east windows of Gloucester Cathedral or York Minster, again a distinctively northern feature as opposed to Mediterranean, where it was necessary to keep buildings as cool as possible, and stained glass – and indeed the whole glass house experience of Late Gothic – never became a significant part of the Italian way of doing Gothic.

At first, the windows were tall, narrow *lancets, like those of Romanesque churches but with pointed rather than rounded heads. Then, as lancets were grouped two or more together under the frame of a wider arch moulding with a simple roundel filling the space between their heads, the wall-space between the lancets could be diminished till it was simply a mullion, provided that it was of dressed stone rather than rubble walling. As two or more lancets were grouped together, more imaginative use was made of the space between the heads of the lancets, and a number of different shapes of geometric design were contrived to fill the space in an essentially Y-shaped frame. Eventually this decorative tracery escaped from the purely geometrical window heads to create tear or flame shapes flowing downwards to fill much of the window, producing the *Flamboyant style on the continent; while English windows, pressing as far up as they could into the corners of the space available, retained the vertical panel as the basic

St Elizabeth, Marburg,
Germany, early
thirteenth century.

Sees Cathedral,
Normandy, late
thirteenth century.

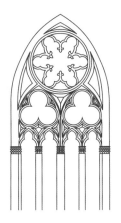

Amiens Cathedral,
France, first half of
thirteenth century.

Chipping Norton,
England, late
fourteenth century.

Below: Squared rose window ending a transept
in Troyes Cathedral.

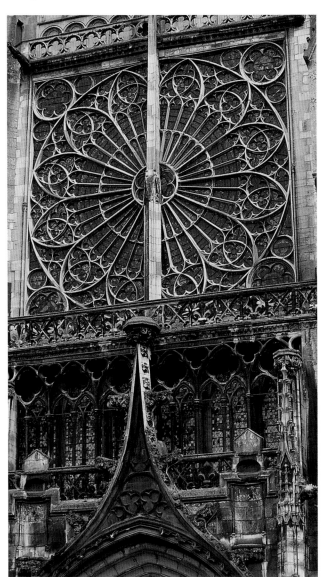

unit and developed the flat-headed four-centred arch
typical of the style known as Perpendicular. Although
it was fashionable to describe these evolving forms
as distinct periods in English architecture – Early
English, Geometric, Decorated and Curvilinear – and
to trace the evolution of the pointed arch in a similar
way, this somewhat rigid classification does not fit
the overall development of Gothic architecture in
Europe as a whole.

The rose window occupies a special place
in the development of glazing. Small roundels had
always had a place in glazing schemes, but enlarging
them so that they entirely filled the upper stage of
a Gothic transept, west end or even a squared east
end was a novel way of flooding the building with
light and at the same time using the circle, that
most perfect of forms. Some rose windows have
stone carvings of figures on the rim that show they
were thought of as the wheel of fortune, in which,
as in the *Magnificat* (Song of Mary), God is praised
for putting down the mighty from their seat and
raising up the poor and lowly. The rose represented
Mary, and the rosary – a string of beads forming a
circle – was a popular aid to meditative prayer. The
rose window in the west end of the nave at Chartres
is the same size as the maze on the floor, another
illustration of the vertical or heavenly dimension
being echoed by the horizontal or earthly.

Left: Unusual fourteenth-century stone tracery fills the chancel arch of Great Bardfield, Essex, to form a screen.

Right: West rose window at Reims Cathedral.

Below: Wooden parclose screens at St Mary's, Dennington.

Tracery was not confined to windows; it was used to fill the opening of a wooden screen, or even to fill the whole of a chancel arch, as at Great Bardfield.

What gave many churches an even greater illusion of height was the lengthening of the clerestory. As the triforium became little more than a shallow gallery above the nave arcade, it was sometimes reduced to a bare wall with stone tracery, as if it was a blank window or the panel of a door. It was a short step from there to drop the clerestory window to embrace the triforium level, dividing each vertical bay into two, rather than three, levels. Larger clerestory windows meant more light in the main body of the nave, not just in the aisles.

In northern Europe, where light was at a premium, larger windows and paler glazing predominated, as in the School of York. In France, where much rich glass from an earlier period survives, notably in Chartres and the cathedrals

of the Isle de France, the colours are darker, and the images in complex scenes that fill the lower lights are smaller, while life-size figures predominate at clerestory level.

By contrast to these great cathedrals, Paris, known with the Isle de France as the cradle of Gothic, produced one of the most perfect examples of a miniature glass house in the Sainte-Chapelle. This small, richly decorated chapel in the heart of Paris was built by Louis IX between 1244 and 1248 for 40,000 livres to house his treasured relic – the crown of thorns. The relic had cost 135,000 livres, and the king was determined to give it a worthy and appropriate shrine. The slender columns preserve their rich polychrome decoration, and the entire glazing system combines with a pinnacled verticality to create a jewel-like glazed shrine, reminiscent of the richly decorated metalwork reliquaries writ large. In contrast, Santa Maria della Spina, a little chapel on the banks of the River Arno in Pisa, Italy, looks oddly out of place, though both chapels use the spikiness of Gothic architecture to write large their *raison d'etre* as reliquaries of the crown of thorns. Similar in its tall, aisleless pattern is the Lady Chapel of Lichfield Cathedral, which was built in 1330 to contain the shrine of St Chad.

Above left: Vivid stained glass from Laon showing the Last Supper and Triumphal Entry.

Below: English glass of the School of York designed to let in light in a northern clime.

Above: The jewel-like Gothic casket of Sainte-Chapelle, Paris.

THE PLAN OF A GOTHIC CATHEDRAL

After Chartres and Notre Dame in Paris, new or rebuilt cathedrals sprang up all over France and England, although Gothic came later to Germany. While the cruciform ground plan was continued from the Romanesque churches, the crossing is less evident in an interior now articulated by the repetitive pattern of cross vaulting. Sometimes, as in Salisbury and Lincoln, there is a second, more easterly crossing that hardly breaks the rhythm of the bays, but for the most part, the geometry of the division of vaulted bays and their subsidiary aisles has an inexorable logic. Although the transept survived as an entrance portal with its own character imparted by the sculpture, as in Laon or Amiens in northern France or Lincoln in England, the logical conclusion was a cathedral such as Bourges, in which the transepts have been entirely

subsumed into lateral porches, and no structural division exists in the long sweep from west to east, where a perfect semicircle of radiating chapels closes the east end, as at Le Mans.

In place of the Romanesque westwerk or narthex, where the worshipper was reminded of his baptismal encounter, attention in a Gothic church is focused on the exterior façade. Some of these, such as Salisbury and Wells as well as the great French cathedrals, have a sculptural programme on the western façade that declares the church to be the new Jerusalem: as you approach, you see a vision of heaven. At Salisbury, there was a weekly procession before the high mass on Sundays that culminated in an entrance through the west doors.

On Palm Sunday, in the Sarum Rite, the canons sang Psalm 24, 'Lift up your heads, O ye gates, and be lifted up ye everlasting doors, and the King of Glory shall come in', as they approached;

Spiky Gothic to house a relic from the Crown of Thorns: Santa Maria della Spina, Pisa.

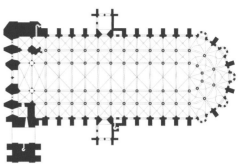

Plan of Bourges Cathedral.

The sweep of the
south side of Bourges
Cathedral.

then the statues seemed to sing, 'Who is the King of Glory?', and the assembly replied, 'The Lord of Hosts, he is the King of Glory' as they entered. In the upper gallery, wooden plugs could be removed in the quatrefoil openings behind the statues on the west front. The rubric instructed seven choirboys to mount the gallery and sing the responses through the apertures, and they still do.

However much the great cathedrals such as Salisbury were designed for the processional rites of the core community rather than to contain a large regular congregation – a relatively modern and utilitarian point of view that would have been incomprehensible to the Medieval cathedral builders – the nature of those processional rites had changed. In early centuries, the major rites were the Easter liturgy and the rites of initiation and incorporation that derived from it. They were the rites of the pilgrim people of God, growing into the faith that had been given them. By the Early Medieval period, processional rites were concerned with marking boundaries between earth and heaven, and patterning the community in the ordered life of the world to come. Rehearsing what God had done for his people in Christ in the dramatic celebrations of the liturgical year and celebrating the lives of the saints in whom that pattern had taken visible root gave an orderly and

prescriptive framework to life. The saints were our friends and forerunners in the faith, and we could enlist their aid. The clergy prayed, many of them in the Benedictine pattern of seven times a day as the psalmist had urged, and this semi-continuous pattern of prayer, known as the Office, was their proper professional care. So, at the heart of the larger churches was a choir, an enclosed area reserved for the clergy, including those who were the musicians, with screens to protect them against the cold.

The Insertion of the Choir

In the choir of a cathedral or collegiate church – a large church supporting a college of priests – were stalls for these clergy or choir monks (to distinguish them from the lay brothers who became more and more necessary for the orderly daily running of the monastery now that choir monks were spending so much time singing the Offices). They might be a college of canons or a community of monks or members of one of the newer orders, such as the Dominicans or Franciscans. No longer surrounding the bishop in the apse, as the altar had moved east to be close to the shrine, the clergy were now seated opposite one another in the choir, with the bishop seated normally on the south side. Some stalls

Right: The choir in Halberstad Cathedral, Germany.

Centre: The west front of Wells Cathedral, England.

faced east along the pulpitum, and this enclosed part of the church had the effect of separating the people from the altar by a considerable distance. Unable to see, except through a narrow aperture in a distant screen, their active participation in the liturgy was considerably reduced, and reduced still further by elaborate music performed by the clergy. The clergy were a class of professionals; in a very hierarchically ordered church, the ordinary lay worshipper must have felt distanced from the heart of the worship. Little wonder that popular devotions – such as praying the rosary, or visiting the shrine or a statue to light a candle and pray for a favour, or even hearing a private mass offered at some subsidiary altar for an intention that you had paid for – seemed a more fruitful exercise than being an onlooker at some distant performance.

In the centre of the choir stood a great lectern large enough for the *Antiphoner, the large volume of vellum sheets with the plainsong chants for the Office, which occupied an increasing amount of a monk's time as the music became more elaborate. The singing monks would gather round this great volume for the more complex chants, and the *Rector Cori*, the director of the choir, pointed to the chant with a long rod. Much of the singing was antiphonal, with verses of psalms and canticles sung from side to side of

the choir, and the monks would know most of the psalms by heart, as the whole of the Psalter was recited each week. While the stalls had seats, the monks had to stand for much of the time. Fixed to the back of the upturned seats were small carved ledges known as misericords – 'may God take pity on us, standing so long' is the thrust of the Latin name – to support them. These carved misericords, normally hidden from sight, provided a wonderful opportunity for some irreverent and occasionally coarse depictions of everyday scenes: men make love to mermaids; asses play the harp; or lay brothers defecate as the woodcarvers cock a snook at the monastic life.

Above: A fourteenth-century misericord from St Mary's, Beverley, England.

Above right: The *coro* in the Cathedral of San Domingo de Calzada, Spain.

In an abbey, or cathedral or collegiate church, such a choir formed the heart of the building, and other worshippers eavesdropped or made their way by the aisles to the chapels round the east end, radiating out from the central point of the high altar and the shrine, where private masses would be offered close to the source of power, the saint whose mortal remains were the conduit between earth and heaven.

In Spain, the *coro* was placed to the west of the crossing – as it is in Westminster Abbey and some other Benedictine foundations – well into the nave. It had a solid west side against which stalls were placed, with the bishop's throne set centrally against the pulpitum facing east, thus reducing the shortened nave to a kind of antechapel. This scheme has the virtue of separating the *coro* from the high altar by a considerable distance, and allowing the worshippers to penetrate the space between the two. Often only a slender walkway links the *coro* in the west to the sanctuary in the east, using fine wrought-iron screens to keep the people, for whom no seats are provided, from invading the space reserved for the liturgical ministers.

In Italy, in such major Gothic cathedrals and churches as there are, the *coro* was frequently placed east of the high altar, whose reredos, and later, an even more substantial altarpiece, provided

An octagonal lantern rises over the crossing at Coutances Cathedral in Normandy.

a screen for the area in which the clergy prayed the Office. Again, this pattern has the benefit of not separating the altar from the people. In Sees, Normandy, the altar at the crossing is two-sided, enabling a choir mass to be said with the celebrant facing west, or a high mass to be sung for a nave full of worshippers with the sacred ministers facing east. At Coutances, on the Cotentin peninsula,

Plan of the cathedral at Tarazona, Spain, showing the *coro* set well to the west of the nave.

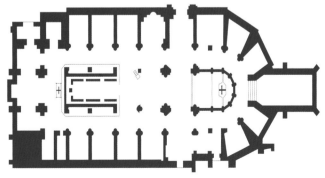

the central crossing space is emphasized by an octagonal lantern.

The Place of the Shrine

The other major factor affecting the plan of the Gothic churches of this period is the placing of the shrine of the founder or patron saint.

While the shrine often remained in the apse behind the principal altar, there was frequently a substantial reredos or *retable to that altar, which was itself the focus of devotion, as in the famous altarpiece commissioned for the cathedral at Siena from Boninsegna Duccio. The base for such an Italian altarpiece was composed of a series of miniature scenes, known as the *predella, and intended for the devotion of the celebrating priest. Above them stood the central panel, or panels, framed in Gothic tracery and flanked frequently by figures of appropriate canopied saints. In the upper niches might be angel musicians. In England, there was more often a substantial screen, sometimes

The Lion Companion to Christian Architecture

132

standing 40 or 50 feet (12 or 15 metres) high, as in Winchester, with canopied niches for a hierarchy of rulers, abbots and bishops, saints and apostles. Sometimes, as in Westminster Abbey, the screen stood no higher than 10 or 12 feet (3 or 3.6 metres), and provided a distinct space for the shrine beyond. Restricted access to the shrine increased its numinous mystery, like being admitted into the Holy of Holies. It was also one more barrier for ordinary lay people.

But screens between the high altar and the saint's tomb were not the only such barriers. Each Lent in Salisbury, a great veil of unbleached linen was suspended between the pillars of the presbytery to represent the veil of the Temple, and a smaller altar was erected in front of it at which the daily choir mass was sung. The well-worn crank that winched up the veil remains to this day. This hints at the way in which the Medieval liturgy used the sequence of spaces to heighten the natural drama of worship, so that at Easter the elaborately decorated high altar would make all the greater impact when at last the veil was drawn aside after forty days.

Not that all shrines were in such close proximity to the high altar; in Whitchurch Canonicorum in Dorset, for example, one of the few undisturbed pre-Reformation shrines in England is set in the end wall of the north transept. When Salisbury's Norman bishop-founder was eventually canonized after a long process in 1457, the splendid shrine of St Osmund was set up in the centre of the Trinity Chapel, in the eastern chapel beyond the retro-choir, only to be entirely destroyed at the Reformation. The canopied shrine of the comparable bishop-founder of the Diocese of Hereford, Thomas Cantiloupe, is in the north transept. In York Minster the tomb of Archbishop Walter de Grey stands perfectly preserved in the south transept: never a shrine, his tomb escaped destruction.

Left: The canopied tomb of Archbishop Walter de Grey in the south transept, York Minster.

Below: Crank for Lenten veil in Salisbury Cathedral.

St Elizabeth, Marburg.

The Gothic Vision: Seizing Space

INTERNATIONAL MOVEMENTS

The cradle of Gothic was northern France. But, by the beginning of the thirteenth century it was not only England in which the majority of the great cathedrals were Gothic; Germany and Italy as well were embracing Gothic forms.

The transition from Romanesque is visible in Germany in churches such as the cathedral at Limburg-an-die-Lahn, and is fully fledged in the pilgrimage church of St Elizabeth in Marburg (begun in 1235), and Cologne Cathedral, from 1248 onwards. More interesting developments include the centrally planned Liebfrauenkirche (Church of Our Lady) in Trier, designed as a rose (1235 onwards), while in Italy the great Basilica of San Francesco at Assisi and the polychrome cathedral at Siena – both built on sloping sites – take the vocabulary of Gothic into a new expression. In Albi, the fortress-like brick cathedral was begun in 1276 but feels as if its wide central span has little in common with the pillars, arches and vaults of northern France. Nor does the open plan of some of the great churches of the new orders, such as San Domenico in Siena or Santa Croce, the Franciscan church in Florence, begun in 1294 and designed for what was then a novel purpose – preaching.

The rise of preaching, the increasing fear of an unshriven death, the terrors of the Black Death and the Hundred Years' War: all were to change the emphasis of the Christian faith and the buildings that embodied it. As a foretaste of the pains of hell became more apparent, the ever-present image of the crucified Christ in the Later Gothic period stressed the distance between sinful humanity and what was experienced as the increasing otherness of God.

The fortress-like cathedral at Albi, in southern France.

Late Gothic

Toppling Splendour, Hanging from Heaven

Il Volto Santo, a much venerated statue of the crucified Christ in the cathedral at Lucca, Tuscany, said to have been carved by Nicodemus from life.

'If one were called upon to give a psychological characterization of the various phases of mediaeval sculpture, one might convey something of the difference, even irreconcilability, of their qualities by saying that Romanesque sculpture was the expression of faith, that Gothic sculpture was the expression of piety, and that the sculpture of the decline was the expression of devotion.

'Romanesque faith, shot through with visions and prodigies, accepted and cherished the mysterious; it moved among superhuman things; it trembled in anticipation of rewards and punishments; the miracle was its law, and the unknowable its nourishment. From these epic heights, round which resounded the thunders of Sinai, the piety of the thirteenth century brings us back to the paths of the Gospel; in God-made-man, it cherished humanity; it loved and respected God's creatures as He loved them; it accepted the benefit which He brought to men of good will – peace on earth – and extended it to include even death, which was no more than a sleep in the Lord. Finally, the devotion of decline, more demanding and perhaps more sensitive in its emotions, replaced this serenity with its own unease, passionately devoted itself to

Right: The wood of the cross on which Christ is crucified becomes the tree of life and sprouts lilies: from St Mary's Westwood, Wiltshire, England.

Centre: Medieval rood screen from St Fiacre, Brittany, holding the image of Christ crucified before the eyes of the worshipper.

the terrible scenes of Calvary, and fixed them, contemplated them, made them live again, suffered them anew, with a dramatic pageantry and mystic power of recreation which conferred holiness even on the accessory and the indifferent object. Iconography, style and technique were all equally expressive of these profound differences.'
Henri Focillon, *The Art of the West*

From the time of Charlemagne onwards, it is possible to chart the shift in the Christian's relationship with God in the Western world through the changes in art and architecture, and the patterns of the church's worship as they developed. Already in the eighth century some major changes were taking place. The priest now had his back to the community as he celebrated mass: no longer did he draw them into the corporate offering of the community to God, into *eucharistia*, or a prayer of thanksgiving, from a congregation whose gifts were elevated during the course of the mass by the actions of the priest into a heavenly sacrificial offering; instead he is the intermediary, who, by the due performances of the proper rites can make the grace of God real. The people are the passive recipients of that grace, which, at the climactic moment of the mass – the consecration – descends to them.

Medieval chest-tomb (c. 1330)
in the Cistercian nunnery of
Maigrauge, Fribourg, Switzerland.

THE PREOCCUPATION WITH DEATH

By the period that Focillon characterizes by 'the
expression of devotion', the goal of religion was
to come to the end of your life – the moment of
death – with enough in the balance in your favour
to secure a passage through purgatory. The prayer
of the devout Christian was that, with careful
tariffs set for each sin like a doctor's prescription,
you might pass through that process of spiritual
refinement in such a way as would not prove
beyond the limits of endurance. By the later
Middle Ages the preoccupation with death was
everywhere. The *Dies Irae* ('Day of Wrath'), the
chilling sequence that forms the second section
of classical settings of the Requiem Mass, had
migrated from being a sequence for Advent, where
it celebrated the second coming of Christ, to the
Requiem for the Departed. The *Danse Macabre* or
Totentanz, the dance of death, was painted on the
walls of churches (as was the Wheel of Fortune)
as a constant reminder of human mortality and
the socially levelling effect of death. The image
of Christ's body being taken from the cross and
being laid in the tomb was everywhere: monks
of a strict monastery would begin to dig their
own graves and practise for death by lying in
them to meditate. While the Hundred Years' War

The rood screen in Halberstad Cathedral.

The damned being drawn into the mouth of hell: detail from the Doom painting over the chancel arch of St Thomas', Salisbury.

And none could be found to bury the dead for money or friendship. Members of a household brought their dead to a ditch as best they could, without priest, without divine offices... great pits were dug and piled deep with the multitude of dead. And they died by the hundreds both day and night... And as soon as those ditches were filled more were dug... And I, Agnolo di Tura, called the Fat, buried my five children with my own hands. And there were also those who were so sparsely covered with earth that the dogs dragged them forth and devoured many bodies throughout the city. There was no one who wept for any death, for all awaited death. And so many died that all believed it was the end of the world. This situation continued [from May] until September.'

(1337–1453) meant that for much of the later Middle Ages armies were roaming Europe in search of provisions, even greater misery was caused by incurable disease, sharpened by the Black Death of 1348–49.

Agnolo di Tura in Siena recorded his experience:

'Father abandoned child, wife husband, one brother another; for this illness seemed to strike through the breath and sight. And so they died.

Where was God in this misery? The prescriptions for spiritual health in an increasingly transactional religion were severe, and this period sees the rise of lay confraternities – sometimes offshoots of the major religious orders – with the same sense of banding together in adversity that characterizes the origin of the Co-operative Societies and Trades Unions, which are their successors. The craftsmen's guilds with their initiation rites and trade secrets, the fraternities dedicated to

Christ, displaying the wounds of his crucifixion, presides over the last judgement in the Doom painting, St Thomas', Salisbury.

charity and caring for the poor and sick, and the preoccupation with the corporal works of mercy all focus on the parable of the sheep and the goats, of the judgement of God, in chapter 25 of Matthew's Gospel. The Doom painting over the chancel arch or rood loft, of which the one in St Thomas', Salisbury, is a fine example, was common; it held before the eyes of the worshipper – as the Archangel Michael weighed souls in the balance – just what the consequences would be if you were found wanting. Only Christ's merits and the regular intercession of those left behind might even the balance and avert the torments of hell. So, making your will and providing for masses for your soul, making a deathbed confession of sin with the crucifix held before your eyes and living a life of charity and good works alone could help to shorten or alleviate the miseries of purgatory.

GOD'S JUDGEMENT AND CHRIST'S PASSION

In a period preoccupied with death, a sense of God's distance – that he was a stern judge of human sinfulness before all else – and that access to his mercies was only granted through the passion and death of his son Jesus Christ did much to shape not only the liturgy but church buildings too. No longer was the rood screen primarily a structural division to emphasize the difference between clergy and lay or religious community and bystanders (and to provide some warmth against the draughts!); it was primarily to hold the *rood, the scene of the crucifixion, before the eyes of the worshipper. Only by entering into Christ's sufferings with him might the penitent have access to the Father's grace. During the Later Medieval period the image of the crucified Christ was everywhere. The figure on the cross on the

139

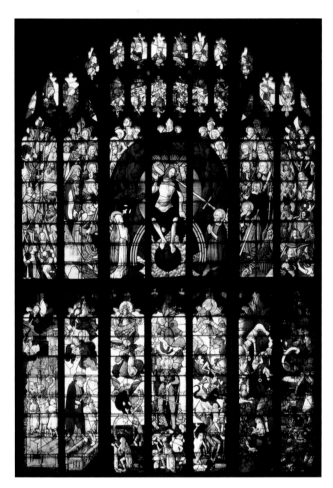

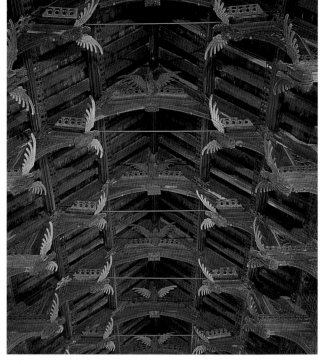

rood became more realistic in its painful contortions, and the Good Friday liturgy shifted subtly from the celebration of the triumph and victory of the cross to personal devotion focused on a theology of atonement that was centred on the payment of the price for human sin. The dominant motif of the Christian life becomes, 'If that is what Christ went through for us, then how can we escape entering his sufferings?' But if worshippers were confronted with the only hope of salvation on the rood, it was frequently in the great west window that they were reminded of the conflict in the coming judgement as they left church, of which the finest surviving example in England is Fairford, Gloucestershire, a church in which a large amount of Late Medieval glass survives. 'From battle, murder and from sudden death, Good Lord, deliver us', prays Cranmer's Great Litany. War was not just one of the miseries of life; it became again an image of the Christian life as it

had for the early desert monks. The world was a battleground, populated by the forces of good and evil in continuous warfare fighting for the souls of God's people. Medieval churches are full of warlike resonances, from the effigies of knights, their helmets and banners to the faces of imps and devils peeping out from the concealing boughs of foliage. Doing battle with the powers of darkness were the hosts of angels visible in the roofs of the churches (in East Anglia in particular, as at March, near Ely) or embroidered on altar frontals and on the vestments of the clergy. In the primers, or personal prayer books of the later Middle Ages, deathbed scenes are represented in woodcuts showing the importance of that last struggle: angels hover around the head of the bed and devils cluster below it, each trying in the last moments of life to win the departing soul.

POINTERS TO HEAVEN

While English examples abound, these ideas were not peculiar to England: the whole of Europe was obsessed with the fear of death. But while this earth might be a continuing battleground and the rituals of death immensely important, there was always the hope of heaven. Pinnacles were everywhere, soaring upwards and pointing people beyond the confines of this earth. Whether this was part of the design of the building as a whole, as in the cathedrals at Milan or Leon, or the chapel on the walls of the chateau at Amboise; or whether it was a prominent spire, like that of Salisbury Cathedral, which was added to the already tall tower, or the western spires of St Elizabeth at Marburg, Germany, the pinnacle or spire with its tapering perspective lifts people's sights above the mundane. On the west front of Bath Abbey is represented Jacob's dream (see page 16), with a ladder linking earth and heaven and the angels of God ascending and descending. Nor was this just an exterior feature. Pinnacles and crocketed canopies adorn the niches of statues and screens alike. The saints may have shared our life, but now they have been drawn up into the life of heaven and open a window into it for us, pointing the way ahead. One form of a hanging *pyx (a vessel suspended above the high altar in which the sacrament was reserved for adoration as a sign of Christ's real presence with his people outside

The cathedral at Leon in northern Spain.

Top: Pinnacled chapel perched on the walls of the chateau at Amboise, France.

Bottom: The angels of God ascend and descend on the ladder (Genesis 28:12), sculpted on the west front of Bath Abbey, England.

Late Gothic

141

the celebration of mass) was a pinnacled turret, like that preserved at Milton Abbey. A hanging pinnacle such as this, suspended from above rather than capping a tower or buttress, emphasizes the descent of God's grace among his people. God gives himself to us; we do not clamber up to grasp hold of him.

These hanging pyxes and suspended tabernacles suggest that the hanging lanterns and suspended vaults that are such a striking feature of Late Gothic architecture may not only be the expression of the architect's skill but also a statement of theological significance. The canopy of heaven descends to earth.

THE EUCHARIST AND THE REAL PRESENCE

In an age of great devotion, protecting the sacrament of the body of Christ itself comes to predominate over access to the sacrament. Infrequent Communion and careful scrutiny of the communicants, the provision of screens and rails to keep people at a distance from the altar and benches at which they might kneel (covered with *houselling cloths lest any small particle from the host might drop) and giving Communion in one kind and directly onto the tongue of the recipient were all signs of the anxiety that the sacrament might be misused for magical or superstitious purposes. The miracle of Bolsena, in which a host in the hands of a priest who doubted the reality of the doctrine of transubstantiation bled onto the corporal, was part of creating an immense devotion to the real presence of Christ in the sacrament. That particular corporal is housed in a substantial Medieval shrine in the nearby cathedral at Orvieto. Everywhere the procession of the consecrated host through the carpeted and flower-strewn streets of the town on the Feast of Corpus Christi became a regular feature of Medieval piety and a focus of the church's power to build community around the sense of Christ's real presence.

Left: A seven sacrament font from East Anglia, England.

Right: A font and its crocketed font cover from Crick, Northamptonshire.

THE FONT AND ITS COVER

It is not only the Eucharistic presence of Christ among his people that is crowned with a heavenward-pointing pinnacle; the sacrament of baptism is similarly a heavenly gift, and fonts in this period are often crowned with elaborately counterweighted pinnacles, like that at Crick in Northamptonshire. The Late Medieval font in the nave of the cathedral at Efurt, Germany, is surmounted by an extraordinary canopy, with interlacing ogee arches. But none is as spectacular as that at Ufford in Suffolk, where the elaborate pinnacled cover dating from the fifteenth century is drawn up telescopically into itself to give access to the font.

But font covers are not there merely to point heavenwards. The church's canon law stipulates that the font must be fitted with a cover that can be locked to protect the water. Protecting the waters of baptism, blessed only once in the year, in the firm belief that holy water has miraculous properties, becomes as important as protecting the Eucharistic host. Sprinkling with holy water becomes an important rite during this period: the congregation were sprinkled during the *Asperges* chant at the start of the Sunday mass, as were the wedding rings of a couple marrying, the houses of

the parish in Eastertide, the body and the coffin at a funeral, among others. In time this leads to the provision of holy water stoups – shallow basins on pedestals or brackets near the entrance of the church from which people can sign themselves with the cross as they enter, as a reminder of their baptism.

Notable in East Anglia in England are a series of octagonal fonts, raised up on a number of steps in the centre of the rear of the nave, with the seven *sacraments of the church carved on the sides. This desire to teach the fullness of the sacramental life from the moment of baptism onwards is a clear indication of the systematic programme that was offered. At least the font, if not the altar, was accessible to the whole congregation, and the life-cycle stages represented on these seven sacrament fonts held these points of transformation before the eyes of the worshippers.

THE LATE MEDIEVAL SACRAMENTAL SYSTEM

In the church's worship a shift is taking place in the whole sense of the sacraments. Sacraments are not so much corporate celebrations of a continuing pattern of transformation in the church as moments when a transaction takes place in an

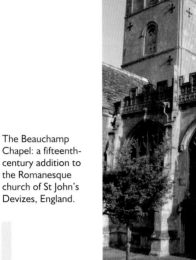

The Beauchamp Chapel: a fifteenth-century addition to the Romanesque church of St John's Devizes, England.

fellow worshippers. So a personal and individual appreciation of the sacrament's power gains in importance over the corporate experience of celebrating together.

This transactional sense of the Eucharistic presence of Christ benefiting the worshipper is paralleled in the other sacraments, notably in baptism, in the sacrament of penance or confession, and in extreme unction, which become tokens of protection in the journey through this world and at the point of leaving it.

CHANTRY CHAPELS

With so much emphasis on individual salvation, perhaps it is not surprising to find that the major additions to many church buildings, whether in the individual. Attention gathers round the precise moment, round the physical and actual change in the substance, and round the power of the ordained priest to effect the change rather than around the quality of the developing relationships. So in the Eucharist what assumes the highest importance is the precise moment at which the bread and wine become the body and blood of Christ – the words of institution in the recital of the last supper narrative in the Eucharistic prayer – and the fact that they are effective just because an ordained priest, who has the power to confect the sacrament, prays them. For the lay people witnessing this daily miracle, the *elevation, the raising of the consecrated host for adoration and the ringing of the bell to tell the world that this has happened, is the key moment. To have seen the risen Christ yourself becomes more important than to have received Communion with your

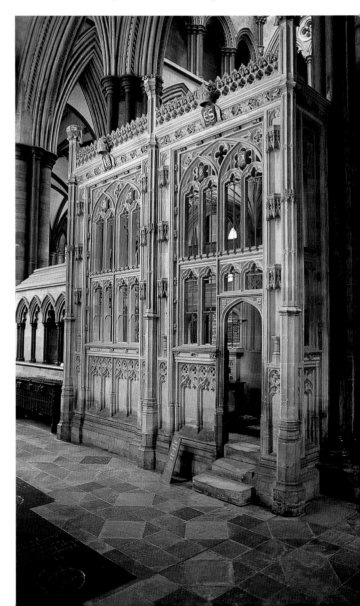

The Audley Chantry in Salisbury Cathedral.

Left: The heraldic roof of the Bayldon Chapel in Bromham, Wiltshire.

Below: Tomb with a lifelike cadaver.

form of additional aisles or *chantry chapels, were rarely made with the good of the whole worshipping community in mind. Frequently they were the result of a pious or powerful individual making what was in effect a private chapel within a church and endowing a priest – or sometimes a whole college of priests – to pray for his soul after death. Sometimes it was as a result of a powerful and important guild or local trade demonstrating their importance and praying for their success. Sometimes, of course, wealthy individuals would be able both to demonstrate their success and to pray to God for favours by entirely rebuilding the church in the modern style.

Sometimes a chantry chapel was built on to an existing church, such as the Beauchamp Chapel in St John's, Devizes, in Wiltshire, or the Bayldon Chapel in the nearby church of Bromham, which was built with the king's permission to offer prayer for the king's majesty and for the souls of two founders. The elaborately decorated roof of the chapel, with its complex heraldry, illustrates the network of alliances in this world that held the families in their place in society. A different style of chantry chapel is illustrated by the Audley Chantry in Salisbury Cathedral. Here a chantry chapel is tucked between two pillars of the north presbytery arcade, so as to lie as close to the high altar as possible. In this position it resembles an

elaborate tomb, and such a position was favoured for the tombs of kings and bishops, whether within a chantry chapel or not. A third kind of chantry chapel is like that at the east end of the south aisle of Cirencester, a large church built on the substantial wealth of the wool trade. Here a simple wooden *parclose screen defines a space at the east end of the aisle for use as a chantry chapel. It is a short journey from such private spaces to the family pews that came to dominate the interiors of many churches in the sixteenth and seventeenth centuries; indeed, sometimes former chantry chapels were hijacked and rebuilt for the purpose, such as the Hungerford Chantry in Salisbury Cathedral which became – and still is – the family pew of the Earls of Radnor.

Not all those who died could afford to endow a chantry priest. Some graves were marked by simple slabs; some – even of notable bishops – eschewed sculptural effigies and were represented by decaying cadavers as a *memento mori*. For some, brasses let into the floor slabs or monumental memorials between the columns of an arcade tell us of their longing for recognition in posterity. In England at least, the tradition of burying the dead around the church provides classic graveyards where the lives of the living and the departed seem closely entwined.

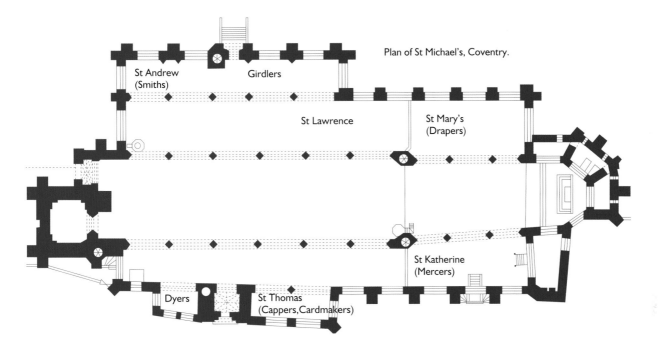

Plan of St Michael's, Coventry.

St Andrew (Smiths)

Girdlers

St Lawrence

St Mary's (Drapers)

St Katherine (Mercers)

Dyers

St Thomas (Cappers,Cardmakers)

CHURCH BUILDING AS A SIGN OF SUCCESS

In parallel to this preoccupation with life as a preparation for death and what stretches beyond lies the whole practice of building churches as celebrations of wealth and achievement being offered to God. The great wool churches of England in the Cotswolds, such as Cirencester, or in East Anglia, such as Lavenham or Long Melford, provide remarkable examples of churches whose size had nothing to do with the needs of a worshipping community but everything to do with the demonstration of the power of wealth.

In today's more narrowly nationalistic frame, it is difficult for us to remember that the potent players in the international scene were not so much the local church or diocese, gathered round its bishop in a specific place and country, but the then equivalents of the multinational corporations, the religious orders. The Cistercians grew a reputation for being astute large-scale farmers, and their monasteries, such as the Abbeys of Fountains or Rievaulx in Yorkshire, became rich and powerful.

Opposite: The ruins of the Cistercian abbey at Rievaulx, Yorkshire.

GUILDS AND SPONSORSHIP

But it was not just the great industries such as wool or wealthy individuals who were seeking the security of a favoured place by beautifying churches. During the Middle Ages, and in particular after the social and economic turmoil produced by the combined effects of the Hundred Years' War and the Black Death, there began to emerge a pattern of guilds with a growing ability to provide social cohesion and political clout based on their trade secrets and their professional loyalties rather than ties of kinship or claims of feudal loyalty. We may think of sponsorship as an essentially twentieth-century phenomenon, but the bell-founders' window in York Minster, in which bells make up a decorative border, and the aisles in St Michael's, Coventry – the Medieval predecessor to Coventry Cathedral – indicate the complex and interrelated pattern of loyalties and interests that made up the civil community of the period and competed for attention before God. In St Michael's, the Smiths, the Girdlers, the Drapers, the Dyers, the Cappers, the Cardmakers and the Mercers all maintained guild altars.

Nor was this patronage by guilds confined to England. In Nuremberg, famous for its metalworkers, the makers of the finest trumpets

The polygonal porch of St Mary, Redcliffe, echoing a market cross: a civic church for rich merchants in Bristol, England.

had a guild whose secrets are still unknown. In Florence, the Orsanmichele, a combination of grain market and oratory built around a wonder-working picture of the Virgin on a pier, was enormously well endowed. The city guilds competed to outdo one another in creating the statuary to adorn it.

With the emphasis on the visual, another way of beautifying the church was to present a painting, often in the form of a retable or reredos. Large paintings or multiple compositions with saints, angels and donors clustering round a central scene were erected behind or on top of altars. They provided a visual focus – a sense of the divine presence – when the sacrament was not being celebrated. Some, like the *Maesta* by Duccio, painted for the high altar of Siena Cathedral between 1308 and 1311, were enormous – over 13 feet wide by 7 feet tall (4 metres by 2 metres); and some, like the Isenheim altar (c. 1510–15) by Matthias Grunewald, painted for the sufferers in a hospital chapel, had a series of complex folding wings and panels that were changed according to the liturgical season or the day of the week. Even small churches might acquire an altarpiece, especially if the donor was represented kneeling in the straw at the manger.

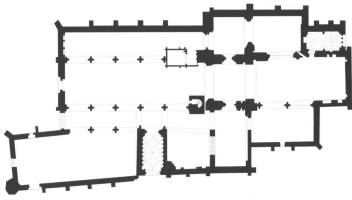

Plan of the parish church at Burford.

Among the great churches of England in the later Middle Ages, such as St Michael's, Coventry, Long Melford in East Anglia and St Mary Redcliffe, Bristol – with its wonderful polygonal porch, shaped for concourse like a great market cross – two churches reveal different aspects of this pattern of development. One is Burford in Oxfordshire, where an older cruciform church with a heavy central crossing has received almost every conceivable kind of addition. There are aisles to the chancel and a vaulted chantry to the north-east corner; between the two-storeyed porch and the south transept a chapel is inserted, and as well as a parclose chantry in the nave, the south-western end of the nave has been demolished and a large additional aisle built at a slight angle. The other is Cirencester, where a large parish church with its splendid perpendicular nave has a series of chapels parallel to the chancel, including St Katharine's with fine fan vaulting, and an additional aisle chapel to the north of the nave, as well as a chantry in the south-east corner. Both churches reveal the individualism of many different benefactors held within the envelope of civic prosperity, as Cirencester's three-storeyed porch indicates. For a more modest interior, South Creake in Norfolk retains the texture of the past, and for intricate, small-scale decoration, the Lady Chapel at Ely is unsurpassed.

By contrast, in Germany and Italy the typical Late Gothic building was more likely to be a wholesale replacement than the piecemeal adaptation and addition that characterized so much of English church development: when a church was felt to be no longer suitable, it was torn down and rebuilt.

THE RISE OF PREACHING AND DRAMA

The pattern of preaching in countries like England dates back to the seventh century, when those who were gifted with the skills of communicating the faith, such as Aldhelm (c. 639–709) in Wessex, used the natural gathering places – such as the bridges crossing rivers – to proclaim the gospel. Such missionary bishops left the security of the monastic communities that sustained them to preach where people were, and frequently preaching crosses mark the sites where friars and other preachers continued this open-air tradition.

In Italy, following the founding of the new religious orders in the thirteenth century, churches with large, open naves began to be built, such as the great brick hall of San Domenico in Siena, where St Catherine of Siena had her visions, and Santa Croce, the Franciscan church in Florence. Here, a

149

shallow apse for the altar in the centre of a T-shaped transept at the east end provided for the liturgical needs. For the rest, the church was a large open hall in which people could crowd round the pulpit – often in origin little more than a portable wooden railed platform to make the preacher both visible and audible over the heads of the throng. Such wayside pulpits or street corner-style preaching may seem unlikely to us, but a large number of preaching crosses that date from the Medieval period remain.

The new orders that sprang up in the thirteenth century were transnational forces within the church: the Dominicans established their presence in many parts of the known world, and became the centres of intellectual life and ferment as their centres in Florence – San Marco, with its famous monastic cells painted by Fra Angelico and Santa Maria Novella – bear witness. The phenomenal spread of the religious orders in western Europe is bound up with teaching, and both the Franciscans, with their fondness for preaching in the open air to engage with the greatest number, and their espousal of worldly poverty, and the Dominicans – the Order of Preachers as they were called, who were often based in a university town – set up their missions wherever the ground seemed fertile. Some early Dominican churches, such as the Church of the Jacobins in Toulouse, were designed like large refectories or lecture halls, with a row of columns down the middle. Sometimes too additional naves witness to this increased function, as at Leominster or in Dorchester Abbey. In Cirencester, the wide nave has one of the best-preserved pre-Reformation 'wine glass' pulpits, painted and gilded and set against a pillar on the north side.

It is too easy to think of the main themes of the gospel being set before an illiterate peasantry solely in wall paintings and stained glass and to overlook the importance in the Later Medieval period of preaching. In the millenarian climate of fear resulting from the terrors of plague and war, preaching took on a new urgency and had a ready audience. Examples such as San Bernardino in Siena and Savonarola in Florence are well known, and begin to create the climate in which reformation could take place.

The polychrome pulpit in the nave of Cirencester parish church.

The organized response to preaching conversion of life lay in the development of fraternities committed to the corporal works of mercy – in Italy, to this day the task of the ambulance service and funeral director is undertaken by a local *Confraternita di Misericordia*. There were also those committed to the care of widows and orphans, and many of the new religious orders concentrated on teaching and nursing. Even today many of those engaged in social work and nursing in Sweden are ordained deacon at the end of their training. Additionally some became flagellants – a movement started as a penitential procession – and undertook personal discipline as a way of sharing in the pains of Christ. From this tradition developed the barefoot processions carrying the cross on Good Friday that are still a feature of the Holy Week celebrations in Spain, as in Seville and Salamanca, for example.

Along with the rise of preaching came the rise of drama. Out of the sequences (strophic hymns sung before the gospel on important feasts)

Below: Preaching outdoors: St Bernardino's banner – an early visual aid.

Below: The Easter Sepulchre in Magdeburg Cathedral, Germany.

Right: Notre Dame de l'Epine: the crocketed spires of the south tower.

developed mini-dramas, such as the *Visitatio Sepulchri*, the visit to the tomb by the women early on Easter day. These quasi-liturgical dramas were designed to bring the gospel events alive and engage people in the drama of the liturgy. This drama centres round the dialogue between the women who bring the spices to anoint the body of Jesus and the angel at the tomb, and was performed by characters in liturgical vestments. Dramas like these, many of which are found in the *Regularis Concordia* of St Ethelwold, were closely linked with developments in the liturgy itself, like burying the consecrated host at the end of the Good Friday liturgy in an

Easter sepulchre of the kind that survives on the north side of the chancel at Patrington in Yorkshire or in the substantial twelve-sided Holy Sepulchre in Magdeburg Cathedral, from which it would be 'resurrected' on Easter day.

Sometimes a church would be founded on the site of a miracle, as was Notre Dame de l'Epine, near Chalons en Champagne. Some shepherds found a statue of the Virgin Mary in the middle of a blazing thorn bush, and built an oratory on the site. Later, a substantial church with pinnacled and crocketed towers, the southern one ringed with a crown of fleurs-de-lys, was raised over it in the Flamboyant style. Inside, the pinnacled shrine sits next to the Renaissance detail of the presbytery screen, and there is a pierced fifteenth-century rood screen, surmounted by a rood beam bearing the rood. The Flamboyant west front has pierced-work gables over the three doorways, the central one containing a crucifix that

Left: The Gothic shrine and a Renaissance screen set side by side in Notre Dame de l'Epine, France.

Right: The south transept and porch of the cathedral in Prague by Peter Parler.

Left: The interior of Plzen in the Czech Republic, a typical hall-church.

looks like an exterior rood screen rising in front of the rose window. The amazing gargoyles were so spectacularly rude that some were replaced altogether in the nineteenth century.

ARCHITECTURAL DEVELOPMENTS

Against this background, architectural developments took place in the High Gothic period that reflect the development of different architectural solutions to solve different problems. For example, the Gothic cathedral of Orvieto has small windows, filled with translucent alabaster panels to keep the interior cool and dark, while in England, maximizing the size of windows to let in more light was highly desirable. Sometimes it was the creation of a jewelled casket within a larger space to define something special – such as the Late Gothic choir with its elaborate stalls, inserted into the great, brick-built fortress of a cathedral at Albi.

In Bohemia, the emperor Charles IV chose Prague as his capital in 1333, and set about building a new cathedral there. Brought up in France, he married the daughter of the King of France and chose a French architect. After his death, one of the most influential architects of the Late Gothic, Peter Parler, was appointed in

1356. Parler is responsible for two major innovations: turning the vaulting through 45 degrees, and creating a hanging boss: where you might have expected a column supporting the springing of a vault, the vault is there, but no column!

Parler's work and that of his family is visible in the south porch and tower of the cathedral at Prague; at Kutna Hora, also in the Czech Republic; in the Frauenkirche at Nuremberg; in the choir – the eastern 'glass house' – at Aachen; and in the pendant boss with flying ribs in the Chapel of St Catherine in St Stephen's, Vienna. These pendant bosses hanging from flying ribs, first seen in Bristol, emerge again at a late stage in churches such as St Leonard in Frankfurt or the Frauenkirche in Ingoldstadt, where they form a decorative web hanging below the primary or structural vault, as they do in a less exaggerated way in Dieppe.

The Hallenkirche

A distinctive contribution from Germany to the Later Gothic period was the Hallenkirche, or hall-church. Aisles of an equal height to the central nave, supported by slender columns, do not diminish the sense of verticality, but they do serve to make the interior a more unified space. When much in the Later Gothic served to emphasize the interior compartmentalization of churches, this Hallenkirche principle serves to emphasize the openness of the space, with the columns and their shafts rising uninterruptedly into the high vaulting, as in this church in Plzen in the Czech Republic (left).

An Italian example of the Hallenkirche style is the Church of San Fortunato at Todi. Built between 1292 and 1460, this large, lofty and well-lit church with wide aisles offers a good liturgical space for both the celebration of the sacraments and for preaching. It has a fine, free-standing Gothic altar whose generous proportions are scaled to the church and indicate that the small altars with *dossals and *frontals known to us from Medieval paintings of the Mass of St Gregory were not necessarily the model for the principal altars in large churches.

Hanging boss in the Church of St James, Dieppe.

In Germany, the rebuilt eastern choir of the cathedral in Erfurt shows that Late Gothic, with tall windows, high vaults and pinnacled buttressing need not be confined to the Hallenkirche, and details like the celebrated triangular porch to the Romanesque north transept reveal a delicacy matched by the rood screen at St Pantaleon in Cologne. But

the most interesting church of the Late Medieval period in Germany is St Anna, in Annaberg, Saxony. This church, built between 1499 and 1525 in Hallenkirche form, has twelve piers, each with eight concave sides and three shallow apses to the east. The double-curved ribs flow from the aisles into the spaces between the buttresses that are incorporated into the interior, so that the columns seem to be suspended from the roof, rather than supporting the vault. The pattern of the vault suggests the petals of a giant flower, hanging in space. Fairly low down, a balcony is constructed between the buttresses, with a continuous frieze sculpted round it, forming small chapels in the recesses below. The pulpit, dated 1516, has naturalistic carvings, including that of a miner, as a reminder of the silver mines on which the town's wealth was based.

A very different roofline is offered by the cathedral of St Barbara in Kutna Hora, a silver-mining town east of Prague in the Czech Republic. Three great pyramidal roofs are supported over the three central aisles of this five-aisled church, held in place by an elaborate system of double flying buttresses, with smaller pyramids over the aisle roofs between the buttresses, the whole looking like a pavilion at a marine trade fair. Inside, the network of flying ribs springs out from the side walls. There are no arches in the arcade, so a continuous pattern of petal shapes covers the entire roof, with the curving ribs intersecting and sometimes hanging down, sometimes rising up.

France and the Flamboyant Style

In France, the Late Gothic is characterized by the Flamboyant style, and though nothing ever outdid Beauvais for height, there are some fine churches, such as the Abbey of St Riquier on the Somme, with its wide nave (43 feet or 13 metres in relation to its height, 79 feet or 24 metres) and a variety of Flamboyant tracery in its windows. There is even

Top: The high Gothic choir at the east end of Erfurt Cathedral.

Bottom: A church for preaching: San Fortunato, Todi, Italy.

Left: The delicate, hanging vaulting in St Anna, in Annaberg.

Right: Mining silver: creation of the wealth that built St Anna, Annaberg, on the steps of the pulpit.

Below: Pinnacles and pavilion roofs of St Barbara, Kutna Hora, in the Czech Republic point heavenward.

finer Flamboyant tracery in the windows and in the delicate stonework of the balustrades of the curved entrance porch of the Church of St Maclou in Rouen, which dates from the early years of the sixteenth century. There the curving lines of the tracery, giving the effect of flickering flames, illustrate perfectly what is meant by 'Flamboyant'. This lacy effect of Late Gothic screenwork is visible in the pulpitum screen of St Pantaleon in Cologne (see page 262). In both of these, the porch effect – perhaps related to the celebrated triangular porch to the north transept of the cathedral in Erfurt – is accentuated by the central section projecting slightly, giving a polygonal plan, and a more substantial central bay. These delicate porches seem to suggest a very fine boundary – like a theatre gauze – between the exterior and the interior of the church, and by implication between this life and the hereafter. The west front of the cathedral at Toul is an example of this. In the lacy screenwork, created between 1460 and 1500, an ogee arch rises over the central portal and comes to a point in front of the rose window. The rose is contained in a pointed arch over which rises an enormous gable, which frames a great crucifix, like some gigantic rood screen. The same effect is visible in the west front of St Ouen, another church in Rouen.

Left and right: The west porch of St Ouen, Rouen.

Below: The west front of Rouen Cathedral.

For sheer complexity, the west front of the Rouen cathedral is hard to equal. From the late 1360s, the thirteenth-century front was overlaid with a series of screens and figurative sculpture behind which a large rose window was constructed. The lateral towers were adapted and completed only in 1507, by which time the design for the central portal and the Flamboyant rose behind it were being planned. The interplay of light and shade on this façade fascinated Monet, who painted it many times in different lights.

The Flamboyant *jubé*, or pulpitum, in the Church of Ste-Madeleine in Troyes is a bridge of three arches, suspended between the columns to the east of the crossing of this originally Romanesque church. The small figures in Renaissance dress entwined among its highly detailed, though finely executed, carving give some sense of the loss of proportion between the liturgy as a whole and personal prayer that characterizes this 'age of devotion'. Renaissance detail is visible right at the end of the Gothic period in the Church of St Pierre at Caen, which has Renaissance candlesticks instead of pinnacles on its flying buttresses.

Spain

In Spain, three remarkable churches illustrate the longing of the Late Medieval spirit to pierce the gloom of this world's misery. The first is the construction of the cathedral at Cordoba, where the first building on the site is a remarkable

mosque, with a courtyard and a fountain, a minaret and a prayer-hall composed of a forest of pillars with red and white arches stretching in every direction (see page 12). This building, begun in 786, was initially shared by both Islamic and Christian communities, but soon the Christians found themselves in their own building. However, with the waning of the Caliphate's power, the building became the cathedral in 1236 under Alonso X. By the sixteenth century, the canons wished for something more sumptuous and obviously Christian in feel so they cut out a cruciform space in the centre of the 850 columns, erected a high vault and set up their *coro*. The emperor Carlos V (r. 1519–56) is said to have been far from pleased with the result: 'You have

Left: The Flamboyant *jubé* in the Church of Ste-Madeleine in Troyes.

Above: The pinnacles and towers of the cathedral at Burgos, Spain.

destroyed something unique,' he said, 'to build something commonplace.' The Late Gothic space is vaulted with a Renaissance stuccoed vault and a *coffered dome, complete with stalls and pulpits in a Baroque style.

Second is the cathedral at Burgos. Here, the cathedral was begun in 1221 and saw a second

major building period in the fifteenth century, when the west front and the spires were added to the towers at the west end and the Constable's Chapel to the east. This chapel, built by Simon of Cologne between 1482 and 1494, is lit by a lacy octagonal cupola with star-shaped vaulting supporting a lantern where some of the web of the vault in the centre has its stone replaced by glass. The eight corner piers are joined at the lower level by decorated arches, from which hang what looks like embroidery in stone. The ogee frames above the arches pierce into the clerestory window zone. In Burgos you can see the interior pattern that is characteristic of Spanish cathedrals, in which the *coro*, with its solid western wall, is set well west in the nave, leaving only a modest 'antechapel' of a few bays. This *coro* is linked to the sanctuary in the eastern arm by tall ironwork screens, allowing the worshippers who are not members of the cathedral chapter a lateral glimpse. Sometimes the *coro* is right at the west end of the nave as in Barcelona, and occasionally – as in Santo Tomas, Avila and San Juan d'Ortega – at first-floor level in a gallery over the westernmost bays.

Third, the cathedral at Granada combines a Late Gothic plan and Early Renaissance architectural detail to produce a massive building which, like

The west front of the cathedral of Burgos.

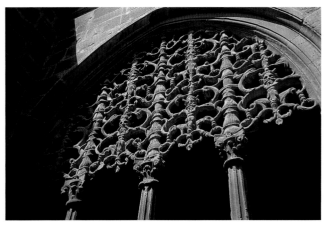

Opposite page: The star vault in the Constable's Chapel, Burgos Cathedral.

Left: The western *coro* in San Juan d'Ortega, Spain.

Below: The Manueline tracery in the cloister of Santa Maria Real Monastery, Najera.

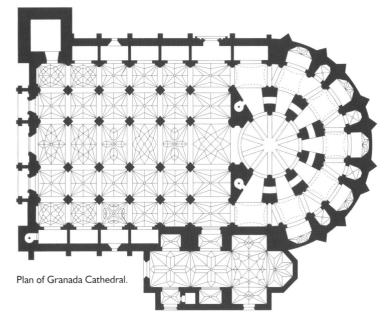

some of the Italian cathedrals, spans these two periods. Here the *Capilla Mayor* or sanctuary is a rotunda, cleverly linked to the nave and its four aisles. This combination of the circular east end with a linear nave, like the pre-Romanesque cathedral of St Benigne at Dijon (see page 87), is echoed by Michelozzo's Renaissance church of the SS Annunciata in Florence, built between 1444 and 1460. In the Iberian peninsula, the distinctive Plateresque style (the use of half Gothic and half Renaissance small-scale relief ornament deriving from the techniques used in metalworking by silversmiths) has a fine example in the cloisters of Santa Maria Real Monastery, at Najera.

Perpendicular Architecture in England

Architecturally, the later Middle Ages drew Gothic to its limits. Reducing walls to their minimum meant the ever-increasing size of windows, whose panels of tracery spill down from the clerestory to cover the walls. This extensive use of window space, whether or not the windows were filled with stained glass, produced the great east window of Gloucester Cathedral, or a west window like that at Southwell Minister, Tewkesbury Abbey or Winchester Cathedral. In these great churches, Romanesque or Early Gothic in origin, the west wall has largely been

removed and a great window inserted to fill as much of the space as possible.

As interiors were unified, a pattern of wall decoration that looks as if a series of wooden panels has been applied to the stonework was developed. The nave of Winchester is an interesting case, as the Perpendicular architecture of its rebuilding in the late fourteenth century by William of Wykeham masks the underlying Romanesque construction, using the thick Romanesque clerestory walls to give a deeply

Plan of Granada Cathedral.

Late Gothic

recessed system of lighting unlike conventional clerestories of the period, which form a single flat panel topping the main arcade. About a hundred years later, the same kind of re-casing was done to the Romanesque abbey at Sherborne. Here the builder clothed the original arcade with a skin of panelling, which then becomes the dominant motif of the tall clerestory – clearly the *piano nobile* to which the arcade serves as a rustic base – which is intimately linked to the fan vault that springs from it. In Sherborne, the whole visual experience is lifted up a layer.

The chief characteristic of the 'Perpendicular' period was this attempt to give the columns, walls, windows, clerestory and vaults a unity, so that the distinction between wall surface and window, between nave arcade and clerestory, was minimized. As the springing of the arcades was delayed till the last moment, the pointed arches of the windows were depressed until they were hardly more than a rectangle, giving way to a four-centred arch, although the east window of the rebuilt abbey at Bath is in fact a complete rectangle, the top corners being filled with small roundels. The vertical mullions of these windows needed the support of horizontal bars from time to time, so large composite windows were designed in repetitive stages made up of a number of smaller units. Such high springing of the vaults led to a flattening of the ceilings, and it was to span these spaces securely that the system we know as *fan vaulting was devised. Here the essential structural ribs or the early, pointed quadripartite or sexpartite vaults, to which lateral infill or *lierne vaults like those at the east end of Tewkesbury Abbey had been added, are replaced by a seemingly gossamer construction of thin webs that seem to float in the air as they carry the panelled surfaces of the walls and windows into the roof.

In England this system of spanning the width of a single rectangular cell reached its apogee in the chapel at King's College, Cambridge. Here the uniform character of the vault throughout the length of the chapel, divided by Henry VIII's substantial pulpitum, carries the

Opposite page: Perpendicular cladding transforms the Romanesque nave of Winchester Cathedral.

Above left: The rectangular east window of Bath Abbey, England.

Above right: Early fan vaulting in the cloisters of Gloucester Cathedral.

Top: The lierne vaults of the apse of Tewkesbury Abbey, England.

Late Gothic

eye from the antechapel, with its low side-chapels tucked between the buttresses that form the lowest stage of the panelled walls, right through to the east end. The fan vault, of which the earliest example is the north range of the cloisters at Gloucester, was built by the architect John Wastell between 1512 and 1515; the richness of the Early Renaissance carving of the woodwork, the well-proportioned Dallam organ case of 1605–06, and the entire sequence of Flemish glass give a better picture of the monumental interior of the early sixteenth century than anywhere else in England. Most astonishing of all – especially when applied to an essentially Romanesque structure like Christ Church, Oxford – are the amazing pendant vaults, with what seem to be hanging lanterns: a lovely star-shaped lierne vault is constructed in the centre of each bay, and thrust out into the space by a lateral rib from which these lanterns hang, as if they were the vestigial traces of some earth-bound support. The only comparable building is the Henry VII Chapel at the east end of Westminster Abbey, where the glittering turreted exterior with its angled windows is complemented by the rich pendant vault above the tomb of Henry VII by the Florentine sculptor, Torrigiani (1472–1528), in an uncompromisingly Renaissance style.

As well as the double *hammer-beam roofs of East Anglia with their carved angels, wood continued to be used, as in the nave roof of St David's Cathedral, Pembrokeshire, or – in combination with plasterwork – as in Edington Priory in Wiltshire.

Top: Henry VII Chapel, Westminster Abbey.

Far Left: The pendant vaults over the choir of Christ Church Cathedral, Oxford.

Left: Sherborne nave.

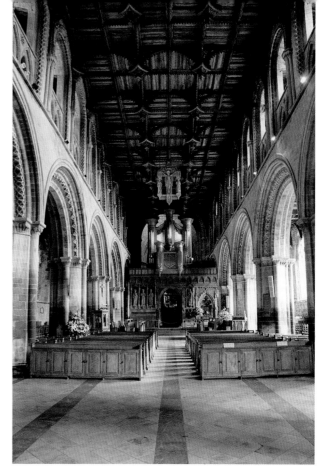

Far left: The brick Gothic cathedral at Uppsala, Sweden.

Above: The wooden roof of St David's Cathedral, Pembrokeshire, Wales.

Left: Medieval crucifix and wall painting in the church at Sigtuna, Sweden.

Scandinavia

The tall spires of the cathedral at Uppsala are a reminder that the Gothic style as well as the Romanesque seeped up through Jutland and into the Baltic states during the Middle Ages. The existence of many largely unrestored and unaltered churches in Sweden is a reminder that there was never a puritan or iconoclastic phase in the adoption of Lutheranism in Scandinavia, which retained most Catholic externals there. Medieval wall paintings and crucifixes, and even Medieval vestments, have continued in unbroken use through the Reformation period until today, even if characteristic Lutheran eighteenth-century additions such as organs, chandeliers and pewing have brought a different feel to the interior (see page 197).

The decorated façade of
Orvieto Cathedral.

LOOKING FORWARD: ITALY

The western façade of the great Gothic cathedral at Orvieto, towering above the Tiber on its sheer outcrop of volcanic rock, creates a two-dimensional end to the cathedral that anticipates the later Baroque façades of city churches. The combination of the carving, the delicate tracery and the mosaics suggests a screen that leads the passer-by from the piazza into the holy space – a screen that is as delicate and easy to pass through as the veil that divides this world from the next.

While the tall interiors of north-western Europe continue the spirit of Gothic, the developments that had been taking place in Italy and central Europe were beginning to point towards the future. Begun in 1296 by Arnolfo di Cambio, the cathedral (or Duomo) in Florence was to be a showpiece outdoing the cathedrals of Florence's great rivals, Pisa and Siena. From the start the Duomo was planned to be stone-vaulted with a central dome. Pisa's monumental group – the Duomo, the Campanile (the famous 'leaning tower'), the Battistero and the Campo Santo (see page 97) – was begun in 1063 and largely completed by the fourteenth century. In the Duomo in Pisa, the central dome was erected over an octagonal crossing space. Siena's project to turn their cathedral through 90 degrees, again using the octagonal crossing as a pivot so that the existing nave would have become just a transept, was halted for ever by the Black Death in 1348. Florence's Duomo was still not completed by the beginning of the fifteenth century. The mosaics in the baptistery date from the thirteenth century and the famous baptistery doors were begun in 1330. The tall, detached *campanile* had been designed by Giotto, and begun in 1334. But the problem of raising the central dome over the octagonal crossing remained. The width of the great octagon was 140 feet (43 metres) across, and no wooden centring could be made large enough to span it. The construction of Brunelleschi's dome began in 1420, building each complete ring of stone on the preceding one, its pointed, rather than

Brunelleschi's Late Gothic dome over the Duomo in Florence.

hemispherical, shape dictated by the necessity of maintaining a downward thrust. Gothic, in the sense that ribs and a pointed arch are used, it none the less bridges the boundary between the Gothic and the Renaissance.

In Milan – although the building period is much longer and the cathedral, though begun in 1386 was not finally finished till 1809 – the

Left: The Classical west front of the cathedral at Pienza, Tuscany.

Right: Turrets and pinnacles of the Duomo, Milan.

style remained utterly and recognizably Gothic, the exterior bristling with pinnacles, statues and parapets. The plan too, though there is a vast crossing space, is recognizably Gothic, with crossing, transepts and an apse raised over the crypt.

The Hallenkirche style took a novel form when it found its way into Italy: Aeneas Piccolomini, who had had a diplomatic career and spent much time in Austria, created a small model city, Pienza, above his birthplace in Tuscany when he became Pope Pius II (r. 1458–64). The centrepiece was a cathedral built in the Hallenkirche style, which is a curious mixture of Gothic forms and Renaissance detail. The plan and the apsidal windows are Late Gothic, but the façade and – more interestingly – the capitals at the top of the columns are Classical. Pius left firm instruction that this remarkable cathedral was not to be altered!

In the cathedrals at Milan, Orvieto, Florence, and Pienza – as in Barcelona – it is possible to recognize that the boundaries between Late Gothic and Renaissance are more fluid than we might expect both in architecture and in the development of the intellectual life that created it.

The western narthex with its elaborate octagonal lantern: Barcelona Cathedral, Spain.

The Renaissance and the Catholic Revival

CHAPTER 7

From Classicism to Baroque – In Touch with God in Our Midst

Although there are a number of fine Gothic churches in Italy such as Santa Maria della Spina at Pisa or the great Basilica of San Francesco at Assisi, or the cathedrals at Siena, Florence, Milan and Orvieto, they do not really feel Gothic in the way that the churches of northern Europe do. Italy's Lombard, Apulian and Tuscan Romanesque is so strong that Gothic hardly seems natural in the landscape of such pervasive Roman character. Brunelleschi's dome at Florence or the dark green and white liquorice stripes of Siena's nave seem a long way from the Gothic of English or French cathedrals, and the interior decoration of cathedrals such as Orvieto and Pienza seems a million miles away from the angular paintings of the Eisenheim altarpiece at Colmar, France, or the

Brunelleschi's dome dominates the cityscape of Florence.

Left: Brunelleschi's Santo Spirito uses Classical forms to clothe an essentially Late Medieval plan.

Right: The geometrically proportioned façade of Santa Maria Novella, Florence, by Alberti.

doom painting at St Thomas, Salisbury. Only one church in Rome – Santa Maria sopra Minerva – remains obviously Gothic.

On the other hand, it is easy to see continuity between the very Classical forms of the Romanesque of the Duomo at Pisa, with its marble entablatures, round-headed arches and detail that feels very Classical, and a church like Santo Spirito in Florence, designed by Brunelleschi in 1434. Although not completed till after his death, this design, with a cruciform plan that looks essentially Gothic, was constructed on Vitruvian principles of proportion (described below) that were being rediscovered in Italy while northern Europe was still firmly in the Gothic world of the later Middle Ages. Brunelleschi studied the writings of Vitruvius, and adopted both the mathematical basis and the stylistic features of the architecture of Classical Rome. Round-headed arches take the place of pointed ones; columns and pilasters with Classical capitals replace clusters of shafts; barrel vaults and coffered ceilings replace ribs and vaulting. This Classical architecture is one of pierced walls with applied decoration rather than a skeletal structure of ribs, shafts and glass. Inside, the dense grey *pietra serena* sandstone is used to accentuate the decorative Classical features against the creamy colour of the stuccoed walls. In

the strong sunlight of Italy, the Classical pattern of decoration articulates the proportions of the façades of churches, which come to look like the backdrop to Classical theatres, and are frequently applied to buildings, rather than growing organically out of them, as at Santa Maria Novella in Florence by Alberti, begun in 1458. For Alberti, design – the visual effect – is more important than structure, and the façade – often a front in a street or piazza – is treated like a stage set.

HARMONIC PROPORTION AS THE BASIS OF DESIGN

Both Brunelleschi (1377–1446) and Alberti (1404–72) learnt from the writings of the Classical Roman architect Vitruvius the importance of a harmonic proportion that was mathematically grounded. The architect took a basic unit, which he multiplied in various ways to produce that plan and the volume of the building. Alberti's façade of Santa Maria Novella (1458–71) is made up of two

Classical detail in the
Romanesque Duomo at Pisa.

large squares, either side of a vertical line, each divisible into four smaller ones, and the upper stage fits into a single square that sits on top of the two below. In Brunelleschi's Santo Spirito, the basic square of the aisles is doubled to provide the width of the nave, and four of these squares form the chancel, crossing and transepts. The aisle height is doubled to provide the height of the nave, and again the clerestory. This sense of proportion provides a calm and measured space that does not point you beyond yourself in the way that Gothic does, nor does it invite you into the space and propel you forward on a journey in the way that Romanesque does. The model here is not of a distant God who summons the faithful out of darkness into his marvellous light so much as the God who comes among us and shares our life. The icon is not a distant altar seen through the rood screen and veiled in clouds of incense so much as God reaching out to Adam a finger's breadth away in Michelangelo's Sistine Chapel ceiling. The human person is made in the image and likeness of God, and the new creation is revealed among us in Christ. The human person is

potentially divine, and if placed in a harmonically perfect space may be enabled to become so. Alberti and Leonardo da Vinci drew their mathematics from the proportions of the human figure, following Vitruvius, and Michelangelo's tombs for the Medici family in the New Sacristy of San Lorenzo in Florence are startling in making the human figure both real flesh and blood and immortal.

A theological stress on the divine in our midst, a theology of incarnation, leads to centrally planned churches rather than linear ones. Although Alberti believed that the circle was the most perfect form, and that all other forms derived from it, like the octagon and the square, were mathematically subsidiary, the suitability

God and Adam within touching distance; detail from the ceiling of Michelangelo's Sistine Chapel.

Bottom of page: Bramante's Tempietto in Rome; the building that became an icon for perfect harmonic proportion.

Below and right: Madonna di San Biagio, Montepulciano.

Below right: Santa Maria del Calcinaio, Cortona.

of such forms for temples (Alberti's term for churches) was strengthened by the belief that many of the circular and polygonal structures from the ancient world had been temples in antiquity. Architects pointed to such survivals as the Pantheon, Santo Stephano Rotundo or Santa Costanza in Rome as examples. This time it is not so much the association of the ancient Roman

mausoleum or the Holy Sepulchre with the baptismal theology of the circular or octagonal baptisteries that derive from them, but more a purely abstract search for the perfect form that shapes these sketches. The notebooks of Leonardo da Vinci as well as the published works of Alberti are full of sketches of centrally planned churches.

Bramante's Tempietto and the Design for St Peter's

For an entirely circular building, rather than a dome raised over a Greek cross plan, we need to look at Bramante's Tempietto of San Pietro in Montorio, raised over the place where St Peter had been martyred in Rome. This monument – it is really a sculptural object rather than a church – was designed to be set in a square courtyard or cloister and was begun in 1502. It was idealized by Palladio as the most perfect building, as it demonstrated 'the unity, the infinite essence, the uniformity and the justice of God'. It is

Left and below: Santa Maria della Consolatione, Todi.

Background image: Ground plan of Santa Maria della Consolatione, Todi.

this mathematical perfection that lay behind Bramante's unrealized plan for St Peter's in Rome (1505). This was to have been a Greek cross plan, surmounted by a dome, with the pattern repeated in the diagonal axes, and the whole enclosed in a square from which only the four apses projected. This centralized plan would express St Peter's position as the central church of the faith. Although this plan underwent significant changes, initially by Michelangelo in 1546, it remained a catalyst for architects all over Italy, where such centrally planned churches begin to appear, most effectively on free-standing sites outside the towns, as at Cortona, Montepulciano and Todi.

The Evolution of the Centrally Planned Churches

These three churches in Tuscany and Umbria illustrate the progression of these ideas from Santo Spirito in Florence in the early stages of the development of the centrally planned form. The basic unit was a Greek cross, with a dome raised over a central square. In Santa Maria del Calcinaio in Cortona, a high dome over a Latin cross was built between 1485 and 1513. The Madonna di San Biagio outside Montepulciano, begun in 1518 by Antonio da Sangallo and consecrated in 1529, has the four short equal arms of a Greek cross

around the central cube, which is surmounted by the dome. It has a polygonal sacristy added to the liturgical 'east' end and a pair of free-standing *campaniles*, of which only one was completed to full height, tucked into the angles between the 'western' and lateral arms. Its sober decoration of honey-coloured limestone against the creamy stucco gives the interior a calm and very classically Roman solidity. Santa Maria della Consolatione at Todi was begun in 1508 but had a much longer building period. Here the central cube surmounted by the dome is supported by a quatrefoil, so the Greek cross element on the plan has virtually disappeared, and the four semi-domes contrive to give the central space a greater plasticity more reminiscent of St Sergius and St Bacchus in Constantinople. Looking from the outside like an elaborate jelly-mould, the interior feels an almost solid space, sculpted by the geometry of the architecture.

Nor is this Classical style confined to a few grand churches, designed by well-known architects. Santa Maria della Carita in Seggiano is a simple country version of these Classical principles. There a cross-shaped church with a central dome and a Classical façade, with its rustic granite architectural details set off against the creamy stucco, stands in an olive grove

Left: Santa Maria della Carita, Seggiano.

Right: Looking into the monastic *coro* behind the high altar in the abbey of San Giorgio Maggiore, Venice.

outside this small hilltop village in southern Tuscany.

In these churches there is little to encourage you to movement. There is no succession of spaces to draw you forward, no screen to pass through, no changes in level or lighting. Once you are in the space, everything is harmoniously ordered around you: it is a space to rest in and enjoy the harmony and order of the proportions. Such churches are places where human beings feel calm, unhurried and at home, as they are drawn to the centre under the dome. Here the harmony of the universe, visible in its mathematical outworkings, envelops the human person. In such a building, our inborn sense of harmony is affirmed as we partake in that vital force that is the mainspring of the universe.

However, although a mathematician and philosopher with affinities to Platonism like Nicholas of Cusa (1401–64) might make a logical case for an altar at the very centre of such a building – it is Nicholas of Cusa who said 'God is a circle whose centre is everywhere and whose circumference is nowhere' – such a liturgical layout was rare in completely centrally planned buildings. A theology of the Eucharist that recovered the early Christian sense of the immediacy of God in the broken bread at the table of Emmaus, where Jesus had appeared to the disciple with whom he

had walked from Jerusalem that first Easter day, would need to wait for the continental reformers. For the most part, the reformers were uninterested in a theology of church building, and so were content to adapt and reorder the spaces they had inherited or use a style of plain meeting room for their liturgies. So, in those centrally planned churches in central Italy, the altar still tended to be placed in a recess opposite the principal door, or at any rate in that arm of a Greek cross shape, as in San Biagio at Montepulciano. The altar gets placed in the centre of the crossing space where the eastern part of a church is centrally planned, but there is an elongated western arm forming the nave, as in Santo Spirito in Florence (see page 168). In addition, churches like this may have a

Left: The façade of San Andrea, Mantua, derived from a Roman triumphal arch.

Right: The west portal of St Trophime at Arles.

coro behind the principal altar in the eastern arm. Such a plan derives from Late Gothic models such as the cathedral at Pienza, built on the orders of Pope Pius II in 1462 as the centrepiece of a model Renaissance city-town above his birthplace in Tuscany (see page 166). The Renaissance façade masks a Late Gothic hall-church building, constructed on the model of an Austrian church the Pope had seen on his extensive travels in his earlier career as an ecclesiastical diplomat. Its capitals are already Classical, and five shallow projections radiate round the east end ambulatory behind the high altar, of which the central one is just such a *coro*, complete with inlaid stalls on three sides grouped around a large choir lectern. Such a plan reappears in Palladio's abbey church of San Giorgio in Venice in a more elaborate form, and contrasts with the Spanish solution of placing the *coro* at the west end, well into the nave, where it functions – though entirely enclosed – more like a Syrian bema.

Alberti's Façades

As well as Alberti's façade at Santa Maria Novella in Florence, with its proportional panels and mathematical precision, there is the façade that combines a temple front – with rows of columns or pilasters under a shallow pediment – and a triumphal arch. Alberti's façade at San Andrea in Mantua, begun in 1470, illustrates this well. Modelled on the Arch of Titus in Rome, with a large central opening and two smaller ones to the sides, Alberti manages to give the impression that the four full-height pilasters that support the pediment are also the four pilasters that form the frame for the triumphal arch. The church is a temple, a sculptural monument to the presence of the divine in our midst. But it is not just to be admired from a distance; it is also a triumphal arch through which the worshipper is summoned to enter, following in the wake of the triumphal procession of Christ the King. Such a combination was never part of the Classical vocabulary, but it has pre-echoes in the twelfth-century chapel of St Gabriel near Tarascon in Provence (see page 99) and in the west portal of St Trophime at Arles, where the echoes – however unconscious – of a Roman triumphal arch with its processions of victors and captives are clearly visible.

Palladio and the Churches of Venice

These façades by Alberti provide an introduction to the churches by Palladio (1508–80). Better known for his villas, and for the influence he exerted through his writings and published drawings

San Giorgio Maggiore.

on architects such as Inigo Jones and others in England, Palladio built two important churches in Venice. The first was the abbey church of San Giorgio Maggiore, begun in 1566 on the island opposite St Mark's. Following Alberti and Bramante, it was Palladio who provided the solution to one of the more intractable problems confronting the Renaissance architects. They believed that the Christian church was the proper successor to the Classical temple, and so wanted to provide the entrance with a Classical portico, a pediment supported on a row of columns. But unlike the Classical temples with a single rectangular space, churches had evolved as basilicas, with a high nave and lower aisles. How could a Classical temple front be applied to such a building?

Palladio's solution at San Giorgio (following his façade at San Francesco della Vigna) was to use two temple fronts, and interlock them: a lower, flatter pediment to embrace the width of the aisles, and a higher, central pedimented portico superimposed on that, with its tall columns and tighter pediment covering the nave roofline.

San Francesco della Vigna.

Façade of Il Redentore.

Inside the church, there is a developing succession of spaces. An aisled nave leads to an initial resting place, a domed crossing, where the semicircular ends to the transepts embrace the worshipper and draw him to the altar beyond. Unusually, and because it is a monastic church, the altar is backed by two tiers of columns, forming both a reredos and a screen for the monastic choir beyond, whose semicircular east end with its central lectern projects the community's prayer back westwards (see page 172). There are some similarities with the kind of liturgical arrangement that St Paul's Cathedral in London offered originally, in which Wren's choir was screened from the dome and nave by a substantial pillared screen, carrying the organ. The difference is that

Interior of San Giorgio Maggiore.

THE COUNCIL OF TRENT AND THE COUNTER-REFORMATION

While Palladio's complex churches in Venice are far removed from the mathematically conceived and centrally planned churches of the early sixteenth century, they represent the ultimate stage in the purely Classical form in which plain walls and architectural decoration form the cerebral setting for the offering of worship. In the turbulent years of that century, the Reformation had removed England and much of Germany from Papal control; France was fighting a civil war; and it was Spain with its zealous reformers and riches from the New World that was emerging as the dominant Western power. As a response to all this, a General Council was called at Trent to reform the church, and Papal decrees began to emerge from 1565 limiting the buying and selling of ecclesiastical offices, abolishing simony, reforming the liturgy and the morality of the church alike. The exemplar of the new style of churchman is Carlo Borromeo, Archbishop of Milan, who, having lived an extravagant life after accumulating ecclesiastical offices from the age of twelve, resigned many of his sinecures, dismissed half his staff, actually took holy orders and set about teaching the faith, establishing seminaries to train priests, calling diocesan synods and founding schools. The seminaries and schools were often run by Jesuits, the shock troops of the Counter-Reformation, an order founded by Ignatius Loyola to fight for the faith and placed at the Pope's disposal.

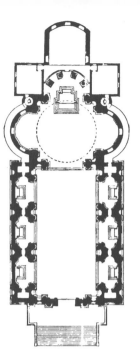

in San Giorgio, the principal altar is west of the screen, while in St Paul's the whole of the liturgical action – not just the singing of the daily Office – took place in the eastern arm.

In the Church of the Redentore, begun in 1576, these ideas are taken further. Again the façade is approached over the water, and to the two interlocking pediments over the nave and aisles is added a third, over the principal door itself. The interior shows Palladio's complete mastery of the spatial elements. Like Alberti's at San Andrea, Mantua, the nave has three deep chapels on each side like the hall of a Roman bath, giving structural stability without external buttressing. The half columns in the darker nave are transformed into pilasters in the apsidal transepts and into free-standing columns in the apse behind the high altar where the light is at its strongest. Each space seems to unfold into the next, and by a series of optical devices such as might be used to create false perspectives in a stage set, worshippers feel drawn beyond where they stand, while there is always a further mysterious space suggested in the distance.

THE BEGINNINGS OF THE BAROQUE AND THE GESU

The zeal unleashed by the Jesuit movement (see box, page 175), partly in reaction to what was felt to be an impious minimalism in the bare churches and spare liturgies of the continental Protestants (see pages 194–96), found its expression in a new piety that was more personal than liturgical. While both the *Missal and the *Breviary were pruned and reshaped, it was in more frequent Communion (and therefore confession) and in more regular reading of the Bible that a new spirit of fervent devotion caught fire. Between 1568 and 1584, Vignola built a mother church for the Jesuits in Rome, Il Gesu, the Church of Jesus.

The interior of the Gesu is a large open space, gathered up under the dome with a shallow apse to the east so that nothing stood between the altar and the people. There are no longer side aisles; they have been incorporated into the chapels between the massive buttresses that support the span of the nave roof, and are linked by passageways pierced through the buttresses. The processions that were a regular feature of Medieval worship, where they were understood as a foretaste of the pilgrimage to the heavenly Jerusalem, are now public civic events, hallowing the spaces of the city, rather than strictly religious

Michelangelo's lifelike *Moses* in Sant' Pietro in Vincoli.

Il Gesu, Rome, showing the large space with its unobstructed views flanked by the lateral chapels.

peregrinations of the church itself round the various side chapels. The church is a place where the faith can be preached dramatically, the liturgy celebrated splendidly and where private masses for special intentions and regular confessions are readily available. The transepts either side of the

dome hardly project beyond the line of the nave walls in this shallow Latin cross-shaped interior, and nothing hinders the congregation from seeing the liturgy or hearing the sermon as the choir of musicians has been banished to a gallery at the rear of the church. Where in the earlier Classical churches all was serenity and calm, now the side chapels and transeptal altars have altarpieces with paintings of the grisly martyrdoms and passionate ecstasies of the saints; and the ceiling is painted with a dramatic representation that draws the imagination beyond the limits of the here and now. In the Gesu the ceiling was painted by Andrea Pozzo towards the end of the seventeenth century. It shows the Jesuits spreading the gospel to many different peoples, as they are drawn up into the central encounter between St Ignatius Loyola, the founder, and the figure of the saviour himself, who holds his cross as he blesses Ignatius.

A favourite theme for these central ceiling panels is the Assumption of the Blessed Virgin watched by the fervent apostles, encouraging worshippers to believe that movement from this world to the next is a real and present possibility. From these representations of ecstasy and fervour, worshippers draw courage and hope in the fight against the powers of darkness, and pray for incorporation into that company of the saints who accompany Christians on their spiritual journey. From the serenity of the abstract and the mathematical order of the Classical buildings, the Baroque propels you into a pattern of swirling movement.

Partly it is being caught up in the drama of the paintings that conveys this sense of movement. In Michelangelo's Sistine Chapel in the Vatican, for example, wherever you look you are invited to enter the world represented there. In the monument for Pope Julius II in San Pietro in Vincoli, his great Moses seems to be present. The sense of being not just onlookers but participants is central to the experience of entering a Baroque church. Churches become dramatic stage sets against which the drama of our salvation is being played in the liturgical action, and the worshipper feels like an extra in the greatest opera company in the world. Even when you step into one of these churches on your own, there is the sense of being drawn into an eternal action that reaches out to enfold you. This participation in the drama of salvation dominates the experience of going into

a church building in Catholic countries for more than three centuries.

The sense of drama is not merely visual. In the confident expansionist mood of the church following the Council of Trent, every art was brought into play. At the start of the seventeenth century, two major musical forms emerged: the opera and the oratorio. While Giovanni da Palestrina (d. 1591) had captured the mood for elegantly proportioned liturgical music, the new churches, planned as great auditoria, took on some of the characteristics of the opera house. The drama of *L'Orfeo, Favola in Musica*, as Monteverdi called the first opera, was paralleled by the musical dramas developed by the Oratorians, the religious order founded by St Philip Neri, whose church Borromini completed in 1640. This genre of musical drama used the dramatic techniques of opera for religious purposes, of which *Jeptha* and *The Judgement of Solomon* by Carissimi – a Roman composer in the musical footsteps of Monteverdi and Cavalli – are two examples from the middle of the century.

ROMAN BAROQUE: BORROMINI

Churches in Rome by the architect Francesco Borromini (1599–1667) display characteristics of the Baroque, in which intellectual genius and a quirky imagination create possibilities never before dreamed of. In San Carlo alle Quatro Fontane (1634–41), the essentially oval plan with the porch at one end and the high altar in the main apse opposite has undulating sides in an S-shape to lead to the shallow recesses for the side altars. This is no longer a centrally planned church designed to create a sense of repose; it is a restless space, pulling the worshipper towards the high altar, but then easing out in the middle. Typically Baroque, there is hardly a straight line on the plan. From a circle, as Alberti showed, you can derive an octagon and a square, each perfectly balanced shapes. Circles are static, but restless ovals have two foci that push and pull in different directions. Just down the road is another oval-shaped church,

Sant'Andrea al Quirinale (1658–70), by Giovanni Lorenzo Bernini (1598–1680). This time the altar stands in a recess opposite the main door on the shallow side of the oval. In this church, the oval is used to provide a sense of embrace – like Bernini's colonnades before St Peter's.

In Borromini's Sant'Ivo della Sapienzia (1642–50) two features are distinctive: the ground plan and the spire. The plan is based on a six-pointed Star of David, the symbol of wisdom, made by two intersecting triangles. Its centre space is a hexagon, the natural form of the cell of a honeycomb, a neat allusion to the Barberini family who commissioned it and whose device was a bee. From the central hexagon three pairs of alternating bays radiate: the bays projecting from one triangle

Sant'Andrea al Quirinale, Rome, by Bernini.

Oppostite page:
Left: The hexagonal interior of Sant'Ivo della Sapienza, Rome.

Right: The restless curves of San Carlo alle Quatro Fontane, Rome, by Borromini.

This page:
Left: The recessed entrance of Sant'Agnese in Agonia, Piazza Navona, Rome, draws the passer-by.

Below: The spiral ramp of the tower of Sant'Ivo della Sapienza pierces the heavens.

end in obtruding semicircles, while the projections of the other triangle end in a concave section of a circle whose centre is outside the building. The whole design is geometrically perfect and balanced, but at the same time exhibits the restless penetration of one triangle by the other. The tower is extraordinary: it is a dynamic spiral, like some ramped ziggurat of a Near Eastern fire-tower; the flames leap out of the bowl on the top and the whole probably symbolizes the ascent of learning towards the truth. The church is not just a space in which certain truths of the faith are illustrated; the building itself embodies that pattern of ascent and change.

The church of virgin martyr St Agnese in Agonia stands in the centre of the Piazza Navona, on the site of the former Roman racetrack. Its façade, dating from the 1650s, has a wide curved front between two *campaniles*, embracing those who wander in the Piazza Navona, one of Rome's largest gathering spaces. The pedimented doorway of Borromini's church is set in the recess, and above it rises the dome, rather as the dome of St Paul's in London rises over the two western towers. Inside, you discover that you have entered the womb-like church in the middle of one of the longer sides of this curved building, which lies parallel to the piazza outside, with its enormous fountain by Bernini. The interior space is related to the public space; the struggle for victory in the Christian life – a parallel that St Paul makes in his epistles – mirrors that of the racetrack.

ST PETER'S AND ITS PIAZZA

After Michelangelo's death in 1564, the design of St Peter's was altered from a Greek to a Latin cross, with an extended eastern arm or nave, giving a sense of processional movement to the interior but concealing Michelangelo's great dome, which is now set much further back from the façade. This linear sense of movement, so characteristic of the Baroque, was accentuated by the addition of a huge piazza by Bernini to the east, dedicated in 1666. This great outside podium, the scene of major Papal occasions today such as the funeral of Pope John Paul II and liturgical celebrations such as Easter or the

Left: Bernini's piazza in front of St Peter's, Rome.

Above: Bernini's colonnades embrace the large gathering space in front of St Peter's, Rome.

clutter by liturgical experts in pursuit of Renaissance humanism's love for clean and unadulterated forms; it was also a tool for unifying the global church under one head, the Pope. This was what Bernini's colonnades around the piazza were designed to express architecturally.

DOMES, CEILINGS AND SHAFTS OF LIGHT

At the heart of the Baroque is a sense of movement, of being on the verge of breaking through into the unseen world. Nowhere is this more evident than in the painted ceilings, where the worshipper looks up through the rim of our world to see the heavens opened, like some great cover drawn back over a football stadium. In SS Giovanni e Paolo in Venice, Piazzetta shows St Dominic being drawn up into the eternal glory, surrounded by a wonderful orchestra. Larger scale and more obviously human figures stand on the rim of the walls of the church; most are gazing up into the skies in rapture, but one looks down to see if we are following. This person – the largest figure and so the one that feels closest to us in

canonization of saints, extends east of the basilica, which forms the reredos or backdrop. The end of the piazza is an oval, with an obelisk at the centre, embraced by twin colonnades of travertine columns.

This piazza is one of the great public spaces in the world, gathering people from every race and nation into the embrace of the mother church of Rome. This sense of the universal church centred on the Pope in Rome was given liturgical reality by the new missal of Pius V in 1570. Within the family of the Western Rites it had been for the local bishop to determine the precise form of the liturgy. But the new rite was not simply purged of its muddle and

Piazzetta's ceiling in SS
Giovanni e Paolo, Venice.

Bernini uses shafts of light to
reveal the *Ecstasy of St Teresa* in
the Conaro Chapel of Santa Maria
della Victoria, Rome.

The crowned dome of Santa Maria della Salute, Venice.

the false perspective of the painting – draws us
into that world to mingle with the saints. This is
at the heart of the Baroque experience. Heaven
is bursting open around us, and whether by
identifying with the ecstasy of the saints in glory
or the Assumption of the Blessed Virgin Mary it
is clear that the veil that divides their world from
ours is very thin.

The theme of heaven breaking open is not
confined to painted ceilings. Shafts of concealed
light are made to fall on altars or tabernacles in
which the sacrament is reserved, or on sculptural
groups such as Bernini's *Ecstasy of St Teresa*
(1644–47) in the Conaro Chapel of Santa Maria
della Victoria in Rome, where a circular hole above
the high altar illuminates it dramatically. This is
very different from the even lighting of the Classical
churches of the Renaissance. In the Baroque,
light is used to gain a deliberately theatrical effect,
like a spotlight. In Spain, Narciso Tome removed
the solid Gothic web in the vaulting of Toledo
Cathedral to flood the Blessed Sacrament Chapel
with light.

A different effect is given by the domes that
crown so many of the churches. In Turin there is
a remarkable dome over the chapel that houses
the *Sindona*, the Holy Shroud, by the architect
Guarino Guarini. Here a series of overlapping and

intersecting arches and ribs gives the impression
of an infinitely tall structure reaching into the
heavens, creating a funnel down which the divine
presence will protect the holy relic and shower the
earth with blessing. A powerful relic, the Blessed
Sacrament, a holy place, even a sculptural group,
are seen as sacramental gateways to the divine. A
different dome, representing the Virgin's crown,
sits on the brow of Santa Maria della Salute, the
church built in thanksgiving for the end of the
plague in Venice from 1630. The Salute sits at the
entrance of the Grand Canal, and, unlike many
city churches, is visible from all sides. The dome
is linked to the octagon on which it sits by a
series of spiral scrolls known as *volutes, and the
projecting chapels are each given a mini-façade,
while an enormous triumphal arch frames the main
portal through which the high altar, mysteriously
lit from behind, is visible. Here again is the
interpenetration of the worlds: the watery green
of the interior penetrated by the shaft of heavenly
deliverance; the striving of this world crowned by
the blessings of heaven.

But the Baroque is not confined to the
principalities, kingdoms and republics that now
make up Italy. One of the finest of the small
Baroque chapels is in the Convent of the Visitation

Above left: The *campanile* of the cathedral in Vieste, Italy.

Above centre: Steps and exterior façade of the church in Noto, Sicily.

Above right: The tiled dome of the Carmine, Palermo, Sicily.

Left: The late ribbed vault in the Convent of the Visitation in Fribourg, Switzerland.

in Fribourg, Switzerland. Here the community found a home after fleeing from the Thirty Years' War (1618–48) in France, and built a new chapel between 1653 and 1656. The design is a centralized one – a Greek cross with four equally apsidal arms, above which rises a central lantern. What is unusual is that on the four great Classical pilasters is raised a complex pattern of interlacing vaulting ribs, in a style that is entirely Gothic, giving the whole chapel a curiously Arabic feel. A small, circular window, or occulus, over the

western apse shed a beam of light on the tabernacle on the high altar at the hour of vespers until a gallery with an organ blocked this in the nineteenth century.

If this chapel is an example of the refined Baroque of an order of nuns, then the country Baroque is as much part of Italy's landscape as the rows of cypress trees that mark the way to the cemeteries. Sometimes these small Baroque churches are set outside the towns, but frequently they are the principal church of the town or village, and their *campanile* marks the high point of the townscape, while their façade is the most imposing feature of the piazza. In Vieste, the small Romanesque cathedral – built on three levels of the steep limestone cliff that marks the end of the Gargano peninsula – is crowned by a splendid Baroque cap to its *campanile*.

SOUTHERN BAROQUE

The Baroque is not confined to mainland Italy. It spread through the kingdom of Naples to Sicily, where some outstanding examples of Baroque churches are to be found in Palermo, such as the Carmine with its tiled dome or San Francesco Saverio with its arched octagonal interior, and the churches of Ragusa and Noto. The steep terrain at Noto in particular gives opportunity for the dramatic use of steps and the creation of façades on different levels. In Lecce in southern Italy, the semi-tropical landscape provides a different context, and one not dissimilar to the area round Goa on the western coast of India, which the Portugese colonized in the sixteenth century. It was from here that St Francis Xavier set out to convert the Far East, and here that his body rests in an extraordinary shrine.

In Spain, the west front of the great cathedral at Santiago de Compostela is one of the most striking Baroque creations, and was completed in 1749. From Spain the Baroque was exported to the New World of the Americas and became the classic idiom of Christian architecture in Mexico, where the shrine of Our Lady of Guadeloupe stands witness to the power of a religion that made devotion to the saints a key part of its teaching. The crowded altarpieces, teeming with naturalistic decoration of exotic fruits and peeping faces like some Hindu shrine, are glowing with vivid colours and burnished with gold.

THE BAROQUE IN SOUTHERN GERMANY AND AUSTRIA

Some of the greatest Baroque churches, many developing the oval as the basic unit of the plan, are to be found in southern Germany and Austria, where the Baroque merges with the *Rococo, a term used to indicate that decoration has overtaken and almost eclipsed the structure.

In the Rococo, the wall surfaces are decorated with bas-relief, plasterwork, carving and sculpture, which seems to merge into the carved and painted architecture itself, so that the distinction between two dimensions and three is blurred. In the Abbey of St Gall, stalls the size of armchairs are canopied with carvings and peopled by saints and angels; organ cases hang from galleries and are draped round windows, with clusters of pipes surmounted by figures beating drums or blowing trumpets. In Zwiefalten, curving galleries project between the nave piers like boxes

The exotic altarpiece in Our Lady of Guadeloupe, Mexico.

in an elaborate opera house; pulpits grow out of naturalistic foliage and are supported on the backs of figures and crowned by angels; tombs and memorials sprout from the walls, the figures of the dead prizing the coffin lids open and tumbling the skeletal figure of death from his throne. This riot of colour and life pushes the boundaries of reality beyond their neat confines: there is no longer a division between this world and the next, between life on earth and the glimpse of heaven revealed

as the lid is lifted, as in the churches of the Roman Baroque. Heaven is fully and gloriously intertwined with our life now in a continuous operatic performance, running at full throttle.

These churches, especially the great pilgrimage churches or abbeys, are often on a huge scale, such as Steinhausen (1728–33), built by Dominikus and Johann Zimmermann, and Ochsenhausen, both of which are based on the oval. Here there are no longer the different zones with horizontal entablatures marking the boundary between walls or columns and the vault or ceiling, but covings that lead from the vertical elements to the horizontal. Side altars prepare you for the high altar and build a pattern of movement towards it, rather than offering separate spaces for private masses. In the pilgrimage church at Diessen, a church of the wall-pillar type found in the Vorarlberg region of Austria, the total space is articulated by the interior buttresses to the nave between which the lateral chapels are formed; the gallery runs through the buttresses at first-floor level. Here the sense of being in an ever-changing stage set is accentuated by it being possible to change the great painting in the high

Left: The stalls and choir organ at St Gall, Switzerland.

Centre: The curved fronts of the nave galleries at Zwiefalten.

Right and plan: The oval interior of Steinhausen.

altar reredos with the changing seasons of the church's year. Perhaps the most splendid pilgrimage church in Bavaria is the Vierzehnheiligen, by Balthazar Neumann, begun in 1743. The austere exterior in ochre sandstone of this shrine church, built to commemorate a herdsman's vision of the Christ child among the fourteen holy helpers, does nothing to prepare the visitor for the complex interior plan formed by a series of interlocking ovals. The pilgrimage altar on the site of the vision, surmounted by the swirling Rococo pyramid of a *baldachino*, or canopy, holding the statues of the fourteen saints, dominates the eastern end of the central oval that forms the nave, where the walls, side altars and tiered galleries all bulge outwards to embrace this remarkable confection. Beyond this object of veneration, and across the transepts, stands the high altar with its towering reredos, secure in its conventional place in the apsidal chancel. Each altar occupies its own space, and the crossing articulates the space between them so that neither obtrudes on the other.

The Lion Companion to Church Architecture

Left: *The Assumption of Our Lady*, sculpted by the Asam brothers in the abbey of Rohr, south Germany.

Right: The Pilgrimage Church of Vierzehnheiligen, Bavaria.

Below left: Ottobeuren Abbey, Bavaria.

Below right: The organ, Weingarten Abbey, Bavaria.

In the Abbey of Ottobeuren (1748–57) by Johann Michael Fischer, a towering high altar and its altarpiece are visible through the great width of the monastic choir, over whose elaborately carved stalls is set the choir organ – one of three quite separate instruments in this vast church. These form a backdrop behind the pilgrimage altar, which forms the focus to the worshipper in the nave, and where mass is offered for the countless pilgrims. These churches offer a total experience rather than a pilgrimage route through a hierarchy of spaces. Here the three-dimensional sculpture melts into the bas-relief of the plasterwork, which in turn is taken up into the two-dimensional painting, so that the surfaces flow from one dimension to the other.

The Abbey of Weingarten was dedicated in 1724. One of the largest classical organs fills the western gallery, and the monumental scale of the building is enhanced by the painted walls of the Baroque plasterers and decorators, the Asam brothers, with their columns, stairs and domes that give the impression that the church is extended into the cloud-capped heavens, where banks of saints await. Here the painted architecture links the worshipper below to heaven above, as it does in Rohr, where Asam's dramatic sculpture of the *Assumption of Our Lady* fills the east end of the abbey (1717–23).

Left: St Nicholas in the Altstadt, Prague.

Above: The pilgrimage church of St Boniface, Fulda.

In Bohemia the Baroque took root as a local vernacular style. Small chapels and wayside shrines used the forms of Baroque to create a colourful sense of the present reality of the Christian faith, and the appropriateness of Baroque as a local style can be seen in the mountain churches of Switzerland. In Prague, the Church of St Nicholas in the Altstadt, where Mozart's funeral took place, provides a restless experience of curves and offers a remarkable organ case. In the cathedral in Prague stands the immense silver shrine of St John Neopmunk, almost blocking the south choir aisle.

Further north, the shrine church erected over the tomb

The silver shrine of St John Neopmunk, Prague Cathedral.

of St Boniface at Fulda was rebuilt from 1704 in a domed Baroque style by Johann Dientzenhoffer. The essentially airy Italian Baroque style is adapted here as a more solid form, in which the way the architecture of the basilica masses externally indicates the significance of what is happening inside. The Hofkirche in Dresden, the capital of Saxony, dates from 1738 and provides a more restrained model of German Baroque. It was built after the conversion of the Albertines to Roman Catholicism – a condition of their acceding to the Polish throne – and there is a fine Silbermann organ (1750–55) in the centre of the curved west gallery, balancing the high altar in the eastern apse. Only a few hundred metres away stands the Frauenkirche, the principal church of the Reformed tradition in Dresden (see pages 214–15).

In Austria, Johann Fischer von Erlach built the extraordinary Karlskirche, with its lofty central dome over the oval church visible above the façade. Here a pedimented central porch curves away to lateral porch-towers, embracing on the way – rather uncomfortably – what look like twin copies of Trajan's Column. Outside Vienna in the Wienerwald is the Abbey of Heiligenkreuz. Here the Romanesque west end of an abbey church,

Left: The Trinity Column in the outer courtyard, Abbey of Heiligenkreuz, Austria.

Right: Les Invalides, Paris.

Below: The Late Gothic interior of Saint-Etienne-du-Mont, Paris.

whose eastern arm was replaced by a Gothic choir and sanctuary at the same time that the abbey received its distinctive Cistercian form in the thirteenth century, projects into a Baroque outer courtyard containing Giuliani's Trinity Column of 1729. In the bright sunlight the juxtaposition of these styles seems perfectly natural, and offers a similar artistic experience to that of a Haydn mass performed in an Anglican liturgy in one of England's Gothic cathedrals.

FRANCE

The interior of Saint-Etienne-du-Mont in Paris, a Late Gothic church built between 1537 and 1624, prefigures the Classical style, with its Classical-feeling *jubé* and later Second Empire fittings. From these beginnings, the classical tradition evolved differently in France. The wonderful church of Les Invalides in Paris by Jules Hardouin-Mansart, consecrated in 1706, combines a two-stage Classical façade with a domed central space that is in the best tradition of Roman Baroque. But in the chapel of the Royal Palace at Versailles, Mansart's tall and elegant Classical columns of the substantial tribune on the first-floor level, where the organ is set above the altar at the east end, make it clear that this is a building in the tradition

of Charlemagne's Imperial Chapel at Aachen: this tribune level is clearly the *piano nobile*, while the stocky ground floor is a working level for the clergy and other minions. A Baroque version of the Sainte Chapelle, a structural support system that is Late Gothic in its conception, is visible in the exterior buttressing.

Later than these are the more strictly Classical churches in Paris, of which La Madeleine, which was begun in 1777 and not finished till after the revolution, is the best known. Its exterior is as close as anything could be to a Classical temple.

Temple of La Madeleine, Paris, in the Greek style.

Right: The Third Empire-style Basilica of Notre Dame, Boulogne.

Below: The chapel of Lulworth Castle, Dorset, England.

Classical churches in a rather heavy style continued to be built in France till well after the middle of the nineteenth century. A fine example of this later style is the Basilica of Notre Dame at Boulogne in northern France, entirely rebuilt between 1827 and 1866, where the dome rises in two stages over the church in the old fortified town above the port. The flattened arches between the pilasters of the second stage of the lantern's drum and the seated statues over the squinches at the four corners of the base connect this landmark back to the stable pre-revolutionary language of the church's Classical architecture.

ENGLAND

In England, the Classical style continued into the late eighteenth century as the norm for recusant buildings. The first church, apart from the embassy chapels, to be built for the Roman Catholic community was John Tasker's chapel in the grounds of Lulworth Castle in Dorset for the Weld family. This chapel, built in 1786–87,

was designed to look from the outside like a cross between a mausoleum and a garden pavilion. Its Classical lines and sash windows conformed to a domestic norm, but inside is a perfect, austere Roman Catholic interior, complete with an organ in the gallery and an altar with suitable relics of the martyrs of the faith. The Classical

Above: Two views of the interior of the chapel at Lulworth Castle.

Right: The Brompton Oratory, London.

tradition continued in the Brompton Oratory in Knightsbridge, opened in 1884 to give smart Londoners a genuine taste of Rome.

The Classical style remained the architectural language of Roman Catholicism in the greater part of Europe until the twentieth century. In England, this Catholic tradition was challenged by Augustus Welby Pugin, the promoter of Gothic as the true style of the Christian religion as opposed – in his mind – to the essentially pagan origins of the Classical style. It is from England that the Gothic Revival, together with an essentially neo-Medieval

theology of the church and its worship, derives in the nineteenth century, and if the story of Classical architecture in the service of the church is essentially Italian and southern continental, then the story of the Gothic Revival is essentially English and northern European.

The Reformation and the Invention of Printing

Radical Reform on the Continent and Evolutionary Development in England

CHAPTER 8

Right: Mural of the Resurrection; Notre Dame des Fontaines, La Brigue, France.

The edifice of Late Medieval religion, with its developed system of transactions and sacramental boundaries, was shot through with various attempts to clarify and simplify the worshippers' relationship with their maker. The complicated series of intermediaries – whether they were the company of the saints or the ranks of the clergy – seemed a far cry from the direct encounter between people and Jesus that the Gospels recorded. From the time of John Wycliffe (d. 1384) in England or John Hus (d. 1415) in Bohemia, attempts to translate the scriptures into the vernacular and give ordinary people access to the narrative of the encounter with God had been viewed with deep suspicion by the institutional church. Loosing control of this access would undermine the power of the church and the clergy, and in the Medieval period reforming movements were put down with a ruthless severity. In the end, it was a combination of two factors that secured a hearing for the alternative view: the rise of the new learning and the invention of printing.

For much of the Medieval period, the church had guarded the story of the faith carefully. The stories of the Gospels and of wonder-working local saints were alike the subject of stained glass windows and murals, and this painted Bible, this essentially visual expression of the faith, was all that many people knew. The dramas of salvation were played out in the liturgy, where the dramatization of the gospel narrative at key festivals had been practised for centuries, and the cycles of Mystery Plays performed by various guilds were an established feature of Medieval England. Pilgrimages to the great shrines such as Canterbury and Compostela, the drama of the rites of Holy Week and Easter and the Corpus Christi celebrations, or processions with the relics of the saint on patronal festivals such as the Pardons in Brittany or when danger threatened the city, all kept the Christian faith in the public domain as an indispensable part of the community's celebration. Only the rhythm of the week and the holy days that punctuated the year provided breaks from the routine of daily labour.

But with the invention of printing, and the encouragement to learn to read for oneself that followed in its wake, the emphasis on telling the Christian story publicly began to change. In many ways, the most complex and interesting Reformation story is that of England, where the initial motive was not a Protestant Reformation as much as freedom from Papal control. When Henry VIII legislated for the Great Bible to be available in each church in 1538, he could not have foreseen the effect of individuals reading

Capitlz XXIII· Qzlr xpſ fvit poſit iŋ moņvmento·

·dimas

Cap·XXV· Qzlr xpſ ịnfernvz eſpoliavit·

the Bible themselves, or later, of portions being read daily by the head of the household at family prayers. Access to Christianity was being opened to lay people, and the faith of the church as delivered to the saints was being subtly transformed into a code for daily living.

On the continent, the Renaissance scholar Desiderius Erasmus was typical of those who wished to see the church renewed through scholarship and good education, and he had begun to publish scholarly texts of the early Christian fathers, which the invention of printing made possible. In his *Enchiridion*, first published in 1503 but not well known till 1515, he laid out a programme for the reform of the church, arguing for a return to the scriptures and the theology of the early fathers, and by implication abandoning the edifice of Medieval theology.

MARTIN LUTHER AND THE CONTINENTAL REFORM

But the prime mover of the continental reform was Luther. Martin Luther (1483–1546) was an overworked and over-conscientious Augustinian friar in Germany. He came to feel that the Medieval system that prescribed every detail of daily life in the name of a God whose primary concern was justice was overbearingly oppressive. His realization that it is faith alone that justifies without the need for dutiful works to prove it was a discovery that changed his life. His escape from this oppressive stranglehold, realizing that it is the gift of God's grace that has freed humans from the tyranny of sin and its consequences, soon led to his determination to reform the church and his questioning of the mediatorial function of the church and the priesthood.

When Luther's claims began to divide the church, he appealed to the German princes to take the reform of the church into their own hands: to abolish taxes to Rome, the celibacy of the clergy and the abuses surrounding Masses of the Dead; and, eschewing the doctrine of transubstantiation, to establish Communion in both kinds,

acknowledging Christ's authority for baptism and the Eucharist alone among the sacraments. Excommunicated in 1521, he spent much of his next years translating the Bible into German and writing hymns that would communicate his insights.

In his approach to baptism, Luther was no *Anabaptist (one who believes in re-baptism in adulthood). He believed that baptism signified death and resurrection and that it should be administered to infants. He rejected the views of those who 'turn the sacrament into a command and faith into a work'.

For Luther, fonts for the baptism of infants remained important, and were often placed at the head of the nave or in close proximity to the pulpit. Worship was the celebration of word and sacrament, and the preaching of God's grace led to baptism and the Eucharist. For the Eucharist he provided a slightly pruned and shortened version of the Medieval rite in 1523, and then a more radical version in German in 1526. Conservative in practical matters, he left the Medieval arrangements of the altar and its furnishings much as they were, and in many Lutheran churches that is how they have remained, at least until the ecumenical consensus that followed the Second Vatican Council of 1962–65.

Other reformers were more radical. The Swiss Ulrich Zwingli (1484–1531) regarded the Eucharist as a memorial meal, an *aide memoire* of Christ's spiritual presence and so a visual aid to the gospel, and consequently thought the prime duty of the clergy was to preach. His liturgies had no music and were focused on the sermon. In Strasbourg, Martin Bucer (1491–1551) pioneered what we might call 'house churches', where reforms in the liturgy were evolving slowly. Unlike Zwingli, Bucer understood the importance of singing, and he had a decisive influence on Calvin and the Reformed French tradition. When new churches were built, rather than existing ones adapted, they were functional auditoria.

By 1530, divisions were beginning to appear between the reformers Luther and Zwingli on the nature of the Eucharistic presence. The humanist-educated Zwingli was suspicious of the ex-scholastic Luther's continuing insistence on the real presence of Christ in the Eucharist, and the substantial Colloquy of Marburg in 1520 left the two on opposing sides. This disagreement over the nature of the sacraments split Germany between a Lutheran north and east and a Reformed south and west.

By 1536 the Frenchman John Calvin (1509–64) was emerging as the leader of the Reformation in Geneva, where by 1541 he was establishing an Old Testament-based religious state, with himself as its leader. 'Four walls and a sermon' was all that Calvin required of a church service, which is hardly a recipe for a theology of worship. This is why no distinctive theology of church building, and only a very meagre liturgical theology, developed in the churches of the continental Reformation, unlike in the Anglican and Lutheran reforms.

The result of these various movements on the continent was dramatic not only in terms of the church's worship: clarity, later to become systematized as the Enlightenment, personal piety, and social and ethical cohesion banded together to produce an intellectual basis for the rise of modern democratic Europe. Areas that embraced reform did so on the authority of local princes: *cuius regio eius religio* ('whose the region, his the religion'), as Luther described it; though the theocratic state imposed in Geneva by Calvin was an autocratic commanderie. The political as well as the religious map of Europe was changing.

BUILDINGS OF THE REFORMED TRADITION ON THE CONTINENT

The Reformation marks the beginning of treating churchgoing not so much as participating in a liturgy as attending a dramatic performance of the word by a preacher, a choir and an organist. This becomes a central thread in Reformed worship, and leads in time to the adulation of particular preachers or choirs. Within this new framework, the focus of devotion shifts from the visual to the aural, from the liturgical to the personal.

Visually, the churches in this Reformed tradition have changed little since the sixteenth century, and look today much the same as they are represented in the Dutch interior paintings by Pieter de Hooch (1629–84) and others. For the most part, the churches were whitewashed all over, so that any figurative painting was hidden. Occasionally, biblical texts – mostly of an improving rather than a liturgical nature – were added in framed panels. 'Wash and be clean' when placed over the font does not offer a theology of baptism! Stained glass, especially if the subjects represented were the lives

Goslar, St Peter and St Paul's:
carved altarpiece.

Left:
Chandelier;
Steeple Ashton,
Wiltshire,
England.

Right:
Emmanuel de
Witte: interior
of Oude Kerk,
Delft, during a
sermon (1651),
in the Wallace
Collection,
London.

of the saints or other non-scriptural scenes, was equally suspect, and frequently removed: clear glass was preferred to let the light of reason illuminate the murk of superstition. In the same vein, in the centre of the spaces there frequently hung large chandeliers – a symbol of the enlightenment provided by unfettered access to the Bible and the new learning. Marvellous examples of these are found in England as well as in the Reformed churches of the continent.

In some of the larger churches, such as St Bavo's, Haarlem, in the Netherlands, for example, a boarded enclosure with raked seating, rather like that erected in fairgrounds for viewing wrestling bouts, was sometimes set up around a pulpit against a nave pillar, making a church within a church. This model of an enclosure with fixed seating takes the idea of the church building as a secular concourse, within which an enclosure for worship can be formed, a stage further, though it has some parallels with the introduction of canopied stalls to enclose a monastic choir in the previous period.

THE LUTHERAN TRADITION

In the Lutheran tradition, it was the singing of congregational hymns or chorales, and the performance, especially in Germany, of elaborate preludes on the chorales by the organist, and later, even cantatas on the chorales such as those of Johann Sebastian Bach in St Thomas, Leipzig, that bedded the new patterns of worship into the hearts as well as the minds of the worshippers. This is a process that was recognized by John and Charles Wesley, the founders of Methodism in the eighteenth century. Although Luther devised a simplified form of Gregorian chant for his order of service, it was the new popular music – the vernacular chorale, with its regular metre and memorable tunes – that formed the link with personal devotion and provided an emotional core to Lutheran piety. 'Why should the devil have all the best tunes?' said Luther of the popular secular tunes of the day. The amazing appeal of the St Matthew and St John Passions by Bach – for many people today a high point of their devotions at Passiontide – witnesses to the continuing power of the sung and spoken word of the biblical narrative, dramatized and coloured by

The elaborate pulpit forms the reredos above the altar in this reformed interior; Stephaniekirche, Westerhausen, Saxony.

A Medieval rood beam and reredos, chandeliers and a statue of Our Lady, as well as a Romanesque crucifix in profile, dominate this Lutheran interior in Sweden.

the commentary of *pietist arias and well-known hymnody. Music and preaching – the emotional power of the word – were becoming the heart of the religious experience. Instead of furnishing their churches with altars, roods and stained glass, the reformers erected pulpits, organs and chandeliers.

In the Lutheran tradition, especially in Scandinavia, some of the fine Late Medieval carved altarpieces or reredos have survived. Frequently, the altars – complete with cross and candlesticks and still set up for celebrations of the Eucharist facing eastward – have become thrones for the Bible, a visible sign of the word incarnate. In the more Calvinistic churches, a Communion table is often set, together with the font, below the pulpit, to show that in their view the sacraments are subordinate to the word of God.

Common to both traditions is the installation, almost always in large west galleries that could accommodate singers and instruments as well, of large and elegant organs. Organs of three or four divisions, including a Ruckpositiv – a division sited behind the player's back and projecting out into the church – and with the pedal pipes in towers at the sides provided a visual as well as a musical focus, and were greatly prized: Arp Schnitger in northern Germany and

Holland; Silbermann in Alsace, lower Saxony and the Rhineland; and Cliquot in France all produced organs of wonderful quality, a number of which have been carefully conserved and are in fine playing order today.

But perhaps the chief change is not just that the worship was more cerebral, more concerned with interior disposition and less with outward expression, but that it was more static. For the most part, except on those occasions when the Lord's Supper was celebrated, worshippers went to their seats and stayed there. Many churches installed solid – and relatively comfortable – fixed pewing. Worship had become an exercise in pious remembering rather than in celebrating the reality of Christ's presence; worshippers kept their hats on and stayed seated to sing the chorales.

ENGLAND AFTER THE REFORMATION

Henry VIII's Reformation in England differed from those of the continental reformers. His motives were less in reforming the church or the liturgy, though the monasteries were easy prey for their financial pickings, than in gaining independence from Rome in order to secure the dissolution of his heirless marriage. While he wished to see English used in the liturgy, especially for the readings and bidding prayers or intercessions, it is unlikely that he would have welcomed the opportunity subsequently taken by Thomas Cranmer, the Archbishop of Canterbury, to shift the reform of worship in a more Protestant direction in the second Prayer Book of Edward VI, published in 1552. In the eyes of Henry and some of his bishops, the Reformation in England was a matter of evolution rather than revolution, emphasizing continuity with the past. The Church of England was Catholic, but Reformed.

However, the arrival in England of the continental reformer, Martin Bucer, undeniably

helped move it in a more Reformed direction. Bucer commented on the first Prayer Book of 1549 and saw its shortcomings. He longed for a more radical return to the round churches of antiquity, where he assumed that the altar had stood in the centre with the congregation gathered round. Worship was to be audible and intelligible. This did not merely mean a liturgy and scriptures in the vernacular, but that the person who led it was, if possible, to be in the nave with the congregation so that there was no division between priest and people in participating directly in the liturgy. Where there was a large nave and a long chancel – as in some former monastic churches now become parish churches – the chancel (as at Wymondham Abbey in Norfolk or the royal foundation at Fotheringay) was pulled

Abbey Dore, Herefordshire; a monastic church rescued by Viscount Scudamore.

down and all worship transferred to the nave. In others, such as Abbey Dore in Herefordshire, the nave was lost and a local landowner, Viscount Scudamore, equipped the choir as the space for the sacrament, and set up a family pew on a gallery in the crossing from where he could look over the benches of the parishioners set up before the screen and pulpit into the old monastic choir, now the sacrament room.

The 1552 Prayer Book was quite explicit in how worship was to be conducted and the churches ordered. A pulpit and reading desk were to be set up in the nave, together with seating. It is important to remember that before this time seeing the host at the elevation was the high point of the liturgy (see page 144). By the end of the Middle Ages, the naves of many parish churches were used as a gathering space for the community where the parish school, the visiting clerk (who could write letters or wills) and parish feasts might happen. Leading off this central space, the various guilds had their aisles or transepts, which served as churches within a church. No doubt on occasion a visiting friar might have preached a mission, but the pattern of fixed pewing we are used to seeing in Medieval churches today was rare. Now that preaching was to be a regular feature of worship, churches needed pulpits for the sermon and lecterns for holding the Bible.

But the chancels were to remain as they had been in the past. Cranmer accepted the existence of rood screens, and clearly thought of the building in Late Medieval terms as a series of spaces. The solemnization of marriage, for example, began with the persons to be married coming 'into the body of the church with their friends and neighbours' for the exchange of vows. The rubric after the nuptial blessing in the 1549 book simply says, 'Then shall they goe into the quier [choir]' during the psalm, but a note after the prayers in the 1552 book makes it explicit that the service continues with the Communion. It was clearly Cranmer's

A pre-Reformation rood screen survives in the remote church of St Margaret's, on the borders of Wales.

expectation that the marriage service should be concluded by the celebration of the Eucharist to seal the union, for which the couple were to move up into the chancel with the priest.

Under the arrangements that Cranmer's liturgy envisaged, the chancel was to become the Communion space, with the stone altar removed from its position against the east wall and a table 'set up in some convenient part of the chancel, within every such church or chapel, to serve for the ministration of the blessed communion', as the arrangements in the Langley Chapel in Shropshire still indicate.

The free-standing holy table in the chancel of the Langley Chapel, Shropshire, England.

The convenience of the communicants was to become the guiding principle, and this soon settled into placing the table lengthways in the centre of the space, around which the communicants could gather. At the Offertory, intending communicants would leave their places in the nave to place their offerings in the chest provided on the way, and remain around the table. The presiding minister, simply robed, would take his place in the middle of the long side of the table, normally on the north, with the newly made Communion cups and flagons for Communion in both kinds before him. Here they remained kneeling until the end of the service, and the sacrament was brought to them. This makes sense of Cranmer's dramatic introduction of the actions of Christ at the Last Supper – taking, blessing, breaking the bread and giving Communion – right into the middle of the Eucharistic prayer. This novel dramatization has not been paralleled in any other Eucharistic rite and seems curious today when – as is normally the custom in Prayer Book Services – the congregation are seated for the whole of the service in the nave, and come up into the chancel only to receive the sacrament. In spite of a brief restoration of the Roman liturgy under the ill-fated Queen Mary, this pattern was largely to prevail for the rest of the sixteenth century and into the seventeenth. The Elizabethan instructions were clear that the screen should remain, and that the minister reading Morning and Evening Prayer should have his seat outside the screen. The 'holy table' was to be 'decently made', and to stand in the place where the altar had stood, 'saving when the Communion of the Sacrament is to be distributed'.

The Lord's Supper, from *A Course of Catechizing*, showing the communicants kneeling round the table set lengthwise in the chancel.

Occasionally, such arrangements survive. There is a chancel with pewed seating on three sides at Deerhurst and – originally – on all four at Hailes, both in Gloucestershire. Different models include that at Coxwold in north Yorkshire, where in a long chancel, crowded with the enormous Fauconberg tombs, the Communion rail extends westward down its length from the altar at the east end to a small semicircular podium from which the priest can speak more easily to the remaining congregation in the nave. A more frequent survival is the three-sided rail, projecting from the east wall with the altar table free-standing, such as at Clodock beneath the Black Mountains in Herefordshire, which does more to preserve the sense of gathering.

LAUDIAN REFORMS

In the second fifty years of the sixteenth century, there was little new church building: mostly the Church of England, as the newly independent church of the British Isles was known, adapted and reshaped its existing buildings for the new Prayer Book worship. In the early years of the seventeenth century, two things happened that brought about changes. First, moving the altar table – particularly if it was solidly made – whenever the sacrament was celebrated became a chore. Second, and more significant, when the church was frequently used as a school and parish meeting room, and dogs came into churches with their owners, it was tempting to use the altar for putting tools and hats on as well as books and papers, and easy for dogs to foul it. The classic case of abuse happened on Christmas day, 1630, at Tadlow in Cambridgeshire. During the sermon a dog stole the bread placed on the table for the Eucharist; and since it was impossible to procure that day 'the best and purest wheat bread' ordered by the rubric, there was therefore no celebration.

As well as these practical questions, the innate sense that the altar demanded a degree of reverence began to lead to a change of attitude, as did the frequent difficulties encountered by the

Three-sided rails round a Laudian-style altar at the east end of Clodock, on the borders of Wales.

clergy in administering the sacrament to people as they knelt in their places with any dignity. So when William Laud, who as Dean of Gloucester had returned the altar in the cathedral to the top of the steps under the window, became Archbishop of Canterbury, the move to return altars to the east end of the chancel and to rail them off gathered momentum. Rather than fence the altar all round, the Laudian churchmen preferred a rail that ran across the chancel from north to south. The rails were originally designed to protect the altar against dogs, as can be seen from the rails at Edington Priory in Wiltshire, where the top of the rails bristles with obelisks and *finials. But soon the rails came to suggest a more convenient way of administering the sacrament to the communicants, who were encouraged to come and kneel at the rails in turn. From the time that he became archbishop in 1633, this pattern of distribution became the norm. The altar was to be 'covered with a decent carpet', and proper reverence was due to it as it was the earthly throne of the Lord of all. As well as restoring the altar to the east end of the church,

Crested altar rails at Edington Priory, Wiltshire, not for the ease of communicants but to protect the altar from dogs.

The chapel at Leweston, Dorset, built for a family's worship.

the Laudians emphasized its significance with a stained glass window, reredos or tapestry behind, and the part of the chancel roof over it with special decoration. There was now a gradual drawing near, a processional approach. The communicants came into the chancel at the Offertory; they approached the altar at the words, 'Draw near with faith…', and they knelt at the rail to receive the sacrament. The worshippers' behaviour in church was to be modelled on their behaviour before their sovereign, whose own worship in his Chapel Royal set such a high standard.

Another factor in shaping the worship of the Church of England in the seventeenth century was the rediscovery, exemplified in Bishop Andrewes' *Preces Privatae* (a personal primer or book of devotions) of the theological and spiritual riches of the ancient church. It was not just to the continental Europe of Luther and Calvin that the English reformers looked if they were dissatisfied with the abuses of Rome; they also had the riches of the Eastern churches to draw upon, with a long and unbroken tradition of worship and spirituality that avoided the perils of papalism. Poets in the tradition of George Herbert and small groups of faithful lay people such as Nicholas Ferrar's community at Little Gidding pointed to an imaginative and reflective response to the

The interior of Leweston, showing the bleached oak panelling, pews and two-decker reading desk and pulpit.

gospel that is a far cry from the slogans and propositional statements of the Augsburg or Westminster Confessions. A small and perfectly preserved chapel, built for the use of his household by Sir John Fitzjames, still exists, complete with all its fittings,

at Leweston in west Dorset. The structure, built in 1616, is Late Gothic but the fittings – all in bleached oak – are Jacobean, complete with bench ends, hat-pegs, two-decker pulpit and altar table. Some of the feel of churches of this period can be gained from the small church at Stanford-on-Avon, where Laud had once been rector. The combination of the Cave family tombs clustering round the altar, the pre-Restoration organ case – expelled by Cromwell from Whitehall – on its Classical columns at the rear of the church, the hatchments against the whitewashed walls and the linenfold panelling and Jacobean embroidery all breathe the language of quiet confidence in the continuity of life and worship, which must have

Top left: 'The handsomest barn in England': St Paul's, Covent Garden, London, by Inigo Jones.

Bottom left: The Cave family tombs in the chancel of Stanford-on-Avon, England.

Above: The whitewashed interior of Stanford-on-Avon, with its hatchments, the pre-Restoration organ on a Classical gallery framing the font and the open nave, breathes the air of gentle pre-Restoration neglect.

seemed so threatened by the turbulent upheavals of the Civil War (1642–51).

The most startling new church in this period was Inigo Jones' St Paul's, Covent Garden. Here for the first time was a significant departure from the Medieval two-roomed church. It was built on the Duke of Bedford's land, and he told Inigo Jones that he did not want to spend much and that he really wanted nothing better than a barn. The architect replied, 'You shall have the handsomest barn in England', and gave him an uncompromising Classical rectangle, with no internal division at all, galleries on three sides, and an altar against the east wall.

Below: The Baroque portal of the chapel at Staunton Harold is framed by the Gothic west window.

Right: The Laudian south porch of the University Church of St Mary the Virgin, Oxford, with its barley-sugar columns and Classical pediment.

Below: Staunton Harold interior.

Oddly enough, it was in the years of the Commonwealth that the most complete Laudian church was built. In the park of Staunton Harold in Leicestershire a small Gothic church stands in a secluded setting next to its house and overlooking a lake. All its furnishings except for the eighteenth-century wrought iron screen are contemporary with the building, which is dated 1653 by this splendid inscription over the Baroque porch, complete with pilasters, angels and drapes:

In the year 1653
when all things Sacred were throughout ye nation
Either demolisht or profaned
Sir Robert Shirley, Barronet,
Founded this church;
Whose singular praise it is,
To haue done the best things in ye worst times,
and
hoped them in the most calamitous.
The righteous shall be had in everlasting
remembrance.

Shirley never saw his church completed. Cromwell was furious when he learnt of it and said that if the man had enough money to build a church, then he could raise a regiment. Shirley refused, and died in the Tower of London within three years, aged twenty-seven.

The church is Late Perpendicular, with square-topped clerestory windows, *crenellated parapets and a tower that is worthy of Somerset. Inside, there is Jacobean panelling on the walls and round the octagonal pillars. The box pews have brass candlesticks, and the three-tier reading pew and pulpit together with the altar are clad in embroidered purple velvet falls. In the gallery stands a small and decorative organ, and the clock faces tell different times.

Laudian principles exerted their influence throughout the period of the Commonwealth and re-emerged after the Restoration: the chapel at Trinity College, Oxford, though not built until 1694, displays the essential setting of the Laudian altar. The chapel has a screen, but at the west end, with stalls returned against it, like the Jacobean screen in Lambeth Palace Chapel. The Baroque south porch of the University Church of St Mary the Virgin in Oxford, built by one of Laud's chaplains, with its twisted 'barley-sugar stick' columns and Gothic fan vault, scandalized the puritans with its figure of the Virgin, framed in a shell-like niche. Another high-church bishop, Cosin of Durham, refurnished several churches as well as the cathedral with a profusion of woodwork in a Late Medieval fashion of which Sedgefield

Above: Limewood carving by Grindling Gibbons frames the Laudian altar of the chapel of Trinity College, Oxford.

Below: The church in the park at Staunton Harold, Leicestershire: a defiant blow for the beauty of holiness in the bleak years of England's civil war.

'in our reformed Religion, it should seem vain to make a Parish-church larger than that all who are present can both hear and see. The Romanists, indeed, may build larger Churches, it is enough if they hear the Murmur of the Mass, and see the Elevation of the Host, but ours are to be fitted for Auditories. I can hardly think it practicable to make a single room so capacious, with Pews and Galleries, as to hold above 2,000 Persons, and all to hear the Service, and both to hear distinctly, and see the Preacher.'

Wren cites his church of St James', Piccadilly, as an example of an ideal plan and size.

Hardly any of Wren's city churches have a screen, and in most of them the pulpit is the most prominent of the fittings. Organs were in the middle of the west gallery, as on the continent, and the altars against the east wall, with rails around and a degree of space in which the communicants may gather. In some, the pulpits are set, as in St Stephen Walbrook, against a pier. In this, the most elegant of his city churches, Wren is successfully combining a centralized, domed structure with nave and

remains the outstanding example after Brancepeth was recently destroyed by fire.

Wren and the Auditory Church

After the Restoration, church building began again – spurred on by the opportunity offered by the Great Fire of London (1666) and the revision that led to the *Book of Common Prayer* (1662). The towering genius of these days is Sir Christopher Wren (1632–1723), who enunciated what has come to be known as the Auditory Principle. In a letter setting out his views, Wren writes:

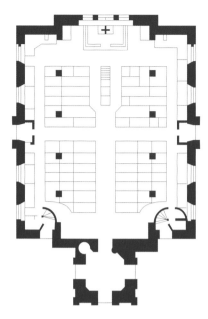

Plan of St James', Piccadilly, by Wren, showing the central pulpit and reading desk.

Wren's domed masterpiece: St Stephen Walbrook, London; now home to Henry Moore's substantial central altar, known irreverently as 'the camenbert'.

A central pulpit and reading desk survive in the unaltered interior of King's Norton, Leicestershire.

choir, aisles and transepts, as he wrestles with the problems he was trying to resolve at St Paul's. In others – and St James', Piccadilly, was one of these until it was altered – the pulpit, combined with the reading desk and with the parish clerk below that, stood centrally, concealing, to our eyes, the altar. A fine surviving example of this plan is King's Norton Church in Leicestershire, which dates from 1770. Here the three-decker pulpit is set two-thirds of the way to the east end in the centre of the aisle. Either side of it are low gates, which carry on the traditional separation of the chancel from the nave. East of this point, the pews are for communicants, and are focused on the altar, set within a rail that runs the width of the church. Churches like this communicate the style of eighteenth-century Anglicanism: lucid, classically balanced, free from excessive emotion and patronizingly charitable.

Some have charged Wren with giving the pulpit prominence at the expense of the altar. But his uncle Matthew was a Laudian bishop and his father Dean of Windsor, and the plans for the high altar at St Paul's included a sumptuous altar under a ciborium like that at St Peter's, Rome. His designs for St Paul's itself passed through many stages, including a more adventurous centrally planned building, the Great Model – a centralized domed structure based on a Greek cross not unlike Michelangelo's St Peter's in Rome – before the present cathedral was built. In the end, without abandoning his centralized design entirely, Wren managed to build a cathedral with the three bays of the choir balancing the three bays of the nave, adding an apse at the east end and a square vestibule bay at the west, with its pedimented porch and lateral chapels. Though St Paul's lost its screen in the nineteenth-century reordering, when the great carved organ case was divided and set north and south, the recent setting of the font in the middle of this western bay has done much to restore the integrity of the western bay as a narthex to the nave proper. While there is sufficient linear movement for St Paul's to be recognizably Anglican, the original design of a space centred round a great domed central area is preserved.

This western bay is interesting for another reason: its width, the two lateral chapels almost providing western transepts behind the great

Left: St Paul's, London: the choir (for the proposed restoration of the organ screen see Chapter 10, p. 260).

Below: Wren's model of St Paul's: a Greek cross with curved sides, preceded by a porticoed westwerk.

Below: 'Queen Anne's Footstool': Archer's church of St John's, Smith Square, with its four towers.

pedimented façade. Wren designated the northernmost of these chapels as the Morning Prayer Chapel, and a number of churches developed subsidiary spaces, not necessarily with altars, for daily prayer. A similar pair of Medieval side chapels in the north-eastern transept at Salisbury is designated the Morning Chapel.

The other remarkable contribution of Wren to London was the skyline. Amid the modern high-rise buildings of the City it is now difficult to appreciate the amazing variety of the towers and steeples of Wren's city churches clustering round the huge dome of St Paul's, which were still visible until the 1960s. Some, like the three-tier

'wedding cake' of St Bride's, Fleet Street, are well known. Others, such as St Vedast, Foster Lane, or St Magnus the Martyr, Billingsgate, are highly original and with their bells – immortalized in the British nursery rhyme 'Oranges and Lemons' – offer an astonishing variety of different summons to worship.

When thinking of Wren's city churches, it is important to remember that some of the most original designs were by his successors. His clerk, Nicholas Hawksmoor, built Christ Church, Spitalfields (1723–29), with its immense Venetian-style portico and soaring tower, and St Anne's, Limehouse (1712–24). In the City itself, he built

Hawksmoor's west front of Christ Church, Spitalfields, compares with Palladio's façades in Venice for invention (see Chapter 7, pp. 174–76).

The Parliamentary congregation in St Margaret's, Westminster: a contemporary print.

St Mary, Woolnoth (1716–27), a compact, square church that seems larger and more sumptuous, with a bulbous pulpit, carved altarpiece and extraordinary exterior, composed of huge rusticated blocks.

More famous to visitors are Gibbs' St Martin-in-the-Fields in Trafalgar Square (1721–26) and Archer's St John's, Smith Square (1713–28). Whatever the truth of the legend that Queen Anne kicked over her footstool and said to the architect, 'Make me a church like that!', the four Baroque towers of St John's rise from elegant pedimented sides, with porticoes to east and west, and this strange church – restored after war damage as a concert hall – still sits as it was designed to in the centre of its square in Westminster.

Worship in England in the Eighteenth Century

These churches reflect an essentially static view of worship. Churchgoing was a social occupation that should do you good, and sermon-tasting – going from church to church in pursuit of a fashionable preacher – was easy in the city. That is not to say that the eighteenth century did not take sacramental worship seriously. Dr Johnson prepared and fasted throughout Holy Week so as to prepare for the annual occasion on which he received the sacrament – at St Paul's on Good Friday. But the combination of the Prayer Book Communion service, which emphasized the sacrificial death of Christ on the cross for the redemption of humankind, mentioning the resurrection only in the Creed, and the infrequency of the celebration of the sacrament (in many churches no more than quarterly) skewed the intended balance in the Church of England between word and sacrament This imbalance can be seen in this print (left) of St Margaret's, Westminster, the parish church of the Speaker of the House of Commons.

However, the Catholic credentials of the Church of England, along with what the liturgy owed to the Eastern tradition, were never entirely forgotten. Incense was still in regular use in Ely

The Lion Companion to Church Architecture

Cathedral till the early eighteenth century, when the sub dean complained that it made him sneeze, and 1722 saw the fourth edition of Wheatly's *A Rational Illustration of the Book of Common Prayer of the Church of England*. 'Wheatly on the Liturgy', as it came to be known, offered a commentary of the rubrics, rites and ceremonies of the church, as well as the texts. The frontispiece to this classic manual of worship showed the disposition – held up as the ideal – of the ancient Syriac church, complete with a bema in the centre of the nave and a free-standing altar in the apse surrounded by a semicircle of 'thrones for the presbyters'. Before the entrance was an open court with the baptistery or font in the centre. The antiquarian ideals that sought to locate justification for the Church of England's practice by appeal to the customs and traditions of the undivided church, and which would eventually lead to the Tractarian revival in the 1840s, were never entirely absent.

Wheatly's comments on fonts and baptism are instructive:

'In the primitive times we meet with them very large and capacious, not only that they might comport with the general customs of those times, viz. of Persons being immersed or put under water; but because the stated times of Baptism returning so seldom, great numbers were usually baptised at the same time… But immersion being now too generally discontinued, they have shrunk into small Fonts, scarce bigger than Mortars, and only employed to hold less Basons with water, tho' this last be expressly contrary to an ancient advertisement of our Church.'

He continues, commenting on the rubric that tells the parents of children to be ready for the baptism after the Second Lesson at Morning or Evening Prayer:

'The reason of which I take to be, because by that time the whole Congregation is supposed to be assembled; which shews the irregularity (which prevails much in some Churches) of putting off Christenings till the whole

Above: Hawksmoor's strongly rusticated St Mary, Woolnoth, faces the Bank of England.

Right: This pedestal font from the chapel of King's College, Cambridge, is no bigger than a stoup or birdbath; by the eighteenth century baptism was administered in a minimalist way.

Service is over, and to reducing them (by the departing of the Congregation) to almost private baptisms.'

It is no surprise therefore to find the typical font of the eighteenth century – though frequently very elegant – no bigger than a birdbath.

The Eighteenth-Century Church in England

The church that more than any other gives the feeling of having grown in a haphazard way as the pews of the wealthy jostle with the benches of the poor is Whitby, in north Yorkshire. This cliff-top church, well above the parish it serves which clusters round the harbour below, has a complete eighteenth-century interior, with pews of every description surrounding the tall three-decker pulpit and reading desk. There is a prominent chandelier and an even more prominent stove, complete with its stove-pipe. Some pews are comfortably, and warmly, equipped. In some, though not in Whitby, there were fireplaces and storage space not only for the family Bibles and leather-bound Prayer Books, but also for bottles. Of the altar, nothing can be seen. It is in fact located in the dark Norman chancel, hidden behind a gallery pew, raised on delicate barley-sugar columns, with the clock on its front. The light nave, pierced with unusually domestic dormer windows, gives way through this dark opening to a chancel that feels as unused as it must have been for the quarterly celebrations of the Holy Communion in the Georgian period.

Its country equivalent is Charlbury in Dorset, where a low, whitewashed Medieval fabric of thirteenth-century origin was comprehensively re-fitted in the Georgian period. There is a west gallery, box pews and a bench in the chancel near the altar, now painted in modern gloss paint. The most interesting feature is the veranda-type screen that divides nave from chancel. It has a Venetian window design with a central arched opening and two flat-headed pew canopies either side that provide seats for squire and clergy. Not far away is the imposing Church of St Peter and St Paul, in Blandford Forum. Blandford was ravaged by a devastating fire in 1731 and largely

Above right: The interior of Charlbury, looking west from the family pews in the chancel through the arched screen to the reading desk, box pew and gallery in the nave.

Right: Chiselhampton, near Oxford, showing the pulpit and reading desk on the north wall and the holy table within a three-sided rail, surmounted by a reredos composed of the Decalogue, the Creed and the Lord's Prayer.

rebuilt in a country classical style by a local family of architect builders, the Bastards. The church (1731–39) is a big, aisled Georgian church, with a west gallery complete with organ, box pews and pulpit, and a shallow apse that was cleverly moved east on rollers when a chancel was inserted in 1893. In Oxfordshire, a modest country church at Chiselhampton shows the relationship between pulpit, reading desk and altar that was standard in the eighteenth century.

Not many of the churches built were circular or octagonal in plan. The preliminary plan for Gibbs' St Martin-in-the-Fields had been circular: it was turned down on the grounds of expense, but Gibbs recorded the design in his book. One fine example is the late church (1790–92) of St Chad's, Shrewsbury, where

originally the pulpit, reading desk and clerk's desk were set – one in front of the other – before the altar at the eastern edge of the circular space. The pews on both ground-floor and gallery level are arranged in concentric circles, and right in the centre stood the font – a fine and substantial marble basin. The church is approached through a circular narthex, out of which the stairs rise to the gallery level. Another church of this period is the elliptical church of All Saints, Newcastle, where the pulpit and reading desk were behind the altar, with the altar in front, an arrangement that 'effected an improvement not generally found, which was in affording the congregation an opportunity of hearing and attending to the communion service as well as to the prayers and sermon'. Interestingly, the clerk's seat was in the centre of the curved congregational seating, facing the reading desk across the sanctuary. Another distinctive feature was the creation of a small chapel on one side of the entrance to balance the vestry on the other with pews, a reading desk and the font, but no altar, so that it could be used either for baptisms or for daily prayer. The pattern of pulpit and reading desk, with that altar in front, is not uncommon in the nonconformist chapels of the period, and re-emerges as a plausible liturgical layout in the middle of the twentieth century in Roger Bastin's design for the chapel of a girls' school.

A different, but liturgically interesting, plan was to put the pulpit over the west entrance, with the reading desk and clerk's stall either side, as at Teigh, in Rutland. The seating of this small church of 1782 was collegiate, with the tiered stalls facing north and south. The altar at the east end, railed on three sides, also supported a small, basin-like font. The congregation could look west to the preacher and east to the altar, and have an uninterrupted view of both. This pattern also found its way to Ireland, where the eighteenth-century reordering of the often quite small cathedrals produced variations on this kind of collegiate plan, with the choir and canons at the west end, the bishop's throne (often facing the judge's seat) among the people and set against a pillar halfway along the choir, and space at the east end for the altar and pulpit, an arrangement not unlike that of the Medieval Spanish cathedrals. This was how Downpatrick Cathedral was reordered in the opening years of the nineteenth century.

Two other features of the eighteenth century are worth recording. The first is to note the

number of churches that were built or rebuilt, whether in the parks near their mansions or in the local villages by the local gentry. There were several consequences to this. First, such churches were frequently influenced by the secular style employed by the local patron: estate churches such as Shobdon in Herefordshire, with its curious Rococo-Gothic interior decoration, owe more to the Gothic of Horace Walpole's Strawberry Hill than to the then-fashionable Robert Adam, or to the Classical architects such as Vanbrugh and Gibbs who built the park and temples at Stowe. Second, such proprietorial moulding of the parish church in the squire's backyard undermined the sense of community ownership to which the layers of building frequently witnessed in Medieval churches, enlarged and reordered as they were from time to time. Third, these were churches for the squirearchy, not for the lower orders, as they would have been called. In a more class-conscious world, in which the Royal Arms had taken the place of the rood above the chancel arch, and a prayer for the sovereign came before the collect for the day in the Communion service, the servants might be given time off to go to the evening service but would not have been at church on Sunday morning. In part – together with what must have seemed very dry and formal worship – this explains why Methodist preaching with its memorable hymns and extempore prayer had such success among the new working classes in the urban world at the beginning of the Industrial Revolution as well as in the countryside.

The second feature is the growing size and importance – again often attached to these family chapels or in the grounds of the large houses – of mausoleums or family burial vaults. Sometimes whole parish churches seem to have become family burial vaults, as the stacked Fettiplace tombs at Swinbrooke in Oxfordshire appear to suggest. In some cases, such as the Gibside Chapel in the north-east, a mausoleum has become a family chapel or sometimes a chapel-of-ease. Here, in

Shobden, Herefordshire: the pulpit is draped in a velvet fall in this complete Rococo interior.

A chapel in Williamsburg, Virginia: a simple meeting house in the vernacular style for the descendants of the Pilgrim fathers.

the centre of this square, domed mausoleum built in 1760, with its trefoiled apses, the Earl of Strathmore in 1812 set up an altar covered in a blue-green velvet cloth in a free-standing, square, railed enclosure with a large three-decker pulpit similarly clad behind.

The chapels of the various nonconformist denominations tended to be plain, rectangular, brick buildings, with simple furniture and clear windows. Quaker meeting houses were in the same vein. The Baptists had tanks for immersion or built their chapels near rivers. The influence of this kind of simple building, using either brick or simple timber-framed construction with clapboarding, can be seen in the United States, especially in New England and in places like Williamsburg, Virginia.

THE REFORMED TRADITION ON THE CONTINENT: GERMANY

The Frauenkirche in Dresden, which was gutted in 1945 – imploding two days after the Allied bombardment – and finally restored only in 2006, is the 'cathedral' of the Reformed German tradition. Built by Georg Bähr from 1722 to 1738, the clarity of form and the sober decoration of this church, with its huge bell-like dome and three tiers of galleries like some enormous opera house

(it can seat 2,200), make a striking contrast to the exuberance of the south German Rococo of the Roman Catholic tradition. Projecting from the centre of the 'stage', where you might imagine the conductor's rostrum in the opera house, is the pulpit, which is backed by an immense organ. This performance area – or *prinzipalstuk* arrangement – gives the building a single liturgical focus, as font and altar are gathered in one space. The effect is similar to being in a great auditorium like the Albert Hall in London. The Frauenkirche is a church in which the 'performance' of the preacher and the professional musicians is the focus of attention, and the emotional response of the individual listener to an essentially cerebral, word-based religion is what the pietist tradition sought to evoke. This is a very different model from that of the Catholic churches, in which the focus of the worship is the drama of the liturgy. But this gathering together of the liturgical foci in one space – which saw a resurgence in the reordering of many churches in the 1970s – while superficially attractive because of its clear visual focus, tends to turn the assembly into an audience and worshippers into spectators rather than participants.

A more modest church in the Reformed tradition is St George's at Eisenach, in Thuringia. Luther studied here, and indeed preached here,

Above: The Frauenkirche, Dresden: entirely rebuilt after allied bombing in the Second World War.

Below: The pulpit in the cathedral at Riga is ornamented with the theological virtues and other allegorical figures.

Above: Galleries in St George's, Eisenach, where the font (in which Bach was baptized) is set in Lutheran fashion below the pulpit at the chancel step.

Right: The font in the cathedral at Aarhus, Denmark, is placed by the pulpit halfway down the nave.

though officially banned in 1521, and translated the New Testament into German in the nearby castle of Wartburg under the patronage of the Duke of Saxony. Eisenach is the birthplace of J. S. Bach, who was baptized in the font at St George's, which is set at the head of the nave on the chancel steps in close proximity to the pulpit. This position for the font is characteristic of the Lutheran tradition, in which baptism into Christ was seen as a response to the challenge of the gospel to die to sin and rise to new

Left: The Medieval seven-branched candelabrum in the Cathedral of Aarhus, Denmark, survived the Reformation to become a symbol of clarity in the Age of Reason.

Right: The Late Medieval reredos in Aarhus Cathedral by Bernt Notke, surmounted by the Coronation of the Virgin, would not have survived Puritan iconoclasm in England.

Below right: A globe of votive lights forms a focus of prayer for the peace of the world in the cathedral at Stockholm. In the dark winters of Scandinavia, candle flames remain a potent symbol.

life in Christ. This Reformation emphasis on personal salvation as a response to preaching means that the font is frequently set just below the pulpit, even when the pulpit is on a pier halfway down the nave. The pews are then grouped so that they face the pulpit and font, regardless of the position of the altar, as in the cathedral at Aarhus in Denmark. When, as at St George's, the font stands at the chancel step, it makes it clear that access to that altar and the sacrament of the Eucharist is through baptism, and that both sacraments are received in response to the all-important word. In St George's, a sixteenth-century aisled hall-church, there are two tiers of galleries above the aisles, while in the chancel a theatre-like box overlooks the monuments to several generations of Landgraves of Thuringia. At the west end, there is room in the tiers of galleries backing onto the tower for a substantial choir and orchestra in front of the fine organ. The word, spoken and sung, is the focus of worship in this church as it is in the Church of St Peter and St Paul in Goslar, in which a fine candelabrum complements the carved pulpit.

SCANDINAVIA

In Scandinavia – essentially the kingdoms around the Baltic – the Lutheran tradition was a development from rather than a revolt against the

Catholicism of Late Medieval Europe. While some fine pulpits were added to the churches, and the fonts were frequently moved away from the west end to the chancel, the altars – including their elaborate carved and painted reredos – remained. In the cathedral in Aarhus in Denmark, the fine polychrome altarpiece by Bernt Notke depicts the Coronation of the Virgin, a subject that would have had the zealous Protestants in England reaching for their axes and hammers. Perhaps in post-Reformation Denmark it was explained as Christ removing the crown from Our Lady's brow! Another feature of Danish churches that is a constant reminder of Denmark's maritime past is the number of votive ships hanging in the churches.

There are also some splendid pulpits, though few as large and colourful as the pulpit in the Cathedral of Stavanger in northern Norway. In the cathedral at Riga in Latvia, there is another tremendous pulpit, complete with the virtues.

In Scandinavian churches, in which there is so little sun during the long winter months, symbols of light have a particular force. On the Feast of St Lucy (13 December) there is a custom of dressing small girls in white and placing a precarious crown of lighted candles on their heads. Not only are there some fine candelabra, but the great seven-branched candlesticks, as in the cathedrals of Lund in Sweden and Aarhus in Denmark, which were once a feature of many churches and survive in places as far apart as Essen and Milan, continue in use. In Stockholm Cathedral a modern globe with lighted candles provides a striking focus of prayer for the peace of the world.

THE UNITED STATES OF AMERICA

America, with its Puritan tradition carried to the east coast by the Pilgrim fathers, provided an astonishing variety of meeting houses, chapels and churches. They were mostly in the Reformed tradition, providing elegant and sober interiors with a pulpit surmounted by a sounding-board on

The interior of Wethersfield Meeting House in the USA illustrates the directness and simplicity of the religion practised by America's founding fathers.

the long side of the building, and galleries on three sides, such as the Wethersfield Meeting House in Connecticut, built in 1764. In 1833, a major shift took place with the building of Charles Finney's Broadway Tabernacle Congregational Church in New York, a large circular building with galleries all round and a large organ backing the substantial platform. According to James F. White:

'In some ways, it was the outdoor camp meeting brought indoors, although large tabernacles continued to be built in rural

A Wesleyan chapel in an Oxfordshire village, one of the many nonconformist chapels that sprang up all over the UK.

regions for camp meeting. Broadway tabernacle soon became the model for thousands of churches, all having balconies to bring the largest number of people close to the platform. Revival preachers could dash about on the platform, seeking to save souls. Sloping floors improved the sight lines and the gradual advent of choirs found a home in a concert stage arrangement behind the pulpit. The Akron plan brought all this to a climax by placing liturgical centres in a corner, with floor and balconies sloping towards them.'

It was a wooden building like this, originally part of a seaside mission, that was set up on Southsea Common in Portsmouth, England, and which was later rebuilt in a more permanent form as St Simon's, Southsea.

This pattern prefigures the mega-churches of the latter years of the twentieth century, such as the 'Crystal Cathedral' in California. Here seating is frequently theatre-style, with tip-up seats. There are few, if any, recognizable liturgical features. The preacher uses a lectern, equipped with various electronic devices, and the choir – now frequently augmented by a band – holds centre stage. Words of the worship-songs or close-ups of the speaker are projected onto vast screens, and all the technological resources available are brought into play to reinforce the message. Participation by the assembly is largely in response to the speaker, and may be by singing together or by coming forward either as an act of witness to a new-found faith or for some gift of healing or grace (see page 258).

THE FUTURE DIRECTION IN THE ANGLICAN AND REFORMED TRADITION

It was in reaction to this person-focused, sermon-centred worship that the revival in the Church of England in the 1830s and 40s, known as the Oxford or Tractarian Movement, shifted the concept of what was the essential nature of the Christian church, and so, in consequence, of what church buildings ought to be like. The Tractarian Movement and the Gothic Revival so closely associated with it provided another shift in the way in which churches were conceived.

The Gothic Revival

CHAPTER 6

The Romance of the Romantic and the Revival of the Church

The first stirrings of the Romantic Movement began in the second half of the eighteenth century. In Germany it burst into flower with Goethe and Schiller, Beethoven and Schubert, and with the rebuilding of the castles on the bank of the Rhine in the Gothic style. In England, well before Wordsworth and Keats, Blake and Turner, and the beginnings of the Industrial Revolution, the stirrings of a free spirit had begun to question the settled order of the Age of Reason. Religion seemed formal, dry and bound up with the establishment:

'The rich man in his castle,
The poor man at his gate,
God made the high or lowly,
And order'd their estate.'

So wrote Mrs Alexander in a verse – not often sung today! – of her popular 'All things bright and beautiful' as late as 1848. It was against the background of such complacent views that the movement of tied labour away from the estates towards the supposed freedom of a job in industry took place. In terms of religion, the success among the labouring classes of Methodism and other more homespun revivals fuelled aspirations for a better world. In the intellectual world too, things were moving. Coleridge and his contemporaries were questioning the social and political structures that they had inherited and began to put their dreams of a better world into what they wrote. But discontent with the established order, the dreams of a new world and the stirrings of the Industrial Revolution were all thrown into sharp relief by the cataclysmic events of the French Revolution, and the dangers this seemed to pose for established patterns everywhere. It is against this background that the coming together of several different strands began to project the Gothic ideals of aspiration and craftsmanship, and prepared the way for a return to the language of Gothic as the proper architectural vocabulary for church buildings.

THE SURVIVAL OF GOTHIC IN ENGLAND

In discerning the mainsprings of change in this turbulent age of *Sturm und Drang* ('Storm and Stress'), it is important to remember the threads of continuity. Throughout the period, when the Classical style had at last reached England, and Inigo Jones had developed a classical west front for Old St Paul's, Gothic had never quite died out. It was, however, seen more as a romantic style of ornament or decoration than as a distinct philosophy of building. In his London churches, built after

Left: Hawkesmoor's west towers for Westminster Abbey marry a Classical pediment over the clock face with Gothic-style arches.

Above: Wren's Tom Tower at Christ Church, Oxford.

the Great Fire from the 1670s onwards, as well as elsewhere, Wren used Gothic, or Gothic-derived, ornament from time to time. St Mary Aldermanbury, St Katherine Cree, and the great Tom Tower over the gateway to Christ Church in Oxford, are all a form of Gothic, like Hawksmoor's towers for Westminster Abbey, which are known all over the world.

In addition, there were small rural churches that continued to be built in a simple Gothic style: it preserved some of the continuity with the past that the more Reformed elements of the Reformation threatened. And it was not always small churches either. The parish church of Tetbury in Gloucestershire, built by Francis Hiorne in 1777,

was an elegant aisled and vaulted structure. And there were extraordinary churches such as Shobdon in Herefordshire (1752–56), which is a Rococo essay in how to work the ogee arch in an essentially Classical village church frame, in which Gothic-chinoiserie was an essentially decorative form. Another Georgian Gothic church at Moreton in Dorset dates from 1776–77. Restored by the Victorians in the 1840s, it was again damaged by bombing in the Second World War and as a result has a remarkable set of engraved windows by Laurence Whistler. Latest in these Gothic interiors is Mildenhall in north Wiltshire, where a Medieval church was entirely refurnished in 1815–16. The box pews have Gothic panelling with ogee arches, and on either side of the chancel arch rises a matching pair of pulpit and reader's desk, complete with gabled and pinnacled *testers. The gallery curves inwards, as do the pews, to make space for the font. The chancel has continuous leaf-crested panelling, incorporating a reredos with the Commandments, Creed and Lord's Prayer under a crocketted ogee cresting. The whole is delightful, and gives a feel of the interior of a church in which the characters of Jane Austen's novels would have felt at home.

Georgian Gothic at Moreton, Dorset.

The graceful interior of Shobden, Herefordshire, one of England's few Rococo interiors.

ORIGINS OF THE ROMANTIC GOTHIC MOVEMENT

But what we know as the Gothic Revival is a movement that has its origins in a more romantic appreciation of the past. Alongside Lord Burlington and his disciples' passion for the plainer Classical architecture, known as Palladian, in which the great houses and domestic buildings of late seventeenth- and eighteenth-century England were constructed, a romantic passion for ruins developed. This was partly inspired by the proximity of the suggestive remains of the great Medieval monasteries, into or alongside which many large private houses were built from the dissolution of the monasteries onwards. But when a ruin such as Tintern Abbey in south Wales was not part of the landscape, wealthy landowners built expensive but impractical constructions known as follies – sometimes as the climax of a long vista and sometimes as a surprise when you turned a corner in a walk or driveway – as they tried to make the landscape of their parks look like a great painting by Claude Lorraine or Poussin. Gothic was not just the language of ruins; it was also the language of a literature interested in the picturesque and the 'horrid' in terms of poetry and literature. In Joseph Addison's paraphrase of

Psalm 23, a typical Gothic landscape is evoked:
'Though in the paths of death I tread,
With gloomy horrors overspread'

There was also a sense that the Gothic was somehow the proper old English style, which had provided continuity through the Reformation and the political upheavals that led to the Civil War and the subsequent changes in sovereignty in the sixteenth and seventeenth centuries. Sober Gothic was seen as a native bulwark against those voluptuous continental excesses of Baroque style that the Roman Catholic Church had espoused after the Council of Trent.

The 'Gothick' Revival – originally an architecture of follies, superficial decoration and garden furniture, as the quaint spelling of Gothick with a 'k' suggests – began essentially as a rich man's diversion, typified in the garden pavilions by architects such as William Kent (c. 1685–1748). But it soon became serious business, under protagonists such as James Wyatt (1746–1813), a thoroughgoing improver. One of Wyatt's major works was the restoration and improvement of the cathedral at Salisbury, where he removed the Medieval pulpitum in order to create a vista right though the length

The Lion Companion to Church Architecture

Fonthill Abbey, Wiltshire; a Gothic folly in the rural landscape.

of the cathedral – a characteristically Gothic move. The most megalomaniacal of his original schemes was Fonthill Abbey, where for the eccentric William Beckford he built a cluster of transepts radiating round an enormously tall central octagon in the middle of Wiltshire. Begun in 1796, Fonthill became a great wonder, but the workmen had skimped on the foundations and it was so badly built that it collapsed in 1825. Among other curiosities was a design by Sir James Hall for a 'wicker cathedral', which appeared in the influential essay 'The Origin, History and Principles of Gothic Architecture' (1813) and drew attention to the naturalistic origin of Gothic in great branched avenues. Designs like these found their fulfilment in the Gothic glass houses, in which the use of cast iron made possible the Gothic ideal of minimal structural members with the wall surface almost entirely of glass, of which the Pitt Rivers Museum in Oxford by Deane and Woodward from 1855 is one of the finest examples.

The Pitt Rivers Museum in Oxford provides a skeletal structure in cast iron and glass to house the skeletal remains of prehistoric animals.

CAST IRON AND THE COMMISSIONERS CHURCHES

It was cast iron that made Gothic the desired architecture of the great new phase of church building in the early years of the nineteenth century. With the enclosure of traditional common grazing land in the eighteenth century, and the beginnings of the Industrial Revolution that was to make England a foremost manufacturing power in the nineteenth, there was a substantial movement of population from the countryside to the new cities. The revival movement in the Church of England that began under John and Charles Wesley sought to make the Christian faith available to working people. In rural England, they hired barns or assembly rooms, though frequently under attack from the local rector of the parish church for stealing his flock and unsettling them with a theology of social justice. But the Methodists were fired by a vision of the kingdom of God coming in the here and now, expressed in William Blake's well-known poem, 'Jerusalem', with its reference to England's 'dark, satanic mills'. The growth of Methodism, with its popular preaching and rousing hymns, only served to highlight the difficulty of, for example, the Vicar of Leeds ministering in one parish church to a city that was expanding rapidly, and where many of the new inhabitants were living in large blocks of cheap back-to-back housing with no access to the church's worship – a form of worship that was still largely directed towards a benevolent but distant deity, who ordered all things well and kept the privileged divisions of the English social system firmly in place.

In spite of some reforming movements within the church, one of which led to the abolition of slavery, for example, the established church's response was slow. Two things changed it: funding for a major expansion of church building was provided by the spoils of victory in the Peninsular War (1808–14); and a number of missionary-minded societies with concerns for the British underprivileged as well as the wealthy inhabitants rose to the fore in a new

age of philanthropy. As yet, and this was to wait until the rise of the Tractarian Movement in the 1840s, there was no comparable development in the church's worship that made new and radical demands on the design of the church building itself. It was just that there should be more of them, that they should celebrate the victory over Napoleon and the French threat with its overtones of radical revolution by being uncompromisingly British, plain and uncomplicated. They were to be churches in which prayers for the sovereign and the well-being of the state could be read with due solemnity, a semblance of respectful order imposed on the worshippers, and the virtues of attention and obedience to the word of God inculcated.

So the greater number of the Commissioners Churches, as they became known, were large rectilinear halls, whose wide roof-spans were frequently supported – as the churches Thomas Rickman built in Liverpool were – by the slenderest of the new cast-iron columns. Sometimes they were given fan-vaulted ceilings, though those vaults were normally of plaster. In the new industrial world, this was as close as you might get to mass-produced prefabricated parts, and other decorative features followed suit. Fretwork decoration was frequently used in place of wood carving on balcony- or pew-fronts, and simple traceried forms were used for repetitive features such as windows and doors. In some churches, such as St George's Everton in Liverpool, the result is splendid; in others the result is simply dull and uninspiring. Rectangular boxes with Gothic-derived decoration, and even some structural members, are not the same as a living Gothic church that has been conceived from the inside outwards. It was partly that the new techniques of mass-production in plasterwork and stone-cutting did not give that degree of life to the raw materials. It was a later generation, inspired by William Morris and the Arts and Crafts Movement, that came to value the craftsman as an artist. For the present, Gothic was preferred by the Commissioners simply as cheaper to build than Classical churches that demanded such expensive stone porticoes.

Top: The interior of St Luke's, Chelsea, continuing the tradition of eighteenth-century galleried interiors.

Above left: St Luke's, Chelsea, illustrates the early Gothic Revival style of the Commissioners Churches.

Right: The cast iron columns and ribs of St George's, Everton, Liverpool, by Thomas Rickman provide an almost unbelievably insubstantial structure.

AUGUSTUS WELBY PUGIN

But a saviour was at hand – one who was neither
a dilettante nobleman with a passion for ruins nor
a jobbing architect who was looking to span large
spaces cheaply. Augustus Welby Pugin (1812–52)
was one of a handful of early Victorians – like
Isambard Kingdom Brunel for bridges and tunnels
– who changed the face of England. He did not
pursue Gothic because it was quaint or cheap but
because it was true. For Pugin, the only proper
architecture for churches was Gothic: Classical
architecture was pagan and therefore pre-Christian.
Nor was his passion for Gothic confined to the
style: it was the techniques and crafts of building
that were equally important. He poured scorn on
the ironwork of the bridge-building engineers and
those who made prefabricated units. He would
have dismissed churches like Ste Clothilde in Paris
(1846–57) and others in that idiom in which the
mechanically precision-cut stonework produces a
curiously lifeless feel.

A child prodigy, Pugin was drawing plates
for his father's *Specimens of Gothic Architecture* at
the age of twelve. In 1836 he produced *Contrasts:
or a parallel between the noble edifices of the fourteenth
and fifteenth centuries, and similar buildings of
the present day; showing the present decay of taste.*
This crusading book contrasted the mean and
ugly buildings of modern industrial England
with the noble buildings of its Gothic past. The
thesis was that architecture is a reflection of
the society that created it; a typical illustration
contrasted a Medieval almshouse with a prison-
style workhouse. Pugin longed for the coherent,
Christian society of the Middle Ages and lamented
the soulless and utilitarian society driven by the
desire for profit. Nor was this a purely intellectual
crusade; Pugin had become a Roman Catholic.
It was the faith of that church and the style of
worship associated with it that coloured his vision.
While Pugin continued to write, publishing *True
Principles of Pointed or Christian Architecture* in
1841, he was a practitioner. Best known today
for his collaboration with Charles Barry on the

St Giles',
Cheadle,
designed by
Pugin for
the Earl of
Shrewesbury:
his richest
church.

Houses of Parliament, where every detail of the
interior was crafted by him, his churches rarely
found a patron with sufficient funds to execute the
rich interiors he longed to see. But with the Earl
of Shrewsbury's support, Pugin built the church
he desired in St Giles, Cheadle. 'Perfect Cheadle,
my consolation in all my afflictions' is how Pugin
described it; and the church shows both the clarity
of his architectural vision and the remarkable
decorative scheme that captured the imagination
of those for whom the established church and its
worship seemed dusty and dry, with little to stir
the imagination or lift the spirits.

CHANGES IN THE CHURCH OF ENGLAND

What changed the outward face of the church
in England was a combination of two factors:
the revival of the sense that the Church of
England was essentially Catholic in its worship
and self-understanding that came though the
Tractarian revival; and a scholarly interest in the
archaeology of church buildings fostered by the
Cambridge Camden Society, which soon became
the Ecclesiological Society (see page 229). While
the Tractarian or Oxford Movement was largely
intellectual in its concern to re-establish sound

principles of worship and theology that derived from the early centuries, it was its practical outworking in the building of new churches and the reordering of older ones that shaped the Church of England's future so completely. Part of the agenda was to restore the dignity of sacramental worship.

As a result, in a number of churches fonts were renewed or replaced to underscore a newly rediscovered theology of baptism, and chancels were enlarged or rebuilt as a visible sign of the importance of Eucharistic worship. Such reordering not only provided a more dignified setting for the altar, set against the east wall with a reredos to frame it and with altar rails before it; another reason for enlarging chancels was to accommodate surpliced choirs. In the Medieval period, organs were rare in parish churches, and

only the larger collegiate churches had clerks who could sing elaborate music. In the smaller churches, the whole chancel or presbytery was a space for the action of the liturgy. Now, taking the model of the cathedral or collegiate church as the norm, those who led the revival argued that dignified worship even in smaller churches should be led by choirs placed in the chancel, and accompanied by the organ. Among these was Hooke who, when he was Vicar of Leeds, rebuilt St Peter's to designs by R. D. Chantrell in 1841, mixing a collegiate arrangement in the centre of the church with a large open space before the altar rails for communicants. It was not only Leeds Parish Church; now even smaller parish churches emulated the 'correct' fashion for surpliced choirs, while in the eighteenth and early nineteenth centuries, worship in village churches

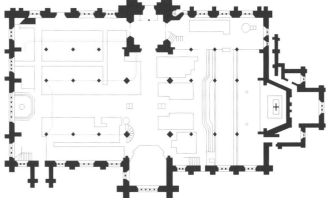

had frequently been led by instrumental bands and groups of singers placed in the west gallery.

This has always been the best position from which to lead the singing of a congregation, and where there was no village band, so valuable in giving an opportunity to build a community, organs had begun to be built in west galleries in eighteenth-century England, as in Germany. Now the choir was vested in surplices and placed in stalls in the chancel; the band was dismissed, and an organ was purchased and installed near them in a side aisle or chapel without any real thought given as to whether it could be heard well or lead the congregation in singing. The replacement of a rustic, male and socially established pattern by a more sophisticated choir of children led by the schoolmistress is well described in Thomas Hardy's novel, *Under the Greenwood Tree*. But it was a thorough revolution. A chancel filled with choir stalls has come to be accepted as the historic norm in the Church of England; but it is a relatively recent innovation with questionable liturgical as well as musical credentials.

Another factor that changed the interiors of English churches considerably was the work of the Incorporated Church Building Society. Even today painted notices in the porches of churches declare:

'This Church was repaired with a grant from The Incorporated Church Building Society, on condition that all sittings in this church should be free.'

In the eighteenth century, country interiors were full of family pews. In other churches, the wealthy could pay rent for their own pews as if they were boxes at the theatre. The result of making all seats free in many churches is still visible today in large acres of wall-to-wall pewing, often in mean pitch-pine. This is a far cry from the normally rather limited seating in Medieval churches, when the nave of the church was a community space. But as churches began to be thought of primarily as places where prayers were read and sermons heard, seating for everyone assumed a significance that it never had in those Medieval churches that were the theoretical models of the Gothic Revival.

During the early part of this period, the pattern of Sunday worship in the Church of England continued to have Morning and Evening Prayer as the principal services, with Holy Communion as an additional (but frequently no more than monthly) service held increasingly at 8 a.m. rather than after Matins. The new interior arrangements facilitated this pattern and provided a more elegant and dignified setting. The many churches built by Gilbert Scott

The chapel at Exeter College, Oxford, by Gilbert Scott, based on the Sainte Chapelle in Paris.

around the courtyard; the whole ensemble signalled the strength of the collegiate life that a foundation like this promoted.

Such a dark, mysterious and exciting church also made it clear that no longer were reason and clarity the most prized sensations. In an England very different from that of the eighteenth century, in which the clergy were rapidly becoming professionals, the church was conscious of its need to appeal to people's emotions and to their longing for mystery and

Above: Butterfield's substantial font at All Saints, Margaret Street.

The rich, dark interior of the iconic Tractarian church, All Saints, Margaret Street, London.

(1811–78) all over England witness to his tireless activity and the rather dull, low-church ideas of 'Common Prayer' that much of the Church of England required. Scott could rise to great heights, however, and between 1854 and 1860 he built a new chapel for Exeter College, Oxford, which was a magnificent replica of the Sainte Chapelle in Paris. However, most of his churches did not serve the growing desire for sacramental worship in many parishes, especially the newly created parishes in the city that were touched by the Tractarian revival. It is William Butterfield's (1814–1900) church of All Saints, Margaret Street, that initiates the development most strikingly. Dating from the 1850s, it has a broad interior, dark with patterned brick, and marks the beginning of a new period of a distinctive Gothic style that owes very little to Medieval originals. On a small, cramped site Tractarian principles are given full expression. Light falls on the richly decorated chancel. The high altar, with its towering reredos, tall candlesticks and hanging pyx (added by Comper later) is visible from anywhere in the church. The font is large and set in its own dignified space. This is a church that signals that it belongs in the Catholic tradition, and speaks in every detail of sacramental – and especially Eucharistic – worship. Butterfield also created the neighbouring vicarage and choir school

THE ECCLESIOLOGICAL SOCIETY AND THE RISE OF CHURCH FURNISHERS

It is difficult for us to realize the immense influence wielded by the Ecclesiological Society, which published reviews of churches and commended the multitude of 'correct' pattern books that their favoured architects produced. While Gilbert Scott was busy working over the majority of England's cathedrals and designing the Albert Memorial – a kind of high Victorian shrine that owed more to Gothic metalwork of the Middle Ages than to architectural examples – other and abler architects were wrestling with the opportunities offered by emerging tastes in worship.

Another feature that was new to the builders of churches was the possibility of mass-produced fittings. Firms like Hardmans of Birmingham, coached by Pugin's workaholic passion for drawing every detail, were able to produce catalogues of metalwork, chandeliers, lecterns and missal stands. Clayton and Bell were the comparable makers of stained glass, producing – together with Kempe – glass more advanced both in technique and artistry than anything available on the continent, where much of the glass painting of the mid- to late nineteenth century is frankly mawkish and sentimental. Little of the glass was in that sense mass-produced, though glassmakers did have certain stock characters and patterns of censing angels to fill in those awkward corners of the upper tracery. The most exotic of the mass-produced wares in England were not furnishings and fittings but whole churches. It was possible to buy, and have shipped out in crates to outposts of the empire, whole churches made in corrugated iron. Like other Gothic fantasy products, they came in different sizes,

The Albert Memorial – a Gothic shrine for a departed hero, if not a saint.

In the colonies – the ogee curves of this church porch in Kerala, south India, look entirely at home in that context.

from 'cathedral' and 'abbey' right down to 'chapel'. But they were all Gothic, and in dry climates they had a remarkably long life. The last cathedral model to survive in England was in use as the school theatre at Radley College, Oxfordshire, until the 1970s.

In the expanding empire, Anglicanism took root in many parts of the world, where the practice and the style of worship at home was followed. In countries where there was a substantial ex-patriot population such as India, large numbers of churches were built. Mostly they were – like those who attended them – properly dressed, that is, Gothic in style, like this church in Kerala (below).

Sometime the eccentricities or limitations of the Victorian church were exported as well as its faith. When Colonel Skinner of Skinners Light Horse came to view St James', Delhi – a church that he had built in fulfilment of a vow he had made when lying wounded on a battlefield – he told the architect that he thought he had made a pretty good job of it, except that his initials were actually JHS, not IHS. Skinner had failed to recognize the sacred monogram – the first three letters of the word Jesus, or IHSUS in Greek – which had been stencilled as a decorative device all over the roof!

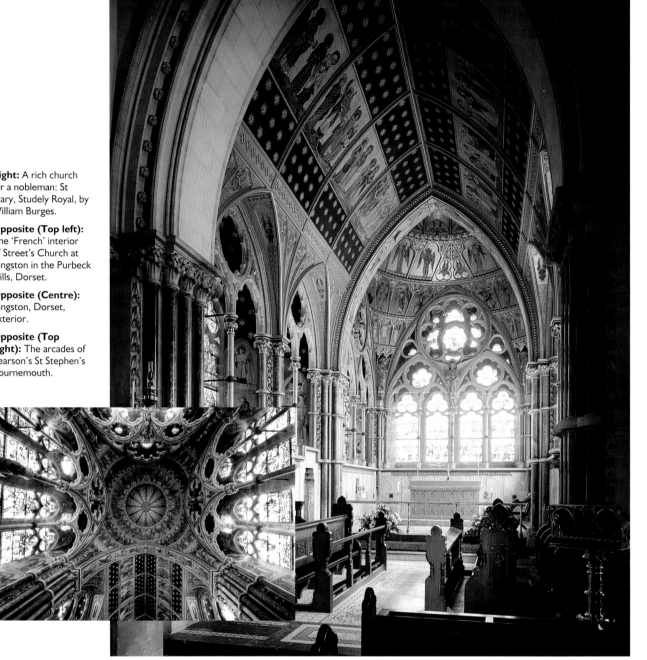

Right: A rich church for a nobleman: St Mary, Studely Royal, by William Burges.

Opposite (Top left): The 'French' interior of Street's Church at Kingston in the Purbeck Hills, Dorset.

Opposite (Centre): Kingston, Dorset, exterior.

Opposite (Top right): The arcades of Pearson's St Stephen's Bournemouth.

transformation. This is what All Saints, Margaret Street, offered them.

In the wake of the Catholic revival, disputes within the church over matters of ritual dragged on until the beginning of the twentieth century. But the appeal of more colourful worship in visually deprived urban parishes and the heroic work of parish priests of the Catholic tradition in the slums of the east end of London in particular made an indelible mark on the Church of England's worship.

CHURCH BUILDERS IN ENGLAND

Several factors combined to make England the leader in this movement. First, in England, more than in the Catholic Mediterranean or the Protestant Germany and Scandinavia, patterns of worship were being challenged and changing. Second, Gothic – the methods of craftsmanship as well as the architectural style – had a philosophical champion in Pugin and his successors. Third, England was for a time the world leader in style, and her burgeoning empire –

an empire of trade and skills as well as of political influence – gave her unrivalled influence.

Among her architects, William Burges (1827–81) built in rich materials, using marbles, glass and metalwork to create rich interiors. His church at Studely Royal, not far from Fountains Abbey in Yorkshire, was designed for a rich patron. In Ireland, he built the magnificent French-style cathedral of St Finbarre's, Cork. The quality of the exterior stone carving is matched by a rich interior, where the liturgical arrangements, with a massive pulpit and lectern at the head of the nave, lead to a choir that leaves little room for any ritual action around the altar, which is set far to the east in the apse.

Less exotic is George Edmund Street (1824–81), perhaps the most 'correct' of all the Gothic Revival architects. Street built churches that have more life in them than Scott's, and among his later churches is a

little gem at Kingston on the Purbeck hills in south Dorset. It is a church that owes more to the Isle de France, with a strong central tower and a vaulted, apsidal chancel, though it is built out of local Purbeck stone and marble. Every detail, including the cast metal screens, is beautifully proportioned, yet it does not feel that it is anything more than a country church for the English religion. This is the same Street that could build St Saviour's, Eastbourne, a large brick church with a canted bay leading into a four-sided apsidal chancel with splendid mosaics.

In the urban areas, some notable churches were built. St Augustine's, Kilburn (1870–80) is one of the churches built by John Loughborough Pearson (1817–97), a master of the early Pointed style. The interlocking vistas of vaults and arches; a triforium gallery running across the transepts and rood screen; the height of the central space in contrast to the low aisles and ambulatory; all these give a sense of

St Saviour's, Eastbourne, one of Street's more exotic churches.

Bodley's great church of St Augustine's, Pendlebury, Manchester.

Bodley's rich chancel in the Holy Angels, Hoar Cross, Staffordshire.

The Holy Innocents, Highnam in Gloucestershire, by Gambier Parry, is frescoed throughout and has a Doom painting over the chancel arch.

The long nave and lofty high altar of St Bartholomew's, Armley, Leeds.

Even the radiators at The Holy Innocents, Highnam, were designed in a Gothic style, as if they were enlarged reliquaries.

scale and spaciousness that lifts worship. The same is true of the way the vaulted processional paths lead the eye to vistas in his St Stephen's Bournemouth (1881–1908). This reveals an architect who understood how to lead the imagination into a sense of the beyond.

A near contemporary of Pearson's, George Frederick Bodley (1827–1907), built a remarkable church at St Augustine's, Pendlebury, in Manchester between 1870 and 1874. This vast church, with its uninterrupted sweep of the nave moving into a chancel delineated structurally only by a rood screen, offers one of Bodley's trademarks: a tall reredos glimpsed through a screen surmounted by a rood. There are no aisles as such; simply a low passageway cut through the buttressed piers that articulate the nave. The church gets its majestic effect by a tall, Perpendicular style of architecture. But there can be no doubt that in this church, the visibility – yet distance – of the high altar by all is what is intended: this is a church for the Catholic faith, newly interpreted. Perhaps the best of Bodley's churches is Holy Angels, Hoar Cross, in Staffordshire (1876). Working for a wealthy patron in the Catholic tradition, Bodley produced a church that was

beautifully proportioned, wonderfully decorated and that was self-evidently a holy place. Marble floor, stone vaults, a richly decorated organ case and all fittings perfectly to scale combine to make this estate church a fine example of high Victorian art.

Another church built for a wealthy patron is Holy Innocents, Highnam, in Gloucester. This is chiefly remarkable for being painted with frescos throughout, including a great doom painting of Christ in Majesty over the chancel arch. The most delightful touch here is the cast bronze cladding of the radiators, for which of course there was no Medieval precedent, making them look as if they are gigantic bell-reliquaries. Recently conserved and cleaned, the paintings are startlingly bright: even on a dull day the effect is overwhelming.

A church of a different character is St Bartholomew's, Armley, in Leeds. The central tower, capped with a French-style spire, rises over a compact east end and forms a landmark in this hilltop suburb of Leeds. Built in 1872 by Athron and Walker, the long and impressive nave with a font placed centrally at the west end culminates in the central tower space that contains the choir, with shallow transepts north and south. The north transept holds a five manual organ by Schulze, originally in a private house. This crossing space prepares the eye for the polygonal east end, raised further and crowned by a wedding cake-style altarpiece. This church now stands alone, and towers over the Victorian Armley Gaol and the remains of the back-to-back housing that once formed its parish.

Towards the turn of the century, rich patrons were able to indulge their architects in the latest styles. The slightly decadent *fin-de-siecle* style of Art Nouveau was never going to be suitable for churches, though the fittings of St Cuthbert's, Philbeach Gardens, in Earls Court in London (1884–87) by Romieu Gough are as opulent as you can imagine, and many sacristies, especially in the seaside towns of southern England, acquired chalices and other vessels encrusted with the amethysts and pearls of elderly widows, such as St Peter's, Parkstone, in Poole. And not only Eucharistic vessels; there are fine examples of crosses and candlesticks as well as chalices by metalworkers such as Omar Ramsden (1873–1939); and Ninian Comper (1864–1960) followed Bodley in designing both fine fabrics and rich embroidery for vestments and frontals, often carried out by anonymous sisters in religious communities. Towards the end of the nineteenth century, the decorative style of the Pre-Raphaelite Movement made some impact, partly though the design of hangings woven by the William Morris school, and partly through some highly original and deeply coloured glass, designed by painters such as Edward Burne-Jones (1833–98), whose work can be seen in the Epiphany Chapel in Winchester Cathedral, for example.

Pre-Raphaelite stained glass of the Annunciation by Burne-Jones in the Epiphany Chapel, Winchester Cathedral.

Chalices encrusted with jewels at St Peter's, Parkstone, Poole.

St Bartholomew's, Armley, Leeds, now isolated from the former back-to-back housing on the top of its hill above the Gaol.

Comper's rich interior at St
Cyprian's, Clarence Gate.

COMPER: A LITURGICAL VISION
BEFORE ITS TIME

The culminating figure among those architects
who worked for the Catholic tradition was Sir
Ninian Comper, who lived until 1960. His
churches are entirely distinctive and he was
capable of designing furnishings and fittings in
a way that made his churches seem at once holy
and splendid. If many Victorian churches are
designed to impress with the slightly gloomy
solemnity of the Almighty, Comper's churches
have a quality that makes the heart rise. After
introducing the 'English altar', complete with
*riddle posts, dossal and side curtains and, if
possible, a hanging pyx for reserving the sacrament

above it, Comper's later churches have a gilded
ciborium – or at least a tester – over the altar. In a
series of pamphlets published throughout his life
he laid out his views on the placing and setting of
the altar as the fundamental element of the design
of the interior of a church. Before it became a
fundamental tenet of the Liturgical Movement in
the mid-twentieth century, Comper realized the
importance of creating the atmosphere in which
the community might be drawn round the altar
to celebrate. Influenced by a visit to the ancient
basilica at Theveste in North Africa, he swept away
the clutter of choir stalls that separated the altar
and its ritual from being seen by the worshipper in
the nave. Singing choirs were located with richly
cased organs in west galleries, and a gilded but
transparent rood screen separated the nave from
the chancel.

In St Cyprian's, Clarence Gate (1903),
probably the best of his London churches, there
are all of Comper's hallmarks: the nave furnished
with chairs, not pews; a font placed centrally and
set forward from the west gallery, surmounted
by a tall, gilded font cover; a richly carved and
decorated rood screen; a large presbytery with an
altar surmounted by a tester; and a hanging pyx
over the altar in which the consecrated host is
reserved.

In 1912 at the Grosvenor Chapel in Mayfair,
the principal altar was brought forward to the heart
of the church and set against a Classical screen.
The proposed ciborium was disallowed, but
Comper created a sense of mystery in the darker
chapel he created behind the screen at the east
end. This was a revolutionary design, and sowed
the seeds that were to bear fruit later in Cosham,
Portsmouth. In his design for Aberdeen Cathedral,
alas never built, he set the stalls of the cathedral
choir towards the west of the nave, a position
similar to that of the *coro* in the Spanish Medieval
cathedral, like Segovia on which it was modelled.

In a simpler style, he re-fashioned the estate
church of the Earls of Shaftesbury at Wimborne St
Giles in Dorset. Against the dark woodwork and
limewashed plaster, the gilded font cover, high

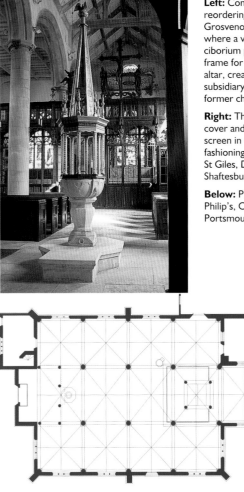

Left: Comper's reordering of the Grosvenor Chapel, where a vestigial ciborium provides a frame for the principal altar, creating a subsidiary chapel in the former chancel behind.

Right: The gilded font cover and a distant screen in Comper's re-fashioning of Wimborne St Giles, Dorset, for the Shaftesbury family.

Below: Plan of St Philip's, Cosham, near Portsmouth.

The Gothic Revival

altar with its tester and organ case stand out. It was his first essay in 'unity by inclusion'.

His largest and richest church is St Mary's, Wellingborough. Here you can experience his principle of unity by inclusion at its richest. Comper was ready to blend the language of Classical columns, pilasters and niches with the vocabulary of Late Gothic. His windows remained traceried Perpendicular, but the columns and pillars might have Classical capitals. A font cover might look like the steeple of one of Wren's city churches, but the font over which it rose was plain Perpendicular. The interior might be light, airy and limewashed like the big wool churches of East Anglia, but the ciborium over the altar might be early Christian in form and richly gilded and painted.

His latest, simplest and in many ways most advanced design is for a church in the suburbs of

Portsmouth, built just before the Second World War. From the outside, St Philip's, Cosham, is a plain, rectangular, brick box, with an apology of a pinnacled bell-turret and vaguely Gothic traceried windows. Inside, the layout is simple, bold and clear. No longer is the high altar behind a screen at the very east end; instead, it stands towards the head of the nave, with space to gather round it on all four sides. Still the sacred space, marked by a gilded ciborium, it is now set in the heart of the building. Behind, like a Late Medieval Italian *coro*, a shallow east end chapel projects, hung in Comper's favourite rose-pink damask. The organ, in a richly decorated case, is in the west gallery, and the only liturgical object of any significance other than the principal altar is the font, under its gilded cover, at the west end of the nave in front of the gallery. All other furnishings – even the

Interior of St Philip's, Cosham, showing the font and organ case at the west end (top right) and the altar with its gilded ciborium (top left and bottom), standing in front of the *coro*. Note Comper's distinctive rose-pink damask hangings.

wooden pulpit – are moveable, like the chairs. The interior, including the columns which have vaguely Classical capitals, is painted a plain white. All the glass in the windows is clear. This is a church in which the dominical sacraments of baptism and Eucharist are celebrated, as the people of God are gathered round the mystery of the word made flesh – in suburban Portsmouth. The design is so pure and so simple that it needs no liturgical adaptation of any kind for contemporary Eucharistic worship, yet it was designed and built thirty years before any such ideas were current.

GOTHIC REVIVAL ON THE CONTINENT AND BEYOND

While England took a leading role in the Gothic Revival, other nations made distinctive contributions, even if they were not expressive of such interesting ecclesiological changes in the patterns and style of worship. Principal among them was Germany, where the major project that captured public attention was the completion of the great Medieval cathedral of Cologne. The east end with the choir and radiating chapels had been built soon after 1248 as the first stage of Europe's largest cathedral. But building finally ground to a halt in 1560, with only the lower stages of the south-west tower of the nave and façade of the rest of the cathedral accomplished. Its completion over a long period from 1840 to 1881 followed the original designs as far as possible, though the nave roof trusses – hidden from view – are of cast iron.

In 1844, the international standing of the English Gothic Revival was signalled by Scott's winning the commission for the Nikolaikirche in Hamburg, built between 1845 and 1863. Another competition won by British architects was that for Lille Cathedral. In collaboration with William Burges, Henry Clutton produced the design in 1855, but was not allowed to supervise its construction as he was not a Roman Catholic.

In France, the Gothic Revival was not married to the same passion for craftsmanship and respect for materials as was the case in the

England of Pugin, Ruskin and Morris. Nor was it the product of a renewed ecclesiology, as was the alliance between clients and their architects in the wake of the Tractarian Movement. The result in France is frequently dreadful: machine-cut stone, slavish copies of thirteenth-century originals; and not having to work hard at a client's demand for a developing pattern of worship produced buildings that feel artificial, such as Gau's Ste Clothilde. What you miss in France is the sense of the church as a palimpsest of the local community – that composite layering of different building periods and architectural styles so characteristic of the pattern of English building. More interesting were the fanciful experiments in iron and stone, such as Louis-Auguste Boileau's (1812–96) proposed iron chapel for Saint-Denis, an eclectic jumble constructed around a cast-iron frame of semi-domes and half-vaults that owes more to Russia, and might have resembled a gigantic jelly-mould, had it been built.

In Germany and Scandinavia, the rediscovered Gothic style was associated with a Medieval romanticism. One of the more interesting essays, marrying the centralized round or octagonal plan that had become a hallmark of Protestant Germany with the vocabulary of Gothic, was the Trefoldighetskirchen in Oslo, built in a brick neo-Gothic style in 1850–58. Another was the Funfhaus Parish Church built by Friedrich von Schmidt (1825–91) in Vienna between 1868 and 1875. This church is centrally planned round an aisled octagon, which rises to a ribbed dome. Hexagonal chapels are grouped round the polygonal apse, and the two west towers set at 45 degrees to the gabled entrance rise to slender octagonal pinnacles that provide a striking contrast to the central dome. These original designs are quite different from anything that could have been built in England, and while the vocabulary is Gothic, the form is a post-Baroque development.

Cologne Cathedral was completed, to its original design, only in the nineteenth century.

The Development of the Rundbogenstil in Germany

When it became inescapably apparent that it was in France, not Germany, that Gothic had originated, many architects were happy to adopt a Rundbogenstil or round-arched style, which owed its life to a synthetic blend of Byzantine and Romanesque elements. If the Gothic was clearly associated with the sacramental worship of the Catholic tradition in Germany, then what would be an appropriate style for the Protestant tradition there to adopt in order to develop a distinctive nineteenth-century equivalent to the Classical forms of eighteenth-century Lutheran churches, with their west-end organs, tiers of galleries and towering pulpits? This novel creation, with the development of the round and the square – so very different from the highly correct early Pointed style of the English architects – reached its most expressive peak not in Germany, but in the United States. In Holy Trinity, Copley Square, in Boston (1872–76) by H. H. Richardson, the German Protestant principle of an open, galleried auditorium, married to this essentially German fusion of round-arched styles, delivered one of the most impressive nineteenth-century churches in the United States. The galleried nave and open transepts of

Holy Trinity, Copley Square, Boston – a bold use of the German Rundbogenstil.

The richly decorated interior of Holy Trinity, Copley Square.

a short-armed Greek cross are spanned by an intricate timber roof. Over the crossing rises a low but massive baronial tower, which looks as if it is modelled on the Romanesque tower of St Martin-le-Grand in Cologne; the altar stands on the chord of the apsidal eastern arm. East of Germany,

A masterpiece of continental Gothic Revival: Steindl's parliament building in Budapest.

where one of the greatest Gothic Revival buildings – the parliament building in Budapest by Imre Steindl (1839–1902) – was built on the banks of the Danube in imitation of Barry's Houses of Parliament in Westminster, the Cathedral of St Stephen that faces it on the citadel opposite was also substantially rebuilt in the Gothic style. Lower down the Danube in Sophia, the old capital of Bulgaria, an immense 'Victorian' cathedral was erected as a nationalist memorial. Its bulbous orthodox style owes more to its continental neighbours than to its orthodox neighbour nearby, the Russian church.

Round-arched Style in England

The round-arched style in England was originally associated with the heavy Norman Romanesque idiom of Ewan Christian (1814–95) and others, and was largely used in the more Evangelical churches for whom pointed Gothic smelt of Pugin and Popery. But the chapel at Wreay in Cumbria, dating from 1840, shows an original treatment of liturgical furnishings in a more centralized plan. Another, more exotic church was built by S. S. Teulon (1812–73) on the banks of the River Wye in rural Herefordshire at Hoarwithy. Using exotic marbles, mosaic and lapis lazuli, Teulon, who was described as the 'fiercest, ablest and most temerarious of

Above left: Nineteenth-century megalomania meets the Orthodox tradition: the Nevsky Cathedral, Sophia, Bulgaria.

Above right: The rich decoration of St Stephen's Cathedral, Budapest, the coronation church.

Left: Teulon's rounded arches and exotic materials give the effect of a Classical ciborium over the altar at Hoarwithy, Herefordshire, England.

239

The cloister-like porch, wrapping round the church, uses Romanesque elements to prepare the worshipper for Teulon's magnificent interior at Hoarwithy.

most significant new church – Westminster Cathedral. This vast and splendid church has a great nave with brick domes, disappearing into incense-laden darkness. The side chapels and the lower walls are covered in marble cladding with mosaics in the apses and barrel vaults, but the vast space of the nave remains plain and mysterious. In many ways, Bentley's ground plan is conventional, and perhaps owes something to the domed churches of Perigueux. He placed the choir at a high level in the eastern apse so that the sound of the boys' voices floats out into the whole building like a choir of angels, and set the high altar under an immense ciborium in the central dome, blending an Italian Romanesque disposition of the raised *coro* with an Italian

contemporary architect adventurers', created a post-Venetian church of great originality. It has an exterior cloistered porch running round two sides of the building, a broad nave spanned by a painted wooden roof in the Italian style and a chancel that gives the feel of an extended ciborium over an apsidal altar that is unparalleled elsewhere. A larger church in the round-arched idiom is St Aidan's, Roundhay Road, Leeds, built in the 1890s. Here a great flight of stairs leads up to an apsidal sanctuary crowned by a large mosaic (1916) in the Art Nouveau style by Sir Frank Brangwyn.

J. F. Bentley (1839–1902) chose a large-scale Byzantine idiom for London's

A flight of steps leads to the raised chancel and Brangwyn's richly decorated apse in St Aidan's, Roundhay Road, Leeds.

Left: The interior of Bentley's magnificent Westminster Cathedral, where the eye is drawn up from the rich marble and mosaic below to the mysterious smoke-blackened brick domes.

Right: Eric Gill's stations of the cross on Westminster Cathedral's nave piers.

Bentley's monumental high altar in Westminster Cathedral, with the choir in the raised apse beyond.

Baroque position for the altar and its setting. Originally designed to be covered in mosaics in the richest Byzantine style, the undecorated brick vaults of the domes make the richness of the great hanging rood cross stand out against the smoky gloom of the vault. The side aisles are little more than processional ways, distinguishing the great space of the nave, which seats 3,000, with an uninterrupted view of the high altar from the lateral chapels, many of which are richly decorated in mosaics in differing styles, contrasting with Eric Gill's (1882–1940) austere but moving stations of the cross set on the piers of the nave. This building, with its distinctive, non-Gothic idiom, marks the emerging confidence of the Roman Catholic community in Great Britain, and complements the Gothic of Westminster Abbey and the Classical of St Paul's. Although built for the liturgy of its period, it remains one of London's finest and most worshipful churches.

Nonconformist chapels used this style too, as the splendid domes of Liverpool's Presbyterian Chapel show.

Continental Developments and Their Influence

Another church showing a distinct continental influence is Quarr Abbey on the Isle of Wight, by Dom Paul Bellot (1876–1944). Using Belgian bricks, this monk-architect built a new church for his Benedictine community – uprooted from their French homeland in the anti-clerical movement of the turn of the century – and contrived an architectural vocabulary by stepping the bricks to form a pointed arch. This unusual building created a spacious square sanctuary under the east-end tower, to which was attached a choir of monastic stalls to the west. This choir was extended at a lower level into a nave for worshippers who were not members of the community, before concluding in a massive western portal. Because the original sanctuary was a square, it has been easy to reorder the space, with a hanging pyx over a free-standing central altar.

Other remarkable examples of a developed Byzantine style include the huge Basilica of Ste Clothilde in Rheims. This large, centralized space shows architects at the turn of the century working to use an idiom other than the essentially longitudinal Gothic to create a different experience for worshippers. Gathering large numbers together for a celebration of the Eucharist was being given architectural expression in an enlarged Byzantine idiom even before the Liturgical Movement of the twentieth century began to exert its influence.

Although owing more to the domed churches of south-west France and the fantastic skyline of the Basilica of St Anthony of Padua, Sacre Coeur in Montmartre – begun in 1875 after the Franco-Prussian War and only completed in 1914 – indicates how far the pursuit of Gothic as a natural vocabulary to conjure up a sense of awe and mystery had developed in the course of the nineteenth century.

The domed skyline of Sacre Coeur, Montmartre, Paris.

Opposite page: Quarr Abbey: the porch and central tower from the west.

Left: The interior of Quarr Abbey, looking down the narrow nave, past the monastic stalls, to the large square sanctuary with its ribbed brick vault.

Right: The Basilica of Ste Clothilde in Rheims: the French–Russian connection.

Above: The domes of the Medieval Basilica of St Anthony in Padua contrast with the domes of the Sacre Coeur in Paris.

Gaudi and the Sagrada Familia

None of the imaginative developments of the Gothic Revival are so remarkable, however, as the extraordinary church – now a cathedral – of the Sagrada Familia in Barcelona by the architect Antonio Gaudi (1852–1926). The building is still unfinished, and has evolved over the years. It was begun on a relatively conventional Gothic ground plan, but the freedom to experiment with free-flowing forms owes as much to tropical vegetation as to conventional Gothic. Gaudi's inventiveness was combined with the potential for improvising and with the possibilities offered by the new ferro-concrete materials. The result is unlike anything else in the world, and its cluster of four Gothic-type spires is a better-known trademark of Barcelona than the city's ancient cathedral. Somehow its unfinished state is an important twentieth-century statement about the inability of the human mind to comprehend, let alone capture, the majesty of God, and contrasts with those Late Gothic statements of majesty and power such as the National Cathedral in Washington, D.C. or Giles Gilbert Scott's Liverpool Cathedral, begun in 1904 and only

The vaults of Gaudi's fantastic Sagrada Familia in Barcelona.

finished – in a somewhat truncated form – in the 1980s. Buildings like these run the risk of dwarfing the human person, and crushing, rather than enlarging, the human spirit, whereas the twentieth century has been more concerned with exploring the unending partnership between the human and the divine.

The spires of the Sagrada Familia have become Barcelona's trademark.

Liturgical Reform in the Twentieth Century

CHAPTER 10

The Search for a Genuine, 'Modern' Church Architecture

Background image:
Schwartz's ground plan in Schloss Rothenfels.

When Dom Prosper Gueranger re-founded the Abbey of Solesmes in 1837 the first steps were taken in the liturgical renewal of the Roman Catholic Church that culminated in the work of the Second Vatican Council (1962–65). Solesmes became known for its revival and performance of Gregorian chant, and these stirrings were confirmed by Pope Pius X's instruction on the chant in 1903. But Pius had wider concerns: he wanted to see a renewed liturgy at the heart of the church's life. He encouraged more frequent Communion from an earlier age, and called for a revision in the lectionary and calendar. From such beginnings, the Liturgical Movement began to grow beyond its monastic origins in the early twentieth century.

The focus of the movement was a recovery of the liturgy as the corporate celebration of the church's sacraments rather than the use of the liturgy as a backdrop to a personal devotional life. The emphasis on corporate celebration was seen in some quarters as 'unspiritual', and major elements in the reform to make the liturgy truly the people's, such as the translation of the Latin rite into the vernacular, had to wait until Vatican II. But the spirit of enquiry into the origins of the church's worship began to provide a new sense of direction when, in the face of the catastrophe of the First World War, repeating old and tired formulae looked increasingly barren.

What was new was the rediscovery of the corporate and the communitarian. The nineteenth and early twentieth centuries had set great store by the value placed on personal freedom and the emerging insights of psychology. This concentration on the individual was given a context – a sense of persons in relation to one another – by studies in social anthropology. Where did the human quest for meaning stand in relation to these new disciplines?

The elements of the church's answer were already there before the First World War. By 1899 Dom Lambert Beauduin was discovering the transforming nature of the celebration of the liturgy for young workers, and in 1906 he joined the Benedictines at Mont Cesar in Belgium, beginning the ecumenical work that was to unite the churches in the study of the origins of worship by the latter part of the twentieth century. By 1913, the Abbey of Maria Laach in the Rhineland was exploring the riches of the Holy Week liturgy with students, and in the 1930s a young architect, Rudolph Schwartz, was employed in setting out the great hall of Schloss Rothenfels for a summer congress organized for

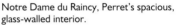
Notre Dame du Raincy, Perret's spacious, glass-walled interior.

The first ferro-concrete church in a Paris suburb, Notre Dame du Raincy, with an impressive tower.

The church of Christ-le-Roi in Fribourg, Switzerland, uses concrete to span a wide, fan-shaped nave, and for the tall columns that support the cupola over the altar.

the Catholic youth of Germany by the inspirational Romano Guardini. The hundred small, black, cuboid stools could be set out in different configurations, and for liturgical celebrations a free-standing altar was placed in front of one of the longer walls of the hall, with the boys surrounding it on three sides. On the fourth side, facing them from behind the altar, was the celebrant. This experience of direct engagement with the Eucharistic action produced a hitherto unknown fervour and a positive sense of unity that those who took part in such celebrations never forgot, according to Schwartz.

THE NEW ARCHITECTURE

Part of the effect of those celebrations was experiencing the freedom from the traditional layout of a church that using a large, whitewashed and unfurnished hall provided. Part was the experience that participating in the liturgy in such a context actually formed the church, the community of faith. Alongside these efforts to uncover the origins of Christian worship and give people an experience of its power, it is important to remember that the Liturgical Movement was accompanied by a parallel architectural movement known as Functionalism. Partly as a reaction to the excesses of Art Nouveau, a trend against ornamentation had developed that was to join hands with a preference for a plain and functional style of architecture that revealed the essential elements of a building's structure and derived its integrity from its form and the materials of which it was built rather than from applied ornament. These principles became dominant in the Bauhaus school of design established in Germany at the end of the First World War, and nurtured architects such as Mies van der Rohe (1886–1969), Dominikus Bohm (1880–1955) and Le Corbusier (1887–1965). With reinforced concrete, almost anything could be built, and interest in church design focused initially on the creation of volumes that spoke of encounter with the divine rather than of liturgical spaces whose structure exhibited a similar structural functionalism.

When the first large concrete church was designed, engineered and built by Auguste Perret in 1922, it caused a shock. The slender columns of Notre Dame du Raincy in an eastern suburb of Paris stand free within the space and the walls – concrete and glass – wrap round them. The simple shuttered concrete vaulting springs from the beams above the columns, and through it all thrusts the western tower. At the east end, the sanctuary is raised by seven or eight steps, and suddenly the liturgical novelty is apparent. Here is a church built not to make an artistic statement, but to serve the worship of the people of God and give them a home.

Structural Functionalism exerted a fascination for architects, and churches like Christ-le-Roi in Fribourg, Switzerland (1951–53), by Fernand Dumas and Denis Honeggar, create a great sense of space, both vertically and horizontally, by exploiting the potential of this material. Here neo-Classical forms are used for the tall columns that support the cupola as it rises over an oval choir surrounded by a dark ambulatory. The fan-shaped nave has a wide central space with a cradle-like roof and lower aisles forming the baptistery and weekday chapel.

Quite different, but also relying on the extraordinary properties of concrete, is Le Corbusier's famous pilgrimage chapel of Notre Dame du Haut at Ronchamp. Ronchamp owes everything to its hilltop site in the Vosges Mountains. The thick, curved roofline, like the cap of some giant mushroom, is visible from a long way off, and the church – part grotto, part surrealist

stage-set with its sloping walls, deeply recessed and asymmetric window apertures, gently sloping floor and conventional liturgical layout – is a throwback to the kind of artistic statement that has little to do with the liturgy or with the pared-down Functionalism of modern architecture. Although this church was not built until the 1950s, it feels self-consciously quaint, like Gaudi's Sagrada Familia, and not part of the taut world of the mid-twentieth century that Perret's Notre Dame du Raincy prefigured. When Le Corbusier worked to a tighter liturgical brief at the Dominican priory of La Tourette outside Lyon, he produced a less famous, but also less eccentric, church.

Strangely, Henri Matisse's (1869–1954) little chapel at Vence above Nice is more successful. Here the collaboration between architect and artist produced a cleaner space, L-shaped in form, with the altar set on the angle. As well as the stained glass, Matisse designed the vestments, vessels and altar ornaments and even the detail of the marble inlay on the steps.

Corbusier's pilgrimage chapel of Notre Dame du Haut at Ronchamp.

Above: Corpus Christi, Aachen: an early church by Schwartz leading all eyes to the distant high altar.

Above right: The interior of St Engelbert, Koln-Riehl (top), with the altar in the well-lit chancel, rather than in the dark, central space. Beneath is the exterior of the church, a centralized octagonal plan by Dominicus Bohm.

NEW CHURCHES IN GERMANY AND FRANCE

The churches built by Schwartz and Bohm around Aachen and Cologne in the 1930s, including Corpus Christi, Aachen (1928–30), by Schwartz and St Engelbert, Koln-Riehl (1930–32), by Bohm find their liturgical fulfilment in post-war churches such as St Anna at Duren (1956) and St Christophorus, Koln-Niehl (1960), both by Schwartz.

In the 1930s, both Schwartz and Bohm were searching for architectural forms that would express a longing for the otherness and majesty of God in Functionalist language. But both architects had grasped the difference between the church as a house for God and the church as a house for the people of God. Corpus Christi in Aachen is a plain, whitewashed rectangle, lit by high windows and vertical strings of clear bulbs. At the east end a simple black marble altar was raised well above the heads of the processional gathering

Left: St Anna, Duren by Schwartz: the font, and beyond it the shrine, are set in a dark space under the low roofs of the side aisle, pierced with shafts of light.

Right: St Christophorus, Koln-Niehl: Schwartz's latest and most severely functional church – a single space with an altar at one end of the rectangle and the substantial font in the side aisle.

of the worshippers. Everyone could see the action of the mass; indeed there was nothing else to see. Schwartz was making a house for divine worship, not an autonomous, architectural expression of religious feeling, even if participation in the liturgy was clearly primarily visual. St Engelbert, in a suburb of Cologne, was quite different. The basic structure is circular in form, created by a ring of eight tall parabolic arches. The entrance is reached by a flight of steps, which gives access into the central space that houses the worshipping community, dark and mysterious under its great arches. From one of them opens a lofty chancel up another flight of steps, which is brightly lit from the sides. The altar is raised and visible, but in a separate space from the assembly, gathered together to witness, but not yet to participate fully in, the offering of the Eucharist.

By the 1950s, the grammar of participation has shifted: the congregation are no longer spectators, however well focused, but participants. In St Anna at Duren, the opportunity to rebuild a pilgrimage church destroyed in the war allowed Schwartz to echo the transcendent values of Corpus Christi at neighbouring Aachen, but with a difference. St Anna is an L-shaped church, with a large nave for pilgrimage gatherings meeting a smaller, parochial nave set at right angles, both focused on the same sanctuary and square altar. Between the two arms is a much lower, shadowy, triangular aisle, lit by glazed domes that create shafts of light over the wide, shallow font and over the shrine and the reliquary. In St Christophorus, the context of an un-churched suburb of Cologne made Schwartz use simple forms, clean, functional lines and indirect lighting, adding to a sense that in this brick rectangle it was the assembly itself that created the sense of holiness and mystery. No longer is the altar lifted up, and the assembly drawn up into a sense of the transcendent; rather, the action of the Eucharistic offering is engaged with the transformation of the day to day doings of the assembly.

DEVELOPMENTS IN ENGLAND

In England, matters were far less advanced theologically. While the Arts and Crafts Movement had campaigned for honesty in building materials, churches such as St Andrew's, Roker, in Northumberland, with its wide arched span, or Fownhope in Herefordshire had remained essentially Tractarian in their ordering. Parliament's rejection of the attempt to make progress with the revision of the Prayer Book in 1928 held the Church of England in a liturgical timewarp until the late 1950s. So although concrete had offered new structural opportunities to the builders of churches in the 1930s, the liturgical plan of many post-war buildings remained much as in the 1860s. The most enterprising buildings (making imaginative use of different levels, as in the Epiphany, Gipton, Leeds, where a semicircular east end articulated by tall columns is surrounded by an ambulatory at the upper level off which is glimpsed a mysteriously lit chapel, and St Francis, Salisbury) were by Cachemaille-Day (1896–1976). For the most part his churches remained

longitudinal, with a firm sense that God was to be discovered in a distant – and lofty – east end, though by the 1960s he had begun to make sorties into a centralized plan, as with Bishop Gorton Church at Allesley Park in Coventry.

This propensity for longitudinal plans lasted through the years of post-war buildings such as Edward Maufe's (1883–1974) Guildford Cathedral until well into the 1960s. Maufe and his contemporaries had indeed studied the work of their continental counterparts, but had looked at them solely in terms of aesthetic composition, not with any assessment of their theological or liturgical basis. With the possibilities of concrete at their disposal, British architects began to experiment with new forms. As a reviewer of *Sixty Post-War Churches* said:

> 'Not for five hundred years have we seen so many new churches going up… Here are churches of all shapes, from a cave to a star, built of anything from aluminium to asbestos… Yet this variety, stimulating as it is, raises a question. Have the architects any clear idea as to the function of the buildings they are designing? Have we who commission them?'

Left: The Arts and Crafts church of St Andrew's, Roker, Northumberland.

The Epiphany, Gipton, Leeds, by Cachemaille-Day shows that he understood how to use stairs and levels to suggest a developing series of spaces, like Palladio's Il Redentore in Venice (see pp. 176–77).

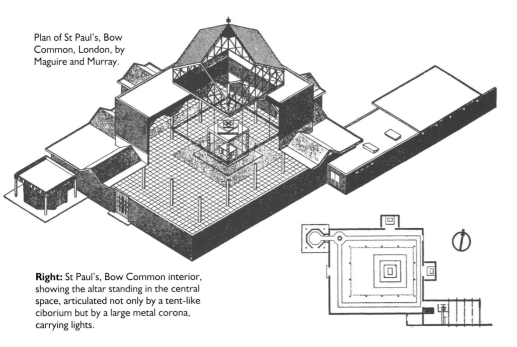

Plan of St Paul's, Bow Common, London, by Maguire and Murray.

Right: St Paul's, Bow Common interior, showing the altar standing in the central space, articulated not only by a tent-like ciborium but by a large metal corona, carrying lights.

St Paul's, Bow Common exterior, showing the glass lantern over the central space.

In 1960 this question began to be answered. A modernist priest-architect, Peter Hammond, published *Liturgy and Architecture*, followed closely by a collection of essays, *Towards a Church Architecture*, in which for the first time the directions of the German Roman Catholic bishops for building churches in the post-war period, issued in 1946, were printed in English. These books were very influential, and began to make common currency of the idea that the church should be a house for the people of God, gathered round the word and celebrating the sacraments of the new creation.

The iconic model in England, owing more to scholarly study of the origins of Christian worship and the German bishops' instructions, was St Paul's, Bow Common (1958–60), in the east end of London, by Maguire and Murray. The congregation enter through an octagonal porch and pass by the font, set in a discrete and darkened walkway, a kind of processional cloister, that runs round the perimeter of the building. In the centre rises a great pyramidal glazed lantern. The altar is free-standing under this lantern, but attention is focused by a ciborium; no one is very distant from the altar, but the benches do not crowd the sanctuary space, articulated by an immense steel corona with its twelve candles. This church was designed from the altar outwards and is a true house for the church.

Developments like St Paul's, Bow Common, pre-date the reforms of Vatican II, but they are an articulation of the common mind that was emerging in the ecumenical alliance between liturgical scholarship, ecclesiology and a number of disciplines related to social anthropology. Inspired by Peter Hammond and the work of Gilbert Cope and J. G. Davies in the Institute for the Study of Worship and Religious Architecture in Birmingham, the Church of England suddenly

St George's, Oakdale, Poole, where Potter and Hare's concrete church of the 1960s expands for the central sanctuary and then contracts towards the east end chapel (above). The font, set at the base of the stairs in the narthex (left).

began to embrace the implications of the Liturgical Movement in its architectural as well as liturgical expression.

Another modern church, St George's, Oakdale, in a suburb of Poole in Dorset, illustrates a different approach. Also reflecting the insights of the Liturgical Movement and the centrality of Eucharistic worship, Potter and Hare built a church in the early 1960s, the climax of which is a free-standing sanctuary at the widest part of this church which has abandoned the strict rectangular form. At the tapering east end there is a subsidiary chapel with a separate altar, and the font is at the west end, tucked under the well of a spiral staircase that leads to the organ gallery. When the church is full, there are people seated on all four sides of the altar, and it is easiest to preach

walking round the central sanctuary; the position for the bishop's chair behind the principal altar, but not raised up, is far from satisfactory. But the church does a fine job of forming the Eucharistic community.

ENGLAND'S POST-WAR CATHEDRALS: COVENTRY'S AND LIVERPOOL'S COMPETING THEOLOGIES

But a decade before the principles advocated in the crusading books by Peter Hammond (see p. 251) had begun to enter the English bloodstream, the question of a new cathedral for Coventry had been raised. The old cathedral, a large Late Medieval parish church, had been bombed in the war, and its ruins still stood. How should a new cathedral relate to the old? What was a cathedral for?

In the early days of Coventry's Reconstruction Committee, different models of the church came to the surface in the discussions over the nature and purpose of the cathedral. The Bishop, Neville Gorton, had been a headmaster before the war, and in the centre of the conventionally arranged school chapel he had set up a free-standing altar, carved by pupils under the direction of the sculptor Eric Gill.

Bishop Gorton had a clear vision of a cathedral being 'built to enshrine an altar' around which the people of the diocese might gather to celebrate the sacraments. As early as 1944, an aspirational statement bore the stamp of his theology:

'This is not a crank idea. It goes back to the very earliest days of the Christian church, and would make the Cathedral in its plan an expression of the very best modern theology and ideas of Christian Liturgy of the present day... The altar does not belong only to the clergy; it belongs to the people. Therefore, set it in the middle of a church and let the people gather round it... Our business then is to go out from there and as a fellowship to witness to God's Truth and give Christian service to others. That is what we want this cathedral to stand for. That is why, connected with the cathedral and its worship, we want a Christian centre of service for the needs of Coventry and its diocese.'

But the Provost had a rather different concept, which triumphed in the brief for the 1950 competition, of a cathedral that would 'speak to us and to generations to come of the Majesty, the Eternity and the Glory of God… It stands as a witness to the central dogmatic truths of the Christian Faith… Architecturally it should seize on those truths and thrust them upon the man who comes in from the street.' Provost Howard hoped for a building that would be noble in size, beautiful in design and inspiring in character.

One model was of a gathered community, drawn around the altar into the body of Christ. The other was of the people, brought to their knees before the majesty of God or – as it turned out – before Graham Sutherland's enormous tapestry of Christ in Majesty, visible through the glass screen from the ruins of the old cathedral. The cathedral was to speak of death and resurrection, of the old and the new, and of Christ's lordship over the whole of Coventry. But as well as the transcendence of God, could it also speak of his immanence?

Some elements of Bishop Gorton's vision remained in the brief:

'The doctrine and worship of the Church of England is liturgically centred in the Eucharist. The cathedral should be built to enshrine the altar. This should be the ideal of the architect, not to conceive a building and to place in it an altar, but to conceive an altar and to create a building [around it].'

The successful architect, Basil Spence, clearly understood the movement from death to resurrection:

'I saw the old cathedral as standing clearly for the Sacrifice, one side of the Christian faith, and I knew my task was to design a new one which should stand for the resurrection.'

Sutherland's tapestry of the ascended Christ dominates the single space of Coventry Cathedral.

What is much less clear is how far he grasped the theology of immanence, so vividly expressed by Bishop Gorton. He fastened onto what the experience of visiting the cathedral might mean to the visitor, rather than the more theological vision of the bishop, and spoke of the building being like a plain jewel casket (see page 255) with many jewels inside, the biggest and brightest jewel being the altar. However, the dominant feature of the interior – cleverly designed to seem larger and more processionally grand than it actually is – is

253

Left: The crown of thorns provides a screen into the Gethsemane Chapel – an intimate space in Coventry Cathedral.

Right: The bridge-like gallery divides the truncated nave from the lofty central spaces in Liverpool's Anglican cathedral by Giles Gilbert Scott.

the great Sutherland tapestry. The long, drab slab of the altar at its foot anchors that great upward sweep that catches you from the moment of your entering into the building, but could hardly be described as a jewel. The focal point of the eastern end is not the altar, but rather the lap of the seated figure. We are not gathered round an altar, but instead are dwarfed – reminded of our humanity – and then drawn up into Christ's embrace. Interestingly, the only space within the cathedral that creates that almost womb-like, immanent experience that Bishop Gorton had at the heart of his vision is the Gethsemane Chapel. Coventry became the last traditional Gothic cathedral, even if in modern dress: although the materials and artefacts are modern, the linear form of the building with its upward sweep and transcendent message about God is Late Gothic in feel.

Liverpool: The Cathedral of Christ the King

Even as Coventry was being built, new ideas were in the air. While the huge post-Gothic Anglican cathedral in Liverpool, with its double crossing either side of the enormous central tower, by Giles Gilbert Scott (who had won the competition to build it in 1902 at the age of twenty-three) was still being built, the Roman Catholic community

in Liverpool decided finally to abandon plans to build the enormous, centralized domed structure designed by Edwin Lutyens (1869–1944) – of which only the crypt had been built – and create a modern cathedral instead. Lutyens, who had designed the Cenotaph in Whitehall, had built – as well as many of the buildings of imperial India – one of the most remarkable religious buildings of the first part of the twentieth century, the great arch at Thiepvalle, as the memorial to those killed in the battle of the Somme. The cathedral at Liverpool, which would have been the largest in the world, was the longed-for peak of his career.

For a thoroughgoing centralized plan, the Cathedral of Christ the King at Liverpool cannot be beaten, though its architect, Frederick Gibberd (1908–84), confessed, 'I have only the slightest knowledge of the new Liturgical Movement.' In ruminating on the problem of building a church, he said, 'churches usually excel over [pubs] for the shallowness of their clichés'. And he continued, 'Church architecture is indifferent because the Church is ignorant of architecture: it does not know how to choose an architect and, having chosen one, it does not understand how to brief him.'

In spite of this, 'Paddy's Wigwam', as it is irreverently called, erected only a short while after Coventry, is an absolutely clear statement of

THE JEWEL CASKET: GLASS, HANGINGS AND PAINTING

Although Spence claimed Coventry as a jewel casket, and John Piper's great baptistery window rising above a hollowed stone from Bethlehem is certainly one of those jewels, it is important to recognize the contribution made to other buildings by stained glass. Notable examples include the glass by Matisse in the east end of the cathedral at Reims, the Prisoners of Conscience window by Gabriel Loire in Salisbury and the Matisse window in another English cathedral – Chichester – commissioned by Dean Walter Hussey. As well as a window by Matisse, Hussey commissioned Piper to make a great tapestry as a brilliant focus for the principal altar in Chichester and designed vestments to go with it, and Sutherland to paint a small picture of Christ appearing to Mary Magdalene as an altarpiece, visible and magnetic – icon-like – down the whole length of the south aisle.

The advantages of commissioning artists of high calibre is obvious: they produce devotional foci that are delivered from the curse of catalogue kitsch. The problem with seeing the church as a jewel casket is that works of art tend to compete with the liturgical action, which is what ought to bring life and colour to the church as the house for the people of God.

The baptistery window in Coventry Cathedral by John Piper.

The east window of the cathedral at Reims by Matisse.

Sutherland's painting of Christ with Mary Magdalene in the garden of the resurrection forms a jewel-like icon at the end of the south aisle of Chichester Cathedral.

John Piper's tapestry of the Holy Trinity makes a vivid reredos to the principal altar in Chichester Cathedral.

Vatican II's ecclesiology and a Eucharistic theology of the church as the body of Christ. Bishop Gorton of Coventry would have been proud of it. But the limitations of such a strongly centralized plan are visible also. First, while the cathedral is entirely suitable for a large-scale celebration of the mass, every other liturgical function, including baptism, is banished to the ring of subsidiary spaces round the perimeter. Second, as everyone is gathered round the altar facing inwards, they have their backs to the outside world. While apparently offering an ideal expression of the church as the body of Christ, there is no sense of movement from the table to engage with what God might be doing in the world. And third, the model is very static: there is nowhere to go. What is the relationship between baptism and the Eucharist, and how does an assembly get any sense of being a pilgrim people? And where in a totally circular building do you set the bishop's *cathedra*, and how do you give significance to the ambo, the focus of the word? Any position for an ambo in the circular sanctuary at the centre of the cathedral is bound to have nearly half the congregation behind the speaker.

The Cathedral of Christ the King in Liverpool by Frederick Gibberd: a thoroughgoing centralized plan.

Addressing the relation between the proclamation of the word and the celebration of the sacrament became one of the problems that new church building had to solve. It is no surprise that the driving force in the Liturgical Movement was the recovery of the Catholic tradition. Balancing word and sacrament proved increasingly difficult, and more sophisticated schemes for both new churches and reorderings began to work with a more complex picture of the church than simply that of the body of Christ gathered round the table of celebration.

Certainly the centrally planned churches such as the Cathedral of Christ the King in Liverpool illustrate how difficult it is to couple word and sacrament in the same space. A sketch by Roger Bastin for the arrangement of the chapel in a girls' college, dating from 1965, shows the altar well forward in the assembly, with five groups of stools arced round it, while the chair for the presider and the ambo are placed centrally, but well back from the altar. This gives the presider, the readers and the preacher good audibility and eye contact with the hearers, but allows the presider to step forward to the altar, where the assembly gathers round on all sides. Though essentially circular in form, this is not unlike the arrangement in some Methodist and Congregational

The interior of the Cathedral of Christ the King at Liverpool, showing all the seating focused on the central altar.

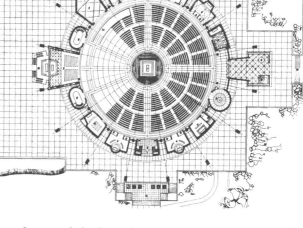

Right: Plan of the Cathedral of Christ the King, Liverpool.

chapels in the late eighteenth and early nineteenth centuries, when the preacher's pulpit, sometimes backed by the deacons or later by the choir and organ, was the dominant feature on what was often the longer wall of a simple rectangle, while the table for the sacrament – in this case less significant – stood on the floor level in front of the pulpit.

BAPTISMAL THEOLOGY

If the rediscovery of how the Eucharist makes the body of Christ shaped the first two-thirds of the twentieth century, and churches were designed primarily as places in which the Christian community met to celebrate round the Lord's table, the last third of the century saw a reawakening of interest in the importance of the sacrament of baptism. In an age preoccupied with death like the Middle Ages, the fear of dying unbaptized loomed large. Since the tenth century the majority of Europeans had been baptized in infancy, and in consequence, fonts had shrunk in size. But in an increasingly de-Christianized world in the West, and with the growth of a highly mission-conscious church in Africa, the

baptizing of new adult disciples emerged as a major opportunity to review how baptism was celebrated. A major impetus to this pastoral concern was the restoration in the Roman Catholic Church of the Paschal Vigil as the major celebration of the baptism of adults in the Christian year in 1952, and of the rest of Holy Week in 1955. No longer was it sufficient to set a traditional font that looked more like a holy water stoup near the church door or a silver rose bowl on a corner of the altar. Adults coming to faith expected a baptismal rite to be celebrated joyfully and substantially in the middle of the assembly, and not in some private side chapel.

As a result, questions arose about what sort of a baptismal font is suitable as well as where it should be placed. Some newer fonts are formed, such as that at Le Dorat in France, in which candidates could stand in the low, square basin with its apse-like eastern projection that stood at the foot of the flight of steps leading down from the west doors of this large Romanesque church. That is a clear statement of baptism as entry into the church. The large, new, tomb-shaped font with the cross-shape cut out of it at Portsmouth Cathedral stands at the narrow junction between the nave and the choir, so that everyone passing by is reminded of their baptism. It also serves

Left: The large cruciform font in Portsmouth Cathedral.

Right: An experimental font basin with four spouts in the centre of the nave in Salisbury Cathedral before the permanent installation in 2008.

as a resting place for a coffin the night before a funeral.

For others, the tradition of the Apostolic Constitutions that says baptisms should be celebrated in running water has suggested a font like that in experimental use in Salisbury Cathedral, in which the four spouts remind the church not only of the four rivers flowing from the garden of paradise (Genesis 2:10–14) but also of the vision in the Apocalypse of John of the rivers of the water of life flowing from the temple of the lamb in the New Jerusalem (Revelation 22:1–2).

For others again, a tiled tank in which submersion can be practised is what has been provided, as in a Baptist chapel, but this is often less suitable for the baptism of infants, and tends to be covered up, so invisible, when not in use.

WORSHIP AS PERFORMANCE

In some churches, especially those in the Protestant tradition, the tendency was to set all the foci of liturgical action on a podium at one end of the room. This was favoured especially in those churches – such as Our Lady of Lourdes at Pontarlier (1959) by Ranier Senn or St Michael's, Hatfield Hyde, a square space that had a diagonal seating arrangement – in which the sightlines

focused on what looked like a stage in one corner. Everything could be gathered there: the table, the ambo, the font, the presider's chair and – especially towards the end of the century, when chorus-singing from the charismatic tradition became the focus of much entertainment-style worship – the band and the 'worship-leader'.

But this gathering of the liturgical foci on a stage, particularly if the seats for the assembly are raked, tends to turn the assembly's worship into a professional performance in which the congregation becomes an audience rather than participants. This is well illustrated in some of the huge glass churches set up by mass evangelists in the United States, such as the Crystal Cathedral in California, built by Johnson in 1980. Worship like this is very different from the liturgical expression of the Christian community's faith-journey that the shapers of the Liturgical Movement had in mind.

One solution is to return to the model of the house church in Dura Europos (see page 21) and place each liturgical focus in a separate space. That is the solution adopted in St Rita's Church, Cottage Grove, Minnesota, in which there is an auditorium-style room for the word and an open hall 'full of celebration' for the Eucharist; the baptistery is in the triangular passageway between one space and another. The same disposition

The many-roomed church of St Rita's, Cottage Grove, Minnesota, has a lecture-theatre-style space for the liturgy of the word, a triangular narthex with the font and a room with no seating and only the altar in the centre for the Eucharist.

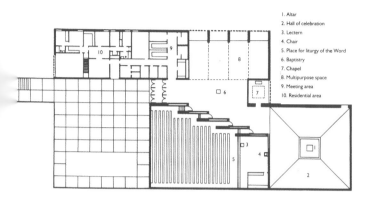

1. Altar
2. Hall of celebration
3. Lectern
4. Chair
5. Place for liturgy of the Word
6. Baptistry
7. Chapel
8. Multipurpose space
9. Meeting area
10. Residential area

The Crystal Cathedral – a great arena for massed performance.

serves the slightly eccentric church of St Gregory of Nyssa in San Francisco, in which the hall for the *Liturgy of the Word has seats angled towards the presider's chair and ambo in a shallow 'V', while the room for the Liturgy of the Table is a lofty octagon with no furniture save the Eucharistic table in the middle, which becomes the table for the party that follows the liturgy. The baptismal font is formed below the grotto shaped against the steep hillside into which the church is built, and this exterior courtyard is visible though the windows of the Eucharistic octagon.

REORDERING OLDER CHURCHES

As well as new churches, many older churches have been reordered for contemporary worship. Sometimes this has meant no more than unthinkingly following the current fashion for celebrating westward by setting up a temporary table poised on a makeshift box at the head of the nave, with little thought for sightlines, or for whether the current furnishings of the church make that a conceivable option aesthetically. Some churches have such complete furnishings and fittings of the period – whether Georgian or Victorian – that any reordering will scream against the character of the building.

The congregation circling the altar in procession in the church of St Gregory of Nyssa, San Francisco; the room for the word is behind them.

Noel Mander's proposal to return the organ to Wren's screen in St Paul's Cathedral, London.

It is hard to imagine that a church like Comper's incomparable St Philip's, Cosham, will ever need reordering (see pages 235–36). Others could be reordered well if a bold opportunity were seized, as it was in the parish church at Cuddesdon, Oxfordshire, which was also used by students at the Theological College. Here Stephen Dykes-Bower set the principal altar under a chandelier in the vaulted crossing of this Medieval parish church in 1941, making it possible for communicants to kneel round it on three sides. He placed a wrought iron screen to the east, turning the long chancel into a subsidiary chapel. How little the groundbreaking significance of this was appreciated can be shown by the clumsy insertion in the late 1980s of a second-hand organ into the north transept, which entirely destroys the sense of gathering round the altar.

In St Paul's Cathedral in London, a scheme to restore Wren's choir screen with the organ on top of it was first mooted by Noel Mander, the organ builder. This would have not only made sense of the choir as a place of worship in its own right, but also created a fine backdrop for a bold altar in the great space under the dome not dissimilar to the relation between the monastic *coro* and the principal Eucharistic space in the Abbey of San Giorgio Maggiore in Venice (see page 172). But even in the 1990s the chapter was not willing to grasp the possibilities offered by such a move that might have united both conservationists and liturgists.

For Southwark Cathedral, London, in which he had done a lot of work on the furnishings, including gilding the reredos in the 1930s, Comper drew up a bold scheme in 1945 for setting the principal altar in the centre of the crossing under a great ciborium. This would have anticipated the directives of Vatican II, and brought some of the insights of St Philip's, Cosham, to a building of cathedral scale. As it is, the opportunity was missed, and the angular neo-Gothic furnishings of Pace and Simms dating from the 1970s are brought out when required, as in so many English cathedrals that have failed to grasp the opportunities of reordered liturgical space.

MAJOR REORDERINGS

Sometimes, but all too rarely, a scheme has been well thought through with an architect and executed in the best materials, so that the result looks as if it was just how the church was originally conceived to be. Examples of good reorderings include St Philibert at Tournus in southern Burgundy; the cathedral at Trier; St Heribert and St Pantaleon, both in Cologne; and the cathedral at Milan. In the English-speaking world, Portsmouth Cathedral by Michael Drury and the Episcopal Cathedral in Philadelphia by Richard Giles provide examples to match the continental ones.

St Philibert, Tournus

The recent reordering of St Philibert, Tournus – a fine Romanesque abbey church with a shrine in southern Burgundy – shows how well Romanesque churches adapt to new dispositions. The principal altar is placed at the crossing with seating for the Eucharistic community on three sides and with the space in the apsidal choir behind the altar

available for the shrine. The design of the liturgical elements – the altar, the ambo, the presider's chair, the cross and the shrine – has been created as a unified work, and the abbey lives again as a coherent liturgical space, with the dark, womb-like narthex providing an appropriate gathering space for the community as it enters for worship.

Trier Cathedral

This is an ancient and complex building, dating from the fourth century onwards. It was closed for many years while archaeological investigations were carried out and is a fine example of the way in which within a cleansed and unified envelope – an interior limewashed in a soft pink – a

major liturgical reordering has been carried out. All the furnishings, fittings, relocated Baroque monuments and subsidiary altars – including the remarkable new altar rising out of its inlaid marble floor representing the four rivers flowing out of Eden and the organ case hanging out of the triforium – are in black and silver. In the centre of the eastern crossing stands the altar, no more than a metre (3 feet) cubed, but sufficient to hold one plate and one cup as the surrounding concelebrants, by their gestures, make the focus of the building and its purpose apparent. Beyond this space, up a flight of curving Baroque steps, lies the eastern reliquary chapel.

St Heribert, Koln-Deutz and St Pantaleon, Cologne

St Heribert, Koln-Deutz, is a large nineteenth-century church in the Rundbogenstil and was reordered by Rudolph Schwartz in the post-war reconstruction. In a way that is frequently successful in a Romanesque-style church, the principal altar has been brought into the crossing and set on an elevated platform, with a raised reliquary chest in the *chevet* behind it. Altar, ambo and reliquary are all designed in the same style. What is distinctive about the reordering is that the trefoiled apse at the east end has been transformed

The shrine behind the altar at the church of St Heribert, Koln-Deutz, reordered by Schwartz.

The nineteenth-century font reset on a very slightly recessed wavy marble floor in the apse of the church of St Heribert, Koln-Deutz, to write it large.

Below: The interior of the reordered Milan Cathedral, showing the high altar set well forward in the crossing, detached from the domed tabernacle screening a secondary altar in the apse beyond.

The reinstated rood screen, seen through the seven branched candlestick, in St Pantaleon, Cologne.

The polygonal Late Gothic rood screen in St Pantaleon provides a ciborium over the modern nave altar by Professor Hildebrand.

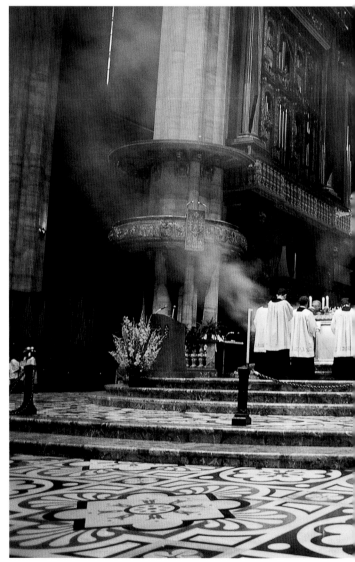

into a baptistery by setting the relatively small font on its pedestal in the centre of a circular pavement of white and green wavy marble, sunk by no more than a few centimetres. The font itself may not be large, but an adult can stand or kneel on the marble pavement, and a great deal of water can be poured over them, so the sacrament can be ministered fully.

In St Pantaleon, an Ottonian basilica with a substantial westwerk, war damage enabled a thorough reordering, as with many of the wonderful churches of Cologne. The Late Gothic pulpitum, moved to the west end to screen the westwerk in the nineteenth century, has been restored to the head of the nave. The pulpitum carries a new organ, and with remarkable trellis-like decoration on its walls and new wrought-iron gates that act like a theatre gauze, it not only screens the Baroque east end with its high altar, but provides a frame – almost a ciborium – for the new sculpted altar by Professor Hildebrand. At the other end of the nave, a large seven-branched candelabrum guards the entrance to the two-storey westwerk, with its echoes of a royal chamber. By reusing existing elements sensitively, an uncluttered and worshipful space has been created.

The Carolingian westwerk of St Pantaleon, Cologne, with its substantial gallery at first-floor level.

Milan Cathedral

Although it did not receive its façade till the early nineteenth century, the cathedral in Milan dates principally from 1386. This double-aisled Gothic cathedral has a wide crossing and an apsidal chancel. After a series of provisional reorderings, the definitive version was established: an oval platform in inlaid marble projects into the crossing with a large altar set forward into the crossing space. The Archbishop's throne is set against the south-east pier of the crossing, while the gospel is read from the northern of the pair of hanging pulpits on the eastern side of the crossing. Set back in the middle of the choir is the lofty tabernacle of the late sixteenth century, but now turned through 180 degrees, so that the arms of the retable that used to embrace the attached high altar today face east, making an enclosed subsidiary worship space for the recitation of the Office and weekday masses in the apse. The whole project has been achieved with the highest standards of workmanship, so that it is difficult to imagine that it was ever otherwise.

Portsmouth Cathedral

In the 1970s, Portsmouth Cathedral was a muddle. The original church had been built in the 1180s, just as the early forms of Gothic had reached England. Dedicated to Thomas Becket, the murdered Archbishop of Canterbury, it had a central crossing with a modest tower, an aisled presbytery, transepts and a short nave of some four bays. During the Middle Ages, the inhabitants of Portsmouth had murdered a bishop of Chichester who had failed to pay them for their services, and so the church had been locked, the font broken and the inhabitants deprived of the sacraments for some sixty years.

Nor was that all. In the Civil Wars of the mid-seventeenth century, the tower had been shelled as a Royalist lookout post, and the church was lying in ruins when Charles II came to meet his bride from Portugal, Catherine of Braganza, at Portsmouth and found no church in which to marry her. Rebuilt in a Classical style with a prod

The completed nave of Portsmouth Cathedral – a square space with raised outer aisles on three sides and no fixed liturgical furniture.

Looking under the tower arch past the new font into the choir.

from the royal household, the church was given a large pulpit, box pews and a west-end tower, complete with Classical cupola.

Altered under the influence of the Tractarian Movement, the cathedral received a directional black and white marble pavement and a Jacobeanesque reredos and tester to its altar to try to give it focus at the beginning of the twentieth century. When it was named as the cathedral of the new diocese in 1927, plans were drawn up for its enlargement. The architect, Sir Charles Nicholson, drew up plans to pierce the west tower to make it a kind of pulpitum or *jubé*, with the organ in the upper stage, and to build a new nave westwards, leaving the Classical nave to the east as a liturgical choir. But only a few bays had been completed before funds ran out and the Second World War broke out. After the war, three unsuccessful attempts to complete the building were made. The building remained dis-ordered,

rather than reordered, and it was not easy to see how it could credibly become the cathedral of the diocese as well as a parish church while also being a centre for spiritual and intellectual leadership. The heart of the worshipping life of the diocese was dysfunctional.

The first task in the reordering of Portsmouth was to create a theological programme for the building, its liturgy, ministry and development. Only the Paschal Vigil could provide the model of that foundational liturgy from which all else would derive, so the architect's brief consisted of nothing other than a description of that act of worship.

Arranging the liturgy to create a unified experience for worshippers, pilgrims and visitors alike gave the detailed plan for using the distinct spaces of the building.

The nave, completed to form a perfect square, was treated as a kind of roofed atrium. The narrow outer aisles were raised to provide a

The sanctuary in the crossing, where the principal altar stands on a platform projected by recessed curves and defined by mosaic edging.

The pyx hanging from Nicholson's colourful tester above a simple stone altar provides a vertical focus to the twelfth-century aisled east end.

cloister-like walkway round this central, well-like space, which is kept free whenever possible. Here, on the night before Easter, the church gathers round the new fire to hear the Old Testament stories of release and new life:

'Fear not, for I have redeemed you; I have called you by name, you are mine. When you pass through the waters, I will be with you; and through the rivers, they shall not overwhelm you; when you walk through fire you shall not be burned, and the flame shall not consume you' (Isaiah 43:1–2).

As the paschal candle is marked, pierced with its five nails and lit from the dying embers, the candidates for baptism are challenged to turn from the darkness of sin and self to say 'yes' to Christ rising in glory.

The processional path funnels the assembly as it moves east through the narrow base of the tower into a person-sized, low-ceilinged space. Here stands the tomb-like font, through whose waters of re-birth the newly baptized emerge into an elegant Classical room, in which the twin poles of lectern and altar, of word and sacrament, nourish the church on its journey.

But the journey does not stop there. When incorporated into the dying and rising of Christ, the pilgrim worshipper has not arrived. There remains an eschatological dimension to Christian life and worship. So beyond the altar, in the space in which the high altar once stood, remains Nicholson's tester or canopy, from which hangs the pyx, a golden vessel counterpoised with a silver crown, containing the Blessed Sacrament. This reminder that the ascension is a necessary prelude to the Pentecostal *Missio* ('Sending out') of the church prepares people for living out their faith in the world.

The Episcopal Cathedral in Philadelphia, Pennsylvania, USA

Faced with a heavy, dark, overfurnished and cluttered cathedral in the Rundbogenstil, an English priest, Richard Giles, who had written about a remarkable transformation in a Victorian church in Halifax in a book called *Re-pitching the Tent*, was asked to become dean and oversee the reordering of the building.

Starting with rebuilding the life of the worshipping community, Giles then set about paring down the framework of the church, clearing out all the existing furniture and paving the cathedral with a stone floor. Placing a stone throne and a semicircular bench for the bishop and his presbyters in the apse and a substantial trough of a font in the south aisle, he set a moveable, free-standing ambo to the west and an altar to the east end of the nave floor space, keeping the whole area free from fixed seating. Members of the assembly bring a stool and set it in an oval round the ambo, moving to re-make the oval round the altar for the Liturgy of the Sacrament. This is a thorough and radical reuse of an old building for a liturgy, which, like Portsmouth's – though in a one-room building in Philadelphia – is essentially a stational liturgy. It compares with the much more furnished reordering of a Classical building by Archbishop Rembert Weakland in Chicago and contrasts with the tendency to build new cathedrals, as in the Roman Catholic Cathedral in San Franscisco.

THE FUTURE

It is difficult to predict the future. Some of the fastest-growing Christian communities are in Africa, and while in the past their style of church-building has often been depressingly derivative of the tradition from which they received the faith, some of the simpler mud-walled and grass-thatched churches in the southern Sudan witness to a desire to create an indigenous style. For large gatherings there, such as an Episcopal ordination or a large confirmation, there is a tradition of

The nave of the new Roman Catholic Cathedral in San Francisco, California, in the shape of an upturned boat.

gathering under a large tree – a safer place than the tin-roofed cathedrals that were easily recognizable targets from the air in the days of the protracted civil war. One fine church in Bor (which no longer exists) was a gigantic quadrilobe *tukel* or local hut – a large, grass-roofed, circular church surrounded by four smaller ones in a cruciform shape. This was built to commemorate the occasion when a whole group of Dinka people burnt their traditional idols on a huge bonfire as they received the Christian faith and were baptized.

Another trend that echoes the desire to build in natural holy places that was noted in the opening chapter is visible in the work of the Finnish architects Kaija and Heikki Siren in the chapel of the Technical University at Otaniemi, near Helsinki. The simple materials – local brick and timber – seek to link the interior and exterior worlds, and the use of a large plate-glass window suggest communion with nature as much as with the Almighty. The sanctuary furnishings are minimal and slender to the point of invisibility, as the worshipper is drawn beyond them into the forest outside, making it feel more like a monastic cell or Zen garden. The techniques are similar to those used by Frank Lloyd Wright in his houses to create an invisible boundary between the inside and the outside. In the Nordic countries, where this elemental sense of cooperation with natural forces seems to be part of the air you breathe, are some of the best crematoria. They combine the function of the reduction of the human body into its primordial dust with a sense that this is merely a speeding up of an entirely natural process.

POSTSCRIPT

What will come next? One of the issues that the world faces is how to build on the slender common ground between Christianity and Islam. This is an issue now not only for those countries in which Christians and Muslims traditionally live side by side such as the Sudan or Syria, but also in countries such as England or Italy, where communities are shaping the same space. In the Tor Tre Teste church built in the outskirts of Rome to celebrate the millennium by the Jewish architect Richard Meier, the three great sail-like wedges of the roofline, reminiscent of the Sydney Opera House, alert us to a vision beyond the local, and to the architect's search for a quality of light that is quite different and more self-consciously derived than Pawson's monastery at Novi Dvur, described below.

More basic, and built out of shuttered concrete, is the church in a new suburb on the outskirts of Grosseto in Italy. It is a circular, semi-domed building, in which the flat ribs meet a central ring as in the narthex in Moissac. Detached, and marking the entrance, is an enormous *campanile* – a cigar-shaped pillar, complete with a gallery ringing its top, just like a minaret. Is this mosque-like building a sign of the future, taking us back to the Great Mosque at Cordoba, a building once shared by Muslims and Christians?

Above: Tadao Ando's Church of the Light at Osaka, Japan, where the cross is inscribed in blinding light on the east wall.

The Episcopal Cathedral in Philadelphia, Pennsylvania, reordered spaciously for a pilgrimage congregation by Richard Giles.

Or does the future lie in the Suomalainen group at Temppeliaukio in Helsinki, and Tadao Ando's Church of the Light at Osaka in Japan? Here a plain rectangle with a window on the right looking onto a blank wall is its only source of

The roofline of Tor Tre Teste Millennium Church in Rome by Richard Meier alerts us to the layered quality of light which characterizes the interior.

The Church of the Holy Family in an estate on the outskirts of Grosseto, Italy, suggests links with Islam.

natural light, save for the cruciform slits in the east wall facing the people that offer an experience of blinding light transcending the cross.

Finally, in the unending search for stillness in the human heart, which has less to do with communion with nature and more to do with exploring the interior life, there is one outstanding church to note. The British architect John Pawson has built a Trappist monastery beside an old hunting lodge on the edge of a remote wooded valley in the Czech Republic. The chapel at Novi Dvur is an entirely plain, whitewashed space. The monks' stalls are of black wood and are very simple. In the centre of the easternmost space is the single block of the altar, with what appears to be an old, battered Romanesque statue of the Virgin and Child perched on a tall, tapering pillar some distance behind; it is the only trace of colour in the chapel. Set in the base of this pillar is the tabernacle. There is no other decoration. The most remarkable thing about the building is the quality of indirect light that floods the chapel. The easternmost space around the altar is lit by some narrow, vertical slits that descend into deep, open embrasures. Over the community's stalls the light is funnelled from high apertures down through the thickness of the wall to spill out at a relatively low level, suffusing this area with a soft, even, indirect light that calms the space. This is the context in which a mixed community from different countries live a life of silent contemplation, drawing their nourishment from the austere but joyful meditation on the mystery of God, who is both Emmanuel – God with us – and at the same time entirely other and unknowable.

This is the contemporary church in which, more than any other, I have found it possible to be entirely still and entirely at peace.

Novi Dvur in the Czech Republic: John Pawson's spacious and calm interior for a Trappist monastery.

Glossary

This includes a number of specialized words used in the text and also some others you may find in guidebooks to churches.

abacus   The square, polygonal or round stone set above a capital.

aedicule   A frame, as for a niche, formed by a pair of columns or pilasters supporting a pediment, gable or barrel vault.

aisle   The side spaces flanking the main nave, divided from it by an arcade, and usually lower in height so that light can reach the main nave through the clerestory (q.v.) windows.

altar   The table – frequently of stone because of the sacrificial associations or resemblance to a tomb – on which the bread and wine of the Eucharist are consecrated.

ambo   An elevated platform, normally in stone with a ledge or desk, at which the reader or cantor stands to proclaim the scriptural readings. See also 'pulpit', 'bema' and 'Exultet'.

ambulatory   The semicircular walkway (Latin *ambulare*: to walk) – usually the extension of the nave aisle – surrounding the columns of the apse at the east end of a Romanesque church, dividing the main space from the radiating chapels and allowing pilgrims to circulate around the shrine set in the apse (see pp. 87–89).

Anabaptist   One who believes in re-baptism on the grounds that only adult believers can express faith, so those baptized in infancy were not truly baptized. This view – that it is an individual's personal faith, rather than the grace of God in Christ, that makes baptism effective – was held by a number of the continental reformers in the sixteenth century.

Anastasis   The icon (Greek) of the resurrection, depicting Christ trampling down the gates of hell.

antependium   Also 'frontal'; the decorative panel, sometimes in metalwork but more usually in fabric, that covers the front face of the altar. A fabric panel above the altar in place of a reredos is called a dossal.

Antiphoner   A book of chants, often so large that it was placed on a lectern, so that a group of singers could cluster round and read as the director of the choir (the *Rector Cori*) pointed to the notes with a long rod.

apse (adj. apsidal)   The semicircular end to a longitudinal or basilica-shaped church, containing the bishop's throne and seats for the clergy. Later, the semicircular end, often surrounded by radiating chapels in a large church, separated from the main space by an ambulatory (q.v.).

arcade   A series of arches on piers or pillars, frequently separating the nave from the aisle(s). A blind arcade is such a pattern of arches set in relief against a wall.

arch   The means of spanning the space between two verticals, other than a flat lintel. Arches may be semicircular, pointed, depressed or ogee in form.

architrave   The cross-member or lintel carried from the top of one column to the next; the lowest member of the entablature (q.v.).

archivolt   The decorative moulding(s) on the underside of an arch.

ark   1. The ark of the covenant made by Aaron's carpenters and metalworkers to house the tablets of the law that Moses had brought down from Mount Sinai, together with a jar of the manna and Aaron's rod, which had sprouted; the focus of God's presence with his people. 2. In a synagogue, the cupboard on the bema at one end of the building in which the scrolls of the law are kept. 3. In the Ethiopian Coptic Church, the low cupboard – not unlike a bedside table – at the centre of the Holy of Holies in which the tabots are kept, and on the top of which they are placed for the celebration of the Eucharist.

armaria   Cupboards, like those illustrated in the mosaic of a sacristy in the tomb of Galla Placidia in Ravenna, in which the Gospel Books were housed when not in use, and that are similar to the arks of the Ethiopian Church.

ashlar Cut stone, shaped to create a smooth wall surface; as opposed to rubble.

Asperges The chant used at the beginning of mass as the celebrant sprinkled the congregation with holy water, from the opening words of Psalm 51: *Asperges me, Domine* – Wash me, O Lord.

atrium The open forecourt of a Roman house, normally with a basin or fountain in the middle and colonnaded porticoes round the sides. The term is extended to cover the open courtyard in front of early Christian basilicas as, for example, at San Clemente in Rome (see p. 37) or San Ambrogio in Milan (see p. 94) and some Romanesque churches, and is paralleled by the great courts and fountains before the prayer-halls in mosques (see p. 17).

aumbry A small safe or cupboard in which the Eucharistic elements are reserved, normally to the north of the altar. See also tabernacle and pyx.

baldachino A free-standing canopy raised above a throne, an altar or a tomb, properly with silk hangings (see p. 95). See also 'ciborium'.

baptistery The room or space, sometimes a separate building from the main church, in which the sacrament of baptism is administered, normally by immersion. In early churches, the baptismal font was sometimes set into the ground in a cruciform or octagonal shape, and accessed by steps leading down. Sometimes an antique bath was reused, as in the Lateran Basilica in Rome, or sometimes a large, raised basin was constructed (see pp. 30–31).

basilica A long, aisled building with the central nave lit by clerestory (q.v.) windows over lower aisles, deriving from a Classical public building, in which transactions carried imperial authority, and often terminating in an apse (see pp. 33–39).

bay The vertical division of the elevation, defined by the space between the piers or pillars, shafts and arches, which creates a spatial unit in the building.

bema A raised platform on the central axis of the nave, and varying how far east it is set. The bema is characteristic of Syian churches, and it elevates and makes audible the reader of the scriptures. It may have derived from a similar platform in the synagogue. Sometimes a crucifix is mounted on the platform, which is called the Golgotha. Occasionally a large ambo (q.v.), with a flight of steps east and west leading to a canopied pulpit, is set in the centre of the nave in the position of a bema, as in the cathedral at Kalambaka in Greece (see illustrations on pp. 39, 54).

boss The block of stone, often elaborately carved, marking the intersection of the ribs of a vault.

Breviary The single volume containing all the texts for reciting the Divine Office or the Liturgy of the Hours. Before the eleventh century, the Psalter, the Hymnary and the Lectionary were normally separate manuscripts.

buttress A mass of masonry built against a wall to support it; hence 'flying buttress', an arch spanning the aisle roofs to a vertical buttress in order to carry the lateral thrust of the heavy vaulting downwards. The decorated pinnacles on the top of such buttresses exert an essential downwards pressure and so are not merely decorative (see p. 122, Le Mans).

campanile The Italian word for a tower, or more properly a bell tower. Early *campanili* on Romanesque churches were sometimes free-standing, such as the famous leaning tower at Pisa (see illustration on p. 97); most had an increasing number of arched apertures at each successive stage, such as the *campanile* at the cathedral at Trani (see illustration on p. 94).

cancelli See 'chancel'.

capital In Classical architecture, the carved cap to a column. In Classical Greek architecture the flat cushion cap is called Doric, the curled rams-horn capital, Ionic, and the acanthus foliage, Corinthian. These orders were developed in Roman architecture, and Renaissance architects used a variety of capitals. In Romanesque architecture some capitals were simple tapered blocks; others were stylized foliage or mythical beasts, while some were intricately sculpted with biblical scenes. Early Gothic capitals tended to be stylized or 'stiff-leaved' foliage.

catechumens The technical name given in the early church to the (adult) candidates who were preparing for baptism at Easter. They had a particularly rigorous period of preparation during the forty days of Lent, at which time they were tested thoroughly, had various preparatory exorcisms performed, and received the key texts of the Apostles' Creed and the Lord's Prayer. Admitted to the *Synaxis* (q.v.), they were dismissed after the homily until they had passed through the waters of baptism at the great Easter Liturgy, been anointed and received the kiss of peace from the bishop, and took their place with their fellow Christians at the Eucharist.

cathedra A Greek term meaning the bishop's throne, hence cathedral – the building in which the bishop has his throne.

cella The inner walled structure at the heart of a temple, surrounded by colonnades.

censer A metal bowl, frequently fitted with a pierced and pinnacled lid, and suspended on chains by which it can be swung, in which incense is burned on live charcoals (also know as a thurible, from *thus*, the Greek for incense).

chalice The cup in which the wine of the Eucharist is consecrated. After the chalice came to be denied to communicants other than the celebrant, chalices shrank in size, having originally been substantial cups, often with handles, containing several litres.

chancel In an early church, the part of the basilica near the altar marked out or railed off (*cancelli*: rails) for those who had a specific part to play in the liturgy. Later the term comes to be used more loosely for the eastern arm of the church, which contains the sanctuary and altar, and sometimes stalls for a choir. See also 'templon'.

chantry A personal endowment that paid a priest to celebrate a mass for a particular intention, normally the repose of the soul of the donor, members of a family or of a confraternity. The mass was normally said at an altar specially set up in a chantry chapel.

chapel Originally part of a large church, or a separate structure attached to it, that housed an altar with a separate dedication. Later, chapels were added to existing buildings as part of the overall design, as, for example, the series of radiating chapels round the *chevet* of an Early Gothic church. This enabled groups of pilgrims to celebrate a mass in close contact with the shrine while the main liturgy took place at the principal altar. Later, parts of the church might be screened off or extra aisles built by guilds or confraternities, or to serve the needs of private individuals. On this principle, a palace, castle or college may have a chapel, or a chapel may be built on the site of a vision or a sacred spring, for example, to serve a particular non-parochial use.

chevet A French word, referring to the semicircular eastern end of a Romanesque or Gothic church, comprising the apse, ambulatory and radiating chapels (see p. 86).

choir The part of a church – properly a cathedral or monastic church – reserved for the community that sang the Office, and furnished with stalls, often with carved misericords (q.v.). In the Middle Ages choirs were frequently enclosed by screens, and separated from the nave by a pulpitum and/or a rood screen. Also spelled 'quire'.

ciborium 1. A canopy over an altar or tomb, normally supported on four columns. See 'baldachino'. 2. A shallow metal vessel on a stem, and fitted with a lid, in which the consecrated hosts are held, either for distribution or for reservation in the tabernacle or aumbry (q.v.).

clerestory The upper stage of the central walls of the nave, above the height of the aisles, pierced with a series of windows to let in light.

coenobitic A pattern of monastic life lived in community, under a common rule and an acknowledged *abuna* or leader.

coffering A term used to describe the cutting away of the thickness of a concrete or stone roof when not structurally necessary to reduce weight, as in the dome of the Pantheon (see illustration on p. 13). It also applies to the spaces left between the cross-members in flat wooden ceilings, giving a similar recessed effect.

colonnade Just as an arcade is a series of arches on columns, so a colonnade is a series of columns supporting an architrave (q.v.), as in Bernini's oval colonnades embracing the piazza in front of St Peter's in Rome (see p. 182).

column Also 'pillar'; a vertical architectural member, either round, fluted, chamfered or shafted, and distinguished from a pier, which is in origin square in section and is a section of a wall, by being set at the diagonal to the main direction of the wall surface. A series of columns, linked by arches, is called an arcade. Columns terminate in Classical architecture in a capital (q.v.), which supports an architrave (q.v.) or round-headed arch, and in Romanesque and Early Gothic architecture by a capital, from which the arch springs. In more developed Gothic, the column – whether diagonal or round – may be surrounded by a cluster of shafts, sometimes in a contrasting material. The shafts

themselves may be capped by rings or capitals or flow straight into the ribs of the vault.

conch A semicircular niche surmounted by a quarter-dome, often fluted like a shell.

confessio The subterranean recess or chamber below the altar, containing the body or relic of a saint. Sometimes a shaft links the confessio to the altar above and sometimes a flight of stairs allows access. Later, a crypt may be developed around the confessio to allow for other burials in close proximity (see p. 29).

corbel A projecting stone, usually carved with a face or foliage, supporting a roof beam or pilaster, or sometimes a sculpted figure. A horizontal member of stone or a wooden beam supported by a series of corbels is called a corbel table.

cornice The projecting decorative moulding that forms the top course of the entablature in Classical buildings.

coro Italian for choir.

Cosmati work The technique developed by members of the Cosmati family in twelfth-century Italy of inlaying small tesserae (q.v.) of marble, porphyry, serpentine or other semi-precious stones to form pavements, panels and even inlays in the characteristic barley-sugar columns used in Italian Romanesque decorative work, especially on altars, tombs, pulpits, ambos, shrines and screens.

crenellated Of a parapet, echoing the pattern of military indentations.

crocket The decorative knobs, carved to resemble bunched foliage, set at regular intervals along a gable or the frame of a door or window, or a pinnacle or spire; they were much used in thirteenth- and fourteenth-century architecture (see p. 120).

crossing The point at which the four arms of a cruciform church meet.

cruciform Cross-shaped.

crypt A vaulted chamber, wholly or partly below ground level and normally at the east end of a church. Frequently the high altar in the chancel or presbytery was raised immediately above the tomb of the founder or saint buried in the crypt (see 'confessio'), as at St Benoit-sur-Loire (see p. 108). The crypt then became a favoured place of burial, as others sought to be buried as close to the saint as possible.

cupola A dome or dome-shaped vault, not necessarily a complete hemisphere.

diakonion In early churches the space, usually to the south of the sanctuary, set aside for the reception of the congregation's offerings, and serving as a store for goods for the needy. Later, a sacristy or archive.

dome A semi-spherical covering for a roof, normally raised over a square crossing, or – especially in south-west France – over a square bay of the nave. The corners of the square were bridged over to form an octagon, and the resulting corners were further bridged over until a perfect circle was achieved, forming curved surfaces that appear to be hanging from the dome, hence their name, pendentives. Sometimes the dome was raised on a cylinder, which might contain windows, known as a drum. The great dome of the Pantheon in Rome, much admired by later architects who tried to imitate its large span, was lightened by its ceiling being coffered (see p. 13). See also 'cupola'.

dossal   See 'antependium'.

elevation   The point in the canon of the mass at which the priest, having just rehearsed the words of institution – as the words of Jesus at the Last Supper 'This is my body' and 'This is my blood' are known – raises the now consecrated Eucharistic host and the chalice for veneration. This point came to be marked by the ringing of a bell and the censing (q.v.) of the elevated elements.

entablature   In a Classical building, the lateral course carried by a series of columns, usually consisting of the architrave (q.v.), the frieze (q.v.) and the cornice (q.v.).

Eucharist   The principal service of worship of the church, also called the mass, the Holy Communion, the Lord's Supper and, simply (especially in Orthodox churches), the Liturgy. The word derives from the Greek *eucharistein* (to give thanks), and recalls the church's obedience to the command of Christ at the Last Supper to take, bless, break and distribute bread and wine in memory of him, finding him present as they did so. The first part of the Eucharist is known as the *Synaxis* or Liturgy of the Word (q.v.), and is focused on the ambo and the Gospel Book (q.v.); the second on the altar and the bread and wine laid on it.

Evangelarium   The Book of the Gospels for liturgical reading at the Eucharist, often illuminated, and frequently bound and decorated with metalwork and precious stones (see illustration p. 81).

exhedrae   Large, niche-shaped units, spanning a right-angle, used to project a quarter-dome from a larger structure.

Exultet   The Proclamation of the Resurrection, traditionally sung by the deacon to bless the paschal candle at the great Easter Liturgy. Especially in churches with a substantial paschal candelabrum (q.v.) opposite the pulpit or ambo, the ambo would be used with its high stone lectern, over which the Exultet Scroll would be unfurled as the deacon sung the Proclamation. Painted on the scroll – but upside down to the deacon so that they could be visible to the congregation standing around – were illustrations of the events of the Easter commemoration, the stories of the exodus, of Noah and of Jonah, which formed the Old Testament background to understanding the resurrection events.

fan vaulting   See 'rib'.

feretory   See 'reliquary'.

ferramenta   The base of the shrine of a saint on which the sarcophagus, feretory or reliquary rested, frequently pierced with apertures so that pilgrims could thrust the affected part of their body into close proximity with the saint.

filigree   A delicate form of metalwork using gold and silver wire to produce a lacy effect.

finial   The pointed peak of a gable or pinnacle, often decorated with bunched foliage.

Flamboyant   The latest style of French Gothic, the name deriving from the curving, flame-like shapes in the window tracery (q.v.) that give an undulating movement to the whole.

font   The basin or tub that holds the water in which a candidate is baptized (see baptistery). With the establishment of Christianity as the official religion, most candidates were baptized in infancy, and the practice of immersion gradually gave way to infusion or sprinkling in the Western church. In consequence, fonts shrank in size till, by the eighteenth century, they were little more than birdbaths in size. See also 'stoup'.

fresco   Wall painting created by using pigments bound with egg whites (tempera) applied directly on to damp plaster, which binds and sets the paint as it dries.

frieze   The middle element of the entablature (q.v.), providing a flat surface that can be ornamented by carving (see p. 99).

frontal   See 'antependium'.

gargoyle   A grotesquely carved rainwater spout, throwing the water clear of the building.

Golgotha   See 'bema'.

Gospel Book   See 'Evangelarium'.

grisaille   A term used to describe glass painted with stylized patterns of foliage in monochrome sepia, in which the patterns of the leading are more prominent.

hammer-beam roof   A system of projecting a horizontal beam from a wall supported by an arched right-angle bracket to narrow a wide span in constructing a timber roof, used a good deal in England. The ends of the projecting horizontal hammer beams were frequently decorated with carved angels (see illustration on p. 140).

hood mould   A moulding projecting above an arch, whether of a window or doorway, designed to throw off water, but frequently also used inside just decoratively.

host   The Eucharistic bread, in the Western tradition made of unleavened bread.

houselling cloth   In Late Medieval England, the name given to the long white linen cloth spread before the communicants as they received the sacrament, so that no crumb might fall; the custom has survived continuously at Wimborne Minster in Dorset.

iconostasis   The screen of icons, with three doors, that separates the *naos* or nave from the bema or sanctuary in an Orthodox church, which developed from the templon.

idiorhythmic   An individualistic pattern of monastic life, for example of a group of hermits living in a locality but without any common rule or collective worship.

jubé See 'pulpitum'.

katholicon A Greek term meaning the principal church in a monastic enclosure.

lancet A narrow window with a sharply pointed arch at the top. Groups of lancets under an arch, with roundels and geometric tracery (q.v.) filling the space at the top, form the basis of Gothic window design.

lantern A low tower with windows set over the crossing of the nave and transepts to provide light.

lectern A stand for the books containing the readings. In the churches of the Reformation, this means the Bible, and the lectern is frequently in the form of an eagle – the symbol of the evangelist John (see 'tetramorph'). In the Middle Ages, the lectern was frequently a large wooden two-sided music desk, supported on a cupboard (see 'Antiphoner').

lierne See 'rib'.

lintel A horizontal beam of stone, set over a window or door. Over a wide door a stone lintel was liable to crack, so a semicircular arch was built to relieve the pressure, creating the semicircular space filled with a sculpted tympanum (q.v.). In addition, the lintel might be supported from below by a carved pillar or *trumeau* (q.v.).

Liturgy of the Word This first part of the Eucharist, after the Introductory Rite that ends with the gathering prayer known as the Collect, contains readings from the Old Testament and New Testament interspersed by a psalm, and the reading of the gospel, preceded by alleluias and followed by the homily or sermon. It is also known as the *Synaxis*, and catechumens (q.v.) were banished from the Eucharistic meal after the homily. The focus of the Liturgy of the Word is the Gospel Book, brought into the assembly in procession by the deacon as an icon of the presence of Christ among his people.

mandorla An almond-shaped halo or frame, usually containing the seated figure of Christ in Majesty, or sometimes the blessed Virgin Mary, and signifying their divinity. Also known as a vesica.

martyr One who bears witness to Christ by likewise shedding their blood.

martyrium A structure built over a site that bears witness to an event in Christ's life or passion, or over the site of a martyr's death or burial.

misericord See 'stalls'.

Missal The single volume for celebrating the Eucharist that began to replace the large number of manuscript texts used by the different ministers in the Early Medieval period, such as the Sacramentary and Graduale. With the invention of printing and a concerted effort to standardize texts in the wake of the Council of Trent, the Missal became the norm in the Roman Catholic Church.

mosaic A form of figurative decoration achieved by setting small cubes of glass or stone (tesserae) into plaster, which developed in the eastern Mediterranean, the characteristic gold background being achieved by cubes of glass backed with gold leaf.

mullion The vertical member dividing a window into two or more lights.

naos A term from Classical Greek meaning temple, and in Modern Greek, a church; used to describe the central liturgical space in a Byzantine church.

narthex An extended porch or portico, providing a liminal space between the outside world and the church itself. Originally a gathering space before a basilica (see 'atrium'), the narthex in a Carolingian or Romanesque church was often the lower stage of a substantial westwerk, as in Corvy or Nivelles (see illustrations on pp. 72 and 90), and distinguished from the interior of the church by its dark forest of columns. Sometimes the site of the baptismal font, the narthex was the place to which the catechumens (q.v.) were banished before they had been baptized, after the Liturgy of the Word (q.v.). In the Orthodox tradition, the narthex is frequently decorated with painting of Old Testament or even pagan worthies.

nave The name given to the main hall-like structure of a church, in which the body of people assemble for worship. It derives from the Latin *navis* (a ship), from its resemblance to an upturned ship, with the ribs and planking of its roof exposed.

niche A recess in a flat surface, framed by a canopy or an arch, usually for a sculpture.

occulus A small, circular window.

octagon An eight-sided figure, so an eight-sided tower or section of a tower as it supports either a dome or a spire.

Office A term from the Latin *officium* (duty); the name given to the pattern of daily prayer, especially that prayed seven times a day in the monastic life at approximately three-hour intervals, which was the prime duty of the choir monk. In the Benedictine tradition, the seven-fold pattern – seven because the psalmist says 'seven times a day will I praise thee' – consists of Matins and Lauds, Prime (at the first hour, so at 6 a.m. in our reckoning), Terce, Sext, None, Vespers and Compline.

ogee (ogive, ogival adj.) An arch formed by two S-shaped curves, used initially as a decorative canopy for a niche, probably originating in the East. Later used also as a frame for a door or window (see p. 118).

Opus Anglicanum English embroidery, famous throughout the world, using delicately shaded silks to give a realistic, almost three-dimensional effect; and combined with back-couching to create a chequered gold background, like an icon. Probably the best surviving example is the cope of Pius II at Pienza in Tuscany (see p. 118).

opus sectile A covering for walls or floors made by cutting marble slabs into a variety of geometric shapes.

Pantocrator   The figure of Christ as the ruler of all, commonly found in mosaic or painting in the central dome of the church (see illustration on p. 43).

parclose   A transparent screen used to enclose an area, usually at the east end of an aisle, for use as a chantry chapel. After the Reformation, such enclosures frequently became family pews.

paschal candelabrum   Some Romanesque and earlier churches have a large, stone column – sometimes in a barley-sugar twist, or decorated with Cosmati work (q.v.) – on which the great paschal candle was set, and burned throughout the forty days of Easter. Opposite the candelabrum was frequently a large pulpit or ambo from which the Exultet (q.v.) was proclaimed as the candle was lit and blessed (see Bominaco, p. 95).

paten   The flat dish on which the host is laid for the Eucharistic prayer. Originally large shallow bowls, the paten shrank in size when it contained only a single host for the celebrant, and small, individual, wafer-like hosts for the people were held in a ciborium (q.v.).

pediment   A low-pitched triangular gable over an aperture, whether door, window or portico of a Classical building.

pendentive   The curved V-shaped surface formed by building from a right-angle corner to the quadrant of a dome (q.v.; see p. 62). See also 'squinch'.

pier   A substantial masonry support, originally square in section, made up of coursed stone (or brick) and originally conceived as a section of a wall between two apertures. See also 'column'.

pietism   A seventeenth-century movement centred on personal devotion to the redeemer aimed at infusing new life into the rather formal German Lutheran Church.

pilaster   Decorative vertical strips in semi-relief, often fluted and projecting slightly from the wall surface, giving the impression of a flattened column.

pillar   See 'column'.

piscina   A shallow basin set in a niche, normally on the south side of an altar, for washing the sacred vessels after mass.

portico   A pediment supported on a row of columns, providing a porch or entrance.

predella   See 'reredos'.

presbytery   Originally, that part of the church reserved for the presbyterate – the college of clergy who surrounded the bishop and sat with him on the semicircular benches or *synthronon* either side of the throne in the apse. Later, that part of the church containing the altar, and so reserved to the officiating clergy. See also 'sanctuary'.

prothesis   The space, usually to the north of the sanctuary, reserved for the preparation of the Eucharistic elements, and for their reservation afterwards.

pulpit   In Later Gothic and subsequent churches, a platform raised on a stem – Late Gothic pulpits are sometimes called 'wineglass pulpits' – from which the sermon is preached or a lecture given. Some Late Medieval pulpits were portable wooden structures, more like the proverbial soap-box. In early Christian churches the bishop normally preached seated in his throne in the apse, after the model of Christ teaching his disciples. In the Romanesque period, the large pulpit-type ambos that are set opposite the enormous paschal candelabra (q.v.), are clearly intended by their iconography primarily for proclaiming the Exultet (q.v.), rather than for preaching (see p. 93).

pulpitum   A substantial and solid screen, normally pierced by a single doorway giving access to the choir. Sometimes combined with the rood screen (q.v.), the solid construction of the pulpitum provides an excellent support for an organ, as at King's College, Cambridge, or at Exeter Cathedral. At St Alban's Abbey, the pulpitum has two doors, with a carved reredos for the nave altar in the centre. A bay to the east of the pulpitum is the rood screen, with a central entrance into the choir. Also known as *jubé* in French.

pyx   A box-like receptacle, frequently circular with a conical lid, in which the consecrated host of the Eucharist is kept (reserved) for the purposes of Communion or veneration outside the celebration of the Eucharist. See also 'aumbry' and 'tabernacle'.

quatrefoil   A geometric pattern made up of four interlocking circles like a four-leaved clover.

quincunx   A fivefold pattern with a square or cross-shape surrounding a central point, which is often more significant.

Rayonnant   A word meaning 'radiating' in French, and properly is appropriate only to the radiating pattern of the rose window, a feature that was rather arbitrarily chosen in the nineteenth century to typify this style of architecture, which grew out of the Gothic style.

Regularis Concordia   The code of monastic observance in England agreed by the Synod of Winchester under St Dunstan and St Ethelwold, c. 970.

reliquary   A casket carrying the relics of a saint, normally fashioned out of precious metals and decorated with enamels and gems, sometimes made in the shape of the relic enclosed, as in head-reliquary or arm-reliquary. A casket designed to be carried in procession is called a feretory, a name that is also applied to the place in which it normally stands.

reredos   A painted or sculpted backdrop to the altar giving a visual focus to the altar – and indeed the whole church – even when no liturgical action is taking place. It may have hinged panels to the sides (wings) which can be closed in penitential seasons. At the foot of the large paintings, visible to the whole congregation, is frequently a base consisting of small panels providing a devotional focus for the celebrant called the predella.

retable   The shelf standing at the back of the altar on which a reredos (q.v.) or altarpiece stands.

rib The structural member of a roof vault, developed in Gothic architecture, that provides the skeletal articulation. Originally simple in form, ribs – like the shafts of columns – developed more complex sections. The ribs that provided the cross links in later vaulting, and were more purely decorative, are known as liernes. Later developments in vaulting, such as fan vaulting, were formed by taking the decorative wall panel and growing it out of the shaft of a column, as in Sherborne Abbey in Dorset (see illustration p. 162) till it forms a semicircular or fan-shaped vault.

riddle posts The four posts surrounding an 'English' altar, made popular by Sir Ninian Comper, from which curtains are hung to the back and sides (see 'dossal'). The four posts are the residual member of a ciborium (q.v.) or *baldachino* (q.v.).

Rococo A term that derives from *rocaille*, that pattern of overall naturalistic decoration with natural elements such as shells and coral that provides a textured surface covering. It was devised by Pierre Le Pautre in the office of Louis XIV's chief architect, J. Hardouin-Mansert, to smooth over the boundary, for example, between wall and ceiling (see pp. 186–87).

rood The figure of the crucified Christ between Mary and John, supported either by a rood beam or a rood screen, and providing a devotional focus for the congregation in the nave who were often in a long Gothic church at some distance from the altar. A nave altar under the rood was frequently dedicated as an altar of the Holy Cross.

rood screen A pierced screen, in stone or wood, dividing the chancel or choir from the nave in order to support the rood (q.v.), often carrying a substantial loft from which the gospel might be sung from a small stone lectern facing east. It is as if the bema (q.v.) or Golgotha was raised, while retaining the same function (see p. 136). See also 'pulpitum', with which it is sometimes combined.

Sacramentary The book developed to contain the texts needed by the celebrant for the celebration of the Eucharist; gradually replaced by the more comprehensive Missal (q.v.).

sacraments The seven sacraments – those determined by the Western church as the recognized means of grace – are baptism, confirmation, the Eucharist, confession, anointing, ordination and marriage. The Reformation churches, seeking clear scriptural warrant, recognized only the dominical sacraments – those referred to in the Gospels as instituted by the Lord himself, that is, baptism and the Eucharist.

sanctuary A term used interchangeably with presbytery, to designate the east end of the chancel, containing the principal altar.

sarcophagus A carved tomb-chest, sometimes reused for Christian burials.

sedilia A row of three seats for sacred ministers – the priest, the deacon and the sub deacon – at high mass, set to the south of the altar and frequently elaborately canopied.

spandrel The triangular space between the curve of the arch and the vertical and horizontal members that frame it.

squinch The arch set diagonally over a right-angle corner of a square tower to form an octagon.

squint An oblique opening cut in the wall of a chancel to enable those in a transept or even – in the case of lepers or hermits – those outside to see the elevation (q.v.) at mass.

stalls Because of the increasing length and complexity of the Office, wooden seats or stalls for the members of the community were provided, with – later, after the invention of printing – sufficient space for the substantial choir books required. Members of the community sat in a disciplined order, with the senior members in the back row, and the leaders or officials in the corner seats. The back row of stalls frequently had tip-up seats to facilitate standing, but fashioned with a small carved ledge, known as a misericord (q.v.), on which the carver could exercise his imagination unseen (see illustration p. 131). The weary monk could thus appear to be standing, while in reality he is supported.

stoa In Classical Greece, an arcaded loggia or shaded walkway used for teaching: disciples walked and talked with their master.

stoup A shallow basin on a pedestal or projecting from a corbel (q.v.) beside the door of a church containing holy water with which those who enter can sign themselves with the cross as a reminder of their baptism. See also 'font'.

string course A horizontal moulding projecting from a wall, sometimes running continuously round a building and embracing door frames and even windows.

Synaxis See 'Liturgy of the Word'.

synthronon The (normally) curved bench or tiers of benches flanking the bishop's *cathedra* (q.v.) in the apse of an early basilica for the presbyters.

tabernacle A small safe, frequently domed, standing on the altar or its retable (q.v.) in which the Eucharist is reserved. A prominent feature on the principal altar in most Roman Catholic churches from the Renaissance onwards, the tabernacle was ordered to be removed from the principal altar when the practice of celebrating facing the people was restored by the Second Vatican Council, and it was placed in a subsidiary space, preferably on a pillar or as an aumbry (q.v.).

tabot The flat stone tables, normally kept in the ark, unless they are laid on it to be used, on which the Eucharist is celebrated in the Coptic Church of Ethiopia. Once a year, they are taken in solemn procession on the Feast of Timkat (q.v.) to the nearest source of water to be solemnly washed.

templon In Byzantine churches, a beamed colonnade closing off the sanctuary (see '*cancelli*'); later hung with icons and developing into the iconostasis (q.v.).

tesserae The small cubes of glass backed with gold leaf or other colours, marble and semi-precious stones used to create mosaics.

tester A canopy suspended over a pulpit, where it frequently has a functional use as a sounding board, or over an altar, where it acts as a hanging ciborium (q.v.).

tetraconch A building of quatrefoil (q.v.) shape, composed of four conches (q.v.).

tetramorph The symbols of the four evangelists – the man for Matthew, the lion for Mark, the ox for Luke and the eagle for John – deriving from the visions of Ezekiel and described in the Revelation to John as surrounding the throne of God. They are frequently shown in the corners of a rectangular panel with a vesica (q.v.) containing a figure of Christ in Majesty.

Theotokos 'God-bearer'.

Timkat The Feast of the Baptism of Christ in the Ethiopian Coptic Church on which the tabots are taken and ritually washed in the nearest river or spring.

tracery The geometrical patterns of cut stone filling the open arch of a window, and later the application of those decorative patterns to stone wall surfaces or to wooden panels, as on doors or the backs of stalls, for example.

transept The north and south arms of a cruciform church, projecting at right angles to the main nave. Sometimes, as in the Romanesque churches of Apulia in Italy, a transept with a small projecting apse ends the church in a T-shape.

trapeza A Greek term meaning a table, so the refectory or dining room of a Greek monastery.

trefoil A geometric pattern made up of three interlocking circles like a three-leaved clover.

tribune A gallery above the aisles or at the end of the nave or transepts. See also 'triforium'.

triforium A low arcade over the aisles and below the clerestory (q.v.) in a Gothic building, designed primarily as a passageway; the triforium grew out of the tribune, and was later incorporated as a slender walkway at the foot of the clerestory.

trumeau The carved column supporting the lintel in large Romanesque portals, as at Moissac or Vezelay (see illustrations pp. 90, 91).

tympanum The semicircular space formed by a relieving arch over a lintel in the doorways of Romanesque churches, frequently elaborately carved. See also '*trumeau*'.

vaulting A system of roofing a building in stone, using the techniques developed in creating an arch by cutting wedge-shaped stones. Extending an arch laterally produces a tunnel vault; raising the tunnel vault on a wall, pierced by a series of arches, is the first step towards a cross vault, in which two tunnel vaults intersect at right angles. Both tunnel vaults and cross (or groin) vaults were used in the Romanesque period to roof buildings, especially when wooden roofs were so vulnerable to fire. But the round-headed tunnel vaults could only be used to roof fairly narrow spans. Too much pressure was exerted laterally when the width to be spanned was too great. Bringing the thrust more vertically was the result of the discovery of the pointed arch. The Gothic style evolved from the Romanesque when four diagonal ribs were added to a simple groin vault to make a quadripartite vault. Sexpartite vaults have six ribs per bay, and cross members between the main ribs are called liernes.

vesica See 'mandorla'.

volute A spiral scroll, based on the scroll of an Ionic capital, filling the triangular space between a vertical and a horizontal.

voussoire A wedge-shaped stone used to build an arch.

web The stone infilling between the ribs of the vault, often of a lighter or semi-porous stone.

westwerk The monumental west end of a Carolingian or Romanesque church consisting of a narthex below with a galleried first floor, modelled on the imperial gallery chapels, flanked by twin towers (see Maria Laach, p. 75; Nivelles, p. 90).

Further Reading

General Books on the Sense of Space and its Relationship to the Sacred

David Brown, *God and Enchantment of Place* (OUP, 2004), esp. Chapter 5

Peter Cobb, 'The Architectural Setting of the Liturgy' in Cheslyn Jones *et al.* (eds), *The Study of Liturgy* (OUP, 1978)

J. G. Davies, *Temples, Churches and Mosques – A Guide to the Appreciation of Religious Architecture* (Blackwell, 1982)

Christian Norberg-Schultz, *Genius Loci* (Academy Editions, 1980)

Edward Norman, *The House of God: Church Architecture, Style and History* (Thames and Hudson, 1990)

R. Kevin Seasoltz, *A Sense of the Sacred – Theological Foundations of Christian Art and Architecture* (Continuum, 2005)

Nigel Yates, *Liturgical Space – Christian Worship and Church Buildings in Western Europe 1500-2000* (Ashgate, 2008)

The History and Development of Worship

John F. Baldovin, S. J., *The Urban Character of Christian Worship*, Orientalia Christiana Analecta 228 (Pontifical Institutum Studiorum Orientalium, 1987)

John F. Baldovin, S. J., *Bread of Life, Cup of Salvation – Understanding the Mass* (a Sheed and Ward Book, Rowman and Littlefield Publishers, Inc., 2003)

Edward Foley, *From Age to Age*, revised and expanded edition (Liturgical Press, 2008)

George Guiver, C. R., *Company of Voices* (SPCK, 1988)

Joseph A. Jungmann, *Christian Prayer Through the Centuries*, originally published as *Christliches Beten* (Verlag Ars Sacra Joseph Muller, 1969); first published in the USA in 1978 by Paulist Press; this edition prepared by Christopher Irvine for Alcuin Club Collections (SPCK, 2007)

Gordon W. Lathrop, *Holy Things – a Liturgical Theology* (Fortress Press, 1993)

The Early Period

Henry Chadwick, *The Early Church*, Pelican History of the Church 1 (Penguin, 1967)

Yves Christie, Tania Velmans, Hanna Losowska and Roland Recht, *Art in the Christian World 300–1500: A Handbook of Styles and Forms* (Faber and Faber, 1982)

Robin Jensen, *Understanding Early Christian Art* (Routledge, 2000)

Richard Krautheimer, *Early Christian and Byzantine Architecture*, Pelican History of Art (Penguin, 1965)

Cyril Mango, *Byzantine Architecture* (Electa Editrice, 1978; first published in Great Britain by Academy Editions, 1979; paperback by Faber and Faber, 1986)

L. M. White, *The Social Origins of Christian Architecture*, (Trinity Press International, 1990)

John Wilkinson, *Egeria's Travels* (SPCK, 1971)

Romanesque and Gothic

The best guides to Romanesque architecture are in the series *La nuit des temps*, published by Editions Zodiaque, the Abbey of La Pierre-qui-Vire, F-89630 St Leger Vauban, France. There are over eighty volumes, covering the whole corpus of Romanesque art and architecture, and are an indispensible resource.

V. T. Atroshenko and Judith Collins, *The Origins of the Romanesque: Near Eastern Influences on European Art, 4th–12th Centuries* (Lund Humphries, 1985)

Jean Bony, *The English Decorated Style: Gothic Architecture Transformed 1250–1350* (Phaidon, 1979)

K. J. Conant, *Carolingian and Romanesque Architecture 800–1200*, Pelican History of Art (Penguin, 1959)

Paul Frankl, revised by Paul Crossley, *Gothic Architecture* (first published by Penguin in 1962; new edition, Yale University Press, 2000)

Louis Grodecki, *Gothic Architecture*, History of World Architecture (Faber and Faber/Electra, 1979)

Colin Morris, *The Discovery of the Individual 1050–1200* (SPCK, 1972)

Erwin Panofsky, *Gothic Architecture and Scholasticism* (A Wimmer Memorial Lecture, Archabbey Publications, Latrobe, Pennsylvania, 1951)

Otto von Simson, *The Gothic Cathedral* (Routledge and Kegan Paul, 1956)

Richard Southern, *The Making of the Middle Ages* (Penguin, 1953)

The Renaissance and the Reformation

G. Addelshaw and F. Etchells, *The Architectural Setting of Anglican Worship* (Faber and Faber, 1948)

Peter Doll, *'After the Primitive Christians': The Eighteenth Century Anglican Eucharist in its Architectural Setting* (Alcuin GROW Joint Liturgical Studies, no. 37)

Diarmaid McCulloch, *The Reformation* (Viking/Penguin 2005)

Peter Murray, *The Architecture of the Italian Renaissance* (Thames and Hudson, 1969; 3rd edition, 1986)

R. Wittkower, *Architectural Principles in the Age of Humanism* (Alec Tiranti, 1962)

Nigel Yates, *Buildings, Faith and Worship* (OUP, 1991)

The Nineteenth and Twentieth Centuries

Kenneth Clarke, *The Gothic Revival* (Constable, 1928)

Frederic Debuyst, *Modern Architecture and Christian Celebration* (Lutterworth, 1968)

Richard Giles, *Repitching the Tent* (Canterbury Press, 1996)

Peter Hammond, *Liturgy and Architecture* (Barrie and Rockliff, 1960)

Henry-Russell Hitchcock, *Architecture in the Nineteenth and Twentieth Centuries* (first published by Penguin in 1958; 4th edition, Yale University Press, 1977)

David Stancliffe, 'Creating Sacred Space', in Brown and Loades (eds), *The Sense of the Sacramental* (SPCK, 1995)

English Churches

John Betjeman, *Collins Pocket Guide to English Parish Churches*, 2 vols (Collins, 1968)

Alec Clifton-Taylor, *The Pattern of English Building* (Faber and Faber, 1972)

Alec Clifton-Taylor, *English Parish Churches as Works of Art* (Batsford, 1974)

G. H. Cook, *The English Mediaeval Parish Church* (Phoenix, 1954)

G. H. Cook, *The English Cathedral through the Centuries* (Phoenix, 1957)

Charles Cox and Charles Bradley Ford, *The Parish Churches of England* (Batsford, 1935)

Simon Jenkins, *England's Thousand Best Churches* (Allen Lane, 2000)

Index of General Terms

The Lion Companion to Church Architecture

Index of Churches

The Lion Companion to Church Architecture